UTILIZATION OF HEALTH SERVICES IN URBAN KERALA

A Socio Economic Study

UTILIZATION OF HEALTH SERVICES IN URBAN KERALA

A Socio Economic Study

DR. K. GANGADHARAN

SERIALS PUBLICATIONS
NEW DELHI

First Published - 2005

ISBN : 81-86771-92-1

Published by

SERIALS PUBLICATIONS

4830/24, Prahlad Street, Ansari Road
Darya Ganj, New Delhi-110002 (India)

Foreword

As an interdisciplinary topic, health economics is now emerging as an important thrust area for research and higher studies in most of the universities in India and abroad. It is with pleasure and pride that I went through the thesis *"Utilization of Health Services in Urban Kerala A Socio-Economic study"*. I am impressed by the way the author has presented the matter. The thesis represents a good piece of research work on utilization of health service consequences of urban Kerala.

The author has taken an important problem on utilization of health services in urban Kerala. He has formed relevant questions, objectives, hypotheses and coceptual frame work to conduct the study. He has collected enormous amount of data, primary and secondary. He has provided an exhaustive and illuminating review of literature. The study is massive in character with logical chapterisation and using flawless and excellent language. The thesis reads like a novel in every department of its execution. Since the study is related to economics, the author provided a store house of useful literature which will lead to the undertaking of many more research projects.

The major findings of the study proved that rapid urbanization is the root cause of all urban health problems. The problem of accessibility of public medical facilities is an important problem in the urban health environment of Kerala. The poverty related health hazards is increasing in the urban setup. Urban morbidity is rising steadily in all the urban centers and it is mainly due to bad living environment. Morbidity and its linkage with various socio-economic variables analysis reveal the impact of socio-economic status on the morbidity pattern.

Since there is paucity of books on the literature on Urban Health Economics in India, this book will prove itself a very useful one for students, researchers and policy makers connected with Urban Health problems. I am sure that this book will fill the vacuum that exists in the field of Urban Health issues.

It is with deep sense of sentiments of pride and gratitude that I heartily congratulate *Dr. K Gangadharan* for the laudable work well done. I do sincerely hope and pray that he wins greater laurels and the book enjoys wide circulation.

I am extremely happy to recommend this book for the students, researchers and policy makers who are interested in Urban Health issues.

Dr. B.A. Prakash

Professor & Head, Department of Economics
University of Kerala, Thiruvananthapuram

Acknowledgement

I am deeply indebted to *Dr. S. Harikumar,* Reader, Dept. of Economics, Pondicherry University, Mahe under whose supervision I have completed this study. Inspite of his tight schedule at the Department, he was the constant source of encouragement, guidance and help throughout the study. Words can seldom fully convey my gratitude, reverence and sincere thanks to him, whatever he has done for me so kindly.

My sincere thanks are due to *Dr.P. Ibrahim,* Professor and Head, Dept. of Economics, Pondichery University, Mahe for his advisory involvement in this work.

I express my sincere gratitude to the office manager *C.M. Sreekala* and other staff members *K.M. Vijayaraghavan, M.P. Preman, Stella Fernandez* of the Dept. of Economics, Pondicherry University, Mahe.

A fellowship under F.I.P. scheme of the U.G.C. has also helped to bring the study within the realm of possibility. I am obliged to them.

I am thankful to *Dr. D. Narayana,* Centre for Development Studies, Thiruvananthapuram, *Dr. B.A. Prakash,* Professor, Dept. of Economics, Kerala University, *Dr. K.T. Shenoy,* Professor, Dept. of Gastro Enterology, Medical College, Thiruvanathapuram, *Dr. V. Ramankutty,* Epidemiologist, Health Action by People, Thiruvananthapuram, *Dr. T.V. Shekar,* Institute for Social and Economic Change, Bangalore and *Dr. T.P.M. Abdul Fareed, Farook* College, Kozhikode for their valuable suggestions and help rendered to me.

I am indebted to the staff of the following libraries and institutions for providing me access to their resources – Centre for Development Studies, Thiruvanathapuram, University of Kerala, Thiruvananthapuram, the Madras Institute of Development studies, Chennai the Connemara Public Library, Chennai, Institute for Social and Economic change, Bangalore, the Medical College Library, Thiruvanathapuram and Kozhikode, the University of Calicut, Thenhipalam and Kannur University, Kannur.

My sincere thanks are due to the Municipal Secretary and other office staff of the Municipal Corporation, Thalassery.

My heartfelt gratitude to my wife *B. Sandhya* who was the main source of strength behind this endeavor. I also acknowledge with a deep sense of gratitude the encouragement received from my parents and also from each and every members of my family.

Last but not least I would like to record my thanks to my colleagues and well wishers. I express my thanks to all respondents in the urban slum and urban areas of Municipal Corporation, Thalassery without whose co-operation I would not have completed this study.

I wish to express my sincere thanks to *Mr. Thanveer, Ms. Saritha* and *Mr. Azeez* of Print O Fast, Bank Road, Calicut for the neat and prompt execution of the printing work of the thesis.

I express my deep sense of gratitude to *Dr.B.A. Prakash,* Professor and Head of the Department of Economics, University of Kerala for providing a foreword and introduction to this book .

Finally with all my earnestness, sincerity and love, I thank 'God Almighty' who has made many impossible and possible in life.

Dr. K. Gangadharan

Contents

Dedicated to

SWAMI AYYAPPA

1

Introduction

The contribution of human capital to the overall economic growth has been universally accepted. The enhancement of this intangible form of capital through the enrichment of human capabilities has received considerable attention in recent times. Improvement of health status plays a vital role in the enhancement of human capabilities (Sen, 1987). The challenge before the developed countries is to maintain a higher level of health status than what they have already achieved. For the developing countries, the challenge is to attain a better health status.

Few subjects can be more important than health as a constitutive element of the well-being and freedom of a nation. And yet health care has been one of the most neglected aspects of development in India. Despite stirring statements in planning documents on the centrality of health and health care, the field has suffered from persistent neglect in public policy in general and development planning in particular (Dreze and Sen 2002). A direct consequence of inadequate official attention to health matters is that, the Indian population continues to be exposed to a high incidence of communicable diseases and readily preventable illnesses. Communicable diseases are seen to be responsible for more than half of the burden of disease in India (Murray and Lopez 1996)[1]. Many basic illnesses that have radically declined in large parts of the developing world in recent decades (such as tetanus, measles, pneumonia, leprosy, malaria, hepatitis, tuberculosis etc) continue to be common in India. To illustrate, India's share of worldwide leprosy cases is estimated to be as high as 68 percent.[2] It is worth noting that the burden of disease falls very unevenly on different sections of the population. Indeed, health inequalities are very sharp in India, in comparison with many of the other countries, even of the poor ones.[3]

Poverty often causes sickness and determines the disease patterns - hence the expression 'diseases of poverty.' The poor can even to some extent become biologically adapted to substandard condition of life and consider their sickness as normal. Access to health system is moreover deeply conditioned by one's possessions and income (Joseph et al 1983). The underlying cause of disease and health among the poor is this cruelly un- equal distribution of wealth of land, of educational opportunity, of political representation and of basic human rights and this in- equality is the primary disease (Joseph et al 1983). Though all varieties of health services are available in our cities, not all sections of the community are benefited by these facilities (Umashankar and Misra 1993).

Health Status Difference : A Global View

Health improvement is influenced by three sets of factors: (a) health factors .which include medical intervention (b) health promoting factors such as housing, water supply, sanitation and hygiene and (c) non health factors which include social and economic factors. Historical analysis shows that the second and third sets of factors had considerable bearing on health improvement.

A comparison of the developed countries and developing countries with respect to some of health status and human development indicators would reveal that, wide disparities exist between these countries basic human development and health status like, life expectancy, infant mortality rate, maternal mortality rate, infants with low birth weight, adult literacy[4] etc. (Refer Appendix 1.1) There exist wide disparities among nations and regions of the world in the basic human development and health status indicators. It can be seen that the population of industrialized economies are almost fully literate, whereas this was only 50.7% in least developed economies. A comparison of many of the human development indices in India with other countries (see Table 1.1) reveals that India is no exception as in the case of other low-income economies and in many cases the indicators are less than the average of the developing countries taken as a whole. However, within the Indian Union, Kerala State is an exception. The health status of Kerala is far advanced and higher than the all India average and is even comparable with advanced countries.

Table 1.1: Human Development Indicators - A Comparison

Sl No.	*Indicators*	*Kerala*	*India*
1.	Literacy rate 1999		
	Male	93	72
	Female	83	44
2.	IMR* 1997-99	14	71
3.	Birth rate 1997-1999	18.1	26.6
4.	Death rate 1997-1999	6.3	8.9
5.	Life expectancy		
	Male	70	62
	Female	76	64

Source: Dreze and Sen 2002. Table A.1 and A. 2.
IMR–Infant Mortality Rate.

In 1999 the Infant Mortality Rate (IMR) for India as a whole is 71, whereas that of Kerala is 14. In the case of adult literacy also Kerala is far ahead of the all India average. Similarly for life expectancy, birth rate and death rate to some extent Kerala is at par with the advanced countries.

Not withstanding the advanced levels of human development of Kerala, the question that arises is whether the fruits of human development are fairly shared by all segments of population. Studies held in this regard revealed that all sections of population have not benefited fully out of the development process. (Kannan K.P. 1991, Kutty VR 1993, Antia 1999, Surekha 1999, Rajan and Navaneetham 1994, Madhava Menon 2000).

The economic status of a family has a significant effect on whether a child is immunized or not. Recent study on Kerala revealed that (Rajan and Navaneetham 1994) only 56% of children were immunized among families without any assets, whereas it was 77% for families who possessed household assets. The highest percentage of children (77%) immunized is among the Christians, among households with highly valuable assets and among mothers whose education exceeds ten years of schooling. The lowest percentage (39%) of immunization is among the children of illiterate mothers. As the immunization is a precautionary measure to prevent the illness among the children, the poor slum folks, due to their low economic status are not utilizing the health services fully and thereby succumb to more diseases.

Urbanization : At the beginning of the 19th century only 3% of the people in the world lived in urban areas. This figure rose to 10% at the turn of the 20th century and increased to 25% in 1950, 46.1% in 1997 and is projected to about 54.4% by the year 2015 (Govt. of Kerala 1997). In India urban population has been growing at a rate of 3.8% during 1971-81, which was higher than that of the 2.4% national growth of population. Urban population, which was 77 million in 1961 (18%), increased to 156 millions in 1981 (23.34%). As per the 2001 census the urban population in India was estimated at 285.3 million that accounts for 27.78% of the total populations.

In Kerala, the degree of urbanization was low in the pre-independence period. It was only 7.11% in 1901 and it has increased to 13.48% in 1951. From 1951 to 1991 the growth of urban population was 31.18% and in the1991 census it accounts for 26.39% of the total population of the state and it reduced slightly to 25.97% in 2001. The degree of urbanization varies considerably from 3.76% in Wynad district to 50.46% in Kannur (Govt. of India, 2001).

The scarcity and contamination of water supplies and the lack of sanitation and appropriate sewage disposal makes the diarrhoeal diseases one of the most important health problems among the poor in urban areas. Environment of urban poverty with its inadequate services, over crowding, poor and dangerous housing, pollution etc. causes a variety of infectious disease and malnutrition to the urban poor. The first and foremost effect of rapid urbanization is the problem of homelessness and it varies from city to city. In some cities such as Bombay and Calcutta most of the population lives in slums. In addition to the large number of slum dwellers there are many people who are completely homeless. Case studies from Calcutta, Los Angels and Manila particularly mention the homelessness. It is very difficult to obtain reliable estimates of the numbers but it is suggested that in Los Angels there may be as many as 30,000 people in this group (WHO 1992). The higher degree of urbanization may lead to problems of housing, sanitation, and drinking water etc. among the urban dwellers. The N.S.S. 44th round revealed that 18.67% in urban Kerala had no latrine facility and another 15.39% were sharing with other households and only 65.94% had latrines for exclusive use. The condition of Maharashtra, another highly urbanized state is pitiable, where 49.1% was sharing the latrine with other households and 23.2% had no latrines at all. In the field of housing it can be seen that 13.79% urban houses in Kerala are Kachcha houses and another 17.55% are semi-pucca type. The link between urbanization, degraded environment, inaccessibility and a deteriorating quality of life is particularly significant. A study by the Centre for Science and Environment in 1988 showed that more than 40% of the drains in the slums are water logged giving rise to intestinal, respiratory and skin diseases. In 1985 nearly 27.1% urban population in India did not have access to safe water and 71.6% were without basic sanitation. It is also estimated that in 1987-88, 25% urban females and 14.6% urban males have no regular employment (Mukhopadhyay, 1997).

Urban malaria, tuberculosis, pneumonia, leprosy, meningitis and preventable infections in children such as measles, whooping cough, diarrhoeal diseases, and intestinal worm infections are some of the most common health problems apart from higher morbidity and mortality due to accidents. The health hazards of the urban poor are directly related firstly to poverty, secondly to polluted and stressful urban environment and thirdly to social instability and insecurity.

The urban health environment in Kerala : The health situation of urban Kerala is different from that of rural one. Due to the existence of large urban slum population, the health problem is severe in urban areas. The number of slums identified in Kerala in 1985 was 705 with a population of 2,78, 674 whereas in 1996 it increased to 1169 slums with a population of 3,58,012 indicating a growth rate of 28.5% in the slum population over a period of 10 years (Govt. of Kerala 1997). The district wise analysis of slum population revealed that (see the table given in appendix) 8.1% of the population in the statutory towns in Kerala belongs to the slum category. The 1981 census revealed that 8.6% of urban population in Kerala were categorised as slum dwellers and this had risen to 15.9% in 1991. It also reveals that at the all India level the proportion of slum dwellers was 17.5% and 21.3% respectively for 1981 and 1991 (Govt. of India 1997). This raises the question, whether the available health services are properly utilized by all sections of urban community. Some crucial problems are mounted in the utilization of health services in urban area. It is to elicit such problems that the study is carried out in the most urban populated district in Kerala.

Another disturbing trend in the public health delivery system is that it is getting alienated from the people and only 30% of the people even from the lower income group seek medical help from Government hospitals (Govt. of Kerala 1998). This is because of the fall in the quality of services at the Government hospitals. The poor state of Government hospitals may be due to lack of political commitment, financial stringency, bureaucratic inefficiency, corruptions at various levels, lack of proper planning etc.

The unprecedented growth of urban slums in Kerala[5] in recent years consequent on the hike in the price of pucca shelter and land in urban centres would ultimately tell up on the general urban health in Kerala (Ratna Raj 2001). The task force appointed by the Government in 1998 to study about the health and sanitation situation in Kerala reveals the hidden dangers that lies behind the health advancement of Kerala and also about the poor health service utilization by people in certain pockets like urban slums in the state (Madhava Menon 2000).

Research Problem

Kerala has achieved outstanding progress in human development, which is reflected in the high level of education and health of its population. Crude death rates, infant mortality rates and life expectancy at birth in Kerala are comparable even to those in the developed countries (World Bank 1993). Though low mortality rate has pushed Kerala into the forefront of other Indian states and developed countries in health status, the people of Kerala, especially the urban slum population is facing the problem of high morbidity both from communicable and non-communicable diseases. Different studies done across the country revealed that, among the urban population, slum dwellers have higher rate of morbidity prevalence and their living condition is extremely worse (Jha 1986, Kumar and Kumar 1987, Bhatnagar Dosajh and Kapoor 1988, Nangia Praveen, Kamla Gupta and Tiwari 1996, Underwood & Marget 1987, Ebrahim 1984, Rossi Espagnet 1984). The incidence of low birth weight babies is much higher in slums as compared to average. Consequently, infant death rate is also higher. Low birth weight babies are three times more likely to die in infancy than babies of normal weight at birth (Kumar and Kumar 1987). From a comparison of children in urban slums with that of children in rural areas, it is clear that urban advantage disappears. Urban slum children suffer higher rates of morbidity and attain growth status comparable to that of rural children (Underwood and Margett 1987). The study held in certain areas of Bombay slum revealed that 36% of the slum dwellers had one or other type of illness (Jha 1986). In a Delhi longitudinal study (Ebrahim 1984), which reviewed the state of health of 100 children during the first 2 years of life, revealed that morbidity and mortality rates increased from higher to lower socio-economic classes of families who mostly lived in poor environmental conditions.

The major health problems identified in the urban slum areas include diarrhoeal diseases, infectious diseases, malnutrition, tuberculosis, malaria and gynaecological disorders. Among the chronic diseases cardiovascular diseases, cancer, and diabetes emerged at the top. As far as the proportion of morbidity is concerned, urban Kerala is subjected to more of non-infectious than infectious diseases. The NCAER study (Shariff 1995) about prevalence of morbidity among different states in India proved that the morbidity rate is very high among the urban male population in Kerala which is recorded as 185 per 1000 population and for female it was 166 per 1000 population, whereas the national average of morbidity rate was 96 for males and

106 for females. The NCAER study also revealed that 42.3% of the diseases of the urban areas are non-infectious in character and 29.5% are infectious and remaining 28.2% account for fevers. The study clearly revealed that urban Kerala suffers from serious problem of morbidity. The study conducted by the population Research Centre of Institute for Social and Economic Change through the rapid household survey under the RCH project revealed that 13.7% children had diarrhoea complaints in urban Kerala. Similarly, 22% of the children in urban area in Kerala suffer from breathing problems due to acute respiratory infections, whereas this was only 14% in rural areas (ISEC 1999). The urban environment is responsible for certain special health problems and high morbidity. The iron deficiency resulting from the attack of hookworm results in the problem of anemia. Waterborne infectious diseases, like dysentery, typhoid, diarrhoea is also common in urban areas and it is mainly due to poor household hygiene resulting from overcrowding, congestion and also due to shortage and interrupted supply of drinking water. Airborne diseases results from air pollution create chronic health impacts among urban people and are responsible for chronic coughing in children (Appaswamy 1993). Diseases spread by solid hazardous waste, rotting garbage and blocked drains are quite common in urban areas. The incidence of cholera is directly related to improper sanitary facilities for human waste disposal (Azurin and Alvero 1974). Malaria, which is a vector disease, is also common in urban areas in Kerala due to stagnant pools of water, water storage system in houses and high population density, which leads to fast spread of diseases. In 1960s the problem of malaria persisted only in hill areas and coastal belt was free from the attack. But the trend in 1990s is that malaria infection is more in coastal region and persist more in urban slum (Govt. of Kerala 1999). In Kannur district alone 1110 cases of malaria (Govt. of Kerala 1995) was reported in 1995 and out of this most of the cases were reported from urban centres.

Slums are pockets of poor houses, poor people and poor environment either in the middle or in the periphery of a big city. Dirt, filth and stink fill the whole terrain. In one room the human beings of three generation are huddled together like sardines. The same room is used for cooking, co-habitation and breeding. The area of health and welfare is conspicuous by its absence. Slum has been variously described as a cancer on the body of a city, a veritable hell and utmost form of human degradation. Crimes, vices, diseases and illiteracy consistently show higher degree of occurrence in such surroundings. There are abundant cases of starvation, malnutrition of children, women and the old, unemployment and under employment, exploitation, torture, delinquency, desertion, and heinous crimes. They are devoid of food, sanitation water, electricity, privacy, quietude, and protection against diseases, health, medical care and above all any help. (Kumar and Kumar 1987).

The health status of urban population is peculiar in character as majority of them are floating population and the awareness of urban slum population about various health problems like curative, maternal and child health differ widely due to differences in their socio- economic set up. The vulnerable sections in the urban areas are suffering from morbidity problems especially diseases of poverty and are not having enough access to health care services. Due to the low income, they provide first priority to food and later only for treatment. Since income being low, they first usually approach the public hospitals, but the poor and inadequate services rendered by them compelled to go for private health care and in certain cases no treatment at all. The availability of physical presence of health functionaries competent enough to handle the user's problem is also crucial. Laboratory facilities and supply of drugs needed for diagnosis and treatment often play a vital role in determining access to health care services. Access to health care systems is deeply conditioned by one's possession and income (World

Bank 1998). The study intends to focus the basic problem faced by the urban slum dwellers regarding the utilization of public health care service system, utilization pattern of health care services by different socio-economic classes of the urban slum and urban area about the perception of these people with regard to various health problem and also on the cost of health care of these people. Though health services in the form of doctors and hospitals may be accessible to slum dwellers, they lack the purchasing power and basic infrastructure like sanitation, housing and pure drinking water. Some crucial social and environmental factors are responsible for the high morbidity in the urban and slum areas and also in the limited utilization of health services. The study is focused on such factors by dividing the households according to their socio- economic status.

Objectives

1. To examine the linkage between morbidity and socio-economic status of the people in urban slum and urban.
2. To identify the important determinants of health status of urban population and to review the problem of urban health in the utilization of health services.
3. To compare the differences in the perception of need for curative care and to find the kind of health services sought, the type of health centres approached by different socio-economic groups to meet their health needs in urban and slum areas.
4. To assess the extent of utilization of maternal and child health services in urban slum and urban areas.
5. To examine the extent of utilization of Government and private health services in urban and slum areas.

Hypothesis

The following are the important hypothesis postulated for the study.

1. As SES status (Socio Economic Status) comes down the overall morbidity prevalence increases steadily.
2. As SES Status comes down morbidity of diseases due to infection increases whereas chronic illness decreases.
3. The living environment is the important determinant of health status.
4. The better the social and economic position better would be the perception of the people about different diseases and higher would be the utilization of health services.
5. The utilization of MCH (Maternal and Child Health) services is high among the urban and high among the higher SES groups.

Methodology

The details of the methodology followed in the study are discussed in detail in the following chapter.

Importance of Investigation

A study of inter relationship of socio- economic conditions of different segments of community with the nature and pattern of morbidity and their medical aid, health needs and their health services utilization is a significant area of exploration. Such a type of an investigation will not only highlight the health and medical problems of a community, but will also provide insight into the understanding of inherent socio-economic disparities in society and its consequences on further aggravating the structural inequalities of the existing socio- economic order.

Health is a major determinant of human development, as it has socio-economic relation with the quality of life. Therefore, health development is an integral part of national development. Though there exist studies which deal with the health status and health care utilization in general (Kannan etal 1991, Panicker and Soman 1984,

Panicker 1985, Irudaya Rajan and Mohanachandran 1999, Irudaya Rajan and Navaneetham 1994), there are no specific studies related to health care utilization of urban and slum communities in Kerala. Though the urban rural disparities are not as severe as that of other Indian states, there are certain urban centers and urban slums where health status is worse. The study is concentrated in one such urban region of the Kannur district in Kerala. The study revealed a clear dichotomy that exists between the urban and slum communities in their perception about symptoms and diseases seeking treatment, morbidity pattern, treatment process and health services utilization.

In the process of urbanization, the cities are swelling due to population growth. This has resulted in further deterioration of physical environment in these cities not backed by adequate expansion of civic amenities as well as health and other service. Though all types of health facilities are available in our cities, not all sections of the society are benefited by these facilities. The worst sufferers in the urban areas are the people belonging to the economically weaker sections of the society. Hence it was thought important to study the impact of socio- economic variables on the health status and health services utilization in the urban context.

Limitations

The study suffers from the following limitations.

1. Since morbidity rates are sensitive to seasonal factors, this raises the issue of reliability of rates reported from the present study based on a single time point. Hence the rates and pattern of illness captured by this study pertains to only a specific period of the year namely the end of summer and starting of monsoon. So the chances of infectious illness may be slight less compared to the monsoon period.

2. Measurements of morbidity are based on self-perceived basis, most of the deprived sections neglects fever of short duration (i.e. one or two days) as acute illness. If it is also included then morbidity rate would have been much higher.
3. The findings of the study cannot be generalized for the state of Kerala as a whole as the study is limited to Thalassery Municipal Corporation area. All the factors responsible for the utilization of health services are not dealt within this study, as the data was collected only from beneficiaries, hospital authorities medical and paramedical personal were avoided from the data collection.
4. The definition and method of SES grouping of the households intended to reflect the socio-economic class (SES Class) of households has been arbitrary though based on Kuppuswamy's scientific method of SES classification for urban families.

Chapter Scheme

The study report is divided into nine chapters for the sake of clear and meaningful presentation.

The first chapter deals with a general introduction, objectives, hypotheses, significance, limitations of the study and also attempts to review the available literature and related studies in the area.

The second chapter presents a conceptual framework for the study and it deals the detailed methodology followed in the study.

The third chapter provides the basic problems and determinants of urban health with special reference to Kerala.

The fourth chapter provides the profile of the study area by giving stress on health infrastructure.

The fifth chapter examines the linkage of morbidity prevalence and socio-economic status of the sample population.

The sixth chapter examines the treatment process and utilization of curative health services.

The seventh chapter examines the utilization of Government and private health services.

The eighth chapter provides the detailed analysis of the utilization of maternal and child health services.

In the last chapter a summary and conclusion of the study is provided.

Review of Literature

A country like India whose people experience adverse health problems in addition to high levels of illiteracy and poverty needs to have consistent and multi pronged strategy and plans to ensure an equitable health status for its people. Resource crunch does not seem to be the prime reason for failure to implement a satisfactory health care system in most countries. India and Kerala is no exception to this (Panicker 1979, Nayar 2000). The WHO has also pronounced the equitable policies and political will are the two important factors for achieving success in improving the health of a nations population (Nayar 2000).

The review of literature on the health care utilization shows that urban health is still a less researched area in the context of its complexities. In the process of urbanization, the cities are swelling due to population growth and migration. This has resulted in further deterioration of physical environment in these cities not backed by adequate expansion of civic amenities as well as health and other services. Though all the varieties of health services are available in our societies, not all sections of the society are benefited by these facilities. The worst sufferers in the urban areas are the people belonging to the economically weaker sections of the society. As part of review of literature important studies reviewed here is mainly related to morbidity, socio-economic status, factors affecting health services utilization including utilization of maternal and child health services, factors affecting the perception of diseases and certain specific studies related to health services utilization in urban and slum areas.

A noteworthy feature of studies on immunization of children in Kerala was that incomes were not the major determinant of immunization. From a study on childbirth in an urban slum and a more prosperous middle class area in Thiruvananthapuram in 1987-88 (Soman et al 1990) concluded that although the morbidity load in the slum was greater, vaccine preventable diseases against which immunization services were freely available did not pose a particular problem in either area. The spread of education especially among the women is the vital factor for improved health awareness and better health services utilization in Kerala (Panicker 1979). The vital factors responsible for better child and general health include a higher average age at marriage, a higher rates of female employment in the organized sector, higher levels of health awareness and information among women about better utilization of maternal health system and greater decision making roles of women in Kerala households. The expansion of literacy among females, higher emphasis on public health and education provided by the Govt. and above all the poor are more aware of their rights to use health, accounts for high utilization of health services in Kerala.

Since Anderson and his colleagues have proposed the structural model for health services utilization, a great deal of research has been carried out in developed countries to examine the factors that influence the health services utilization. Wan and Soifer (1974) had found that the most important factors related to health services utilization are the need for care (illness level) average cost per visit, health insurance coverage and age. Other variables either have an indirect or negligible effect.

Haynes (1991) examined the relation ship between socio- economic status and health service use. He found that morbidity was related to housing tenure and care availability, rather than to occupational status. He also found that age adjusted morbidity ratios were higher for females in multiple occupancy dwellings in inner city areas.

Anderson and Adey (1978) found that in a national US survey for non-institutional population in 1975, health services are equitably distributed and that age and level of illness are the main determinants of health service use.

Brink and Nader (1981) examined the pattern of primary care utilization in tri-ethnic–urban school children in Galvestno, Textas USA. They found that social class and ethnic group have a strong relationship with the use of medial services. Brink and Nader also found that Anglican's with a low socio- economic status used the service less often than others. Gesler and Meade (1988) examined the relationship between the health service use and distance and socio- economic status. They found that the distance from home to the regular source of care was relatively more important factor for inner city residents than for suburban and urban residents. There was no clear difference by race sex age and occupation.

Health needs at different ages influence utilization patterns. A study conducted in Tunisia, found 'U' shape utilization pattern with peaks at both extremes of age (Benyoussef and Wessen 1974). High morbidity rates in the very young and the elderly explained this study.

Sundar (1995) in her study based on NCAER data of 1992 revealed that the utilization of health services depends on the availability of quality health care services at a reasonable distance and on the ability of the people to utilize health services effectively. The provision of appropriate health infrastructure is a necessary but not a sufficient condition for health care utilization. A number of socio- economic factors such as financial status, caste, occupation, education and gender have great influence on the perceived need for medical care and affect the access to health care facilities. The study categorically proved that with an increase in the level of education, utilization of private health facilities goes up and the utilization of public health facilities comes down.

The impact of socio-economic status on health services utilization is clearly revealed by Shariff (1995) by analyzing the NCAER data of 1992 on health services utilization and expenditure. The first and formost index of better health services utilization is with regard to treatment procedure adopted for curative care on morbidity. At the all India level 8.5% of the reported morbidity in urban areas are untreated. In the urban areas highest percentage of untreated morbidity was reported from Andhrapradesh (16.1%) followed by Karnataka (11.9%) and then Kerala (10.8%). In the problem of untreated morbidity, the urban Kerala is above the national average, which reveals the proportion of poor living in the urban areas in Kerala and their inability to pay for health care and denied of health care services.

Yesudian (1981) studied the health behaviour of four social classes - high, middle, low and very low in the utilization of health services in Bombay city. He observed that as the low and very low social class households are educationally backward, their knowledge, level of diseases, available health services, and their perception, desire to seek health services are found to be lower than that of middle and high class households. The low and very low social classes use mostly the Government health services because of their poverty. They are also not aware of all the services available in General hospitals and as a result their use is restricted to out patient department mostly. In the caste wise utilization of health services in India, the awareness of medical facilities is the lowest among scheduled castes and scheduled tribe groups. They prefer Government hospitals; choose a place where treatment is offered free of cost and rarely to go a private practitioner (Rao 1981).

Heller (1969) revealed that social stratification refers to the arrangement of various groups in a hierarchy indicating the relation of superiority or inferiority with respect to property status and power. It provides differential status and roles to individuals and groups to constitute a basis for human behaviour in relations to each other. Mukherjee (1971) discussed about sanitation and water supply and give a list of diseases, which incapacitates a person for less than a week and those for more than a week. The structural constraints like poor image of primary health centre due to lack of medicines, over crowding long queues and cultural and social gap between the health worker and the patient also limits utilization of health services (Banerjee 1973).

K. Sureender (2000) in a field study in the slum areas of Bombay revealed that squalor, filth, overcrowding and environmental pollution are the root causes of many diseases leading to high mortality in slum areas. Though the health facilities exist in adequate measure, the needy do not utilize them sufficiently due to the ignorance about health issues. Women and children suffered from malnourishment and anemia were mostly underweight. Gastroenteritis, typhoid, malaria, measles, and hepatitis and tuberculosis were the major diseases engulfing the area. Due to overcrowding, inadequate drainage system, unplanned house structures and shortage of potable water, infectious diseases of all types were rampant. The study proved that the project undertaken with the object of improving the health status and health services utilization of the urban slum dwellers through a package measures resulted in bridging the gap that exist between health problems and health services utilization.

Sundar (2000) in her field study conducted in Dakshinpur a low-income re-settlement colony of Delhi reveals the under utilization of Government health services by the slum dwellers. Poor environment and living conditions have given rise to high incidence of diseases like tuberculosis, respiratory tract infection, worm infestation, and diarrhoeal diseases. The study revealed that poor health status of population is mainly due to ignorance and a greater reliance on traditional practices than due to lack of purchasing power or non- availability of health services. The study pin points that the health project undertaken for the area with the objective of improving awareness of family planning, antenatal care, post partum care and checking malnutrition succeeded in spreading general awareness among the target population about the need for practicing family planning and importance of maternal and child health care. The study proved that the reason for under utilization of health services mainly rests with an array of functionaries involved in the health care system and their dedication is a must for the success of any health services utilization programme.

Inequalities in medical care access are a severe problem in the utilization of health services in both urban and rural areas. A study on inequalities in access to medical care (here access stands for empirical relationship between the need and probability of using the health care system for treatment) where the need use probability relationship for one population group which was compared with that of another in Canada, England, Finland, Poland and USA revealed that the findings for the adult varied considerably. The access differentials among children were surprisingly consistent and unrelated to health care system and structures. It appeared that higher family income was associated with greater access to health care among children at all levels of need (Salvekar David 1975).

The significance of socio-cultural factors, behaviour and beliefs in the utilization of health services is increasingly being recognized. In the United States it was found that black children make substantially less use of health services than their white counterparts and this was due to differences in beliefs, related to illness (Tangerose et al 1984). The social status of family has also vital influence in the degree of utilization of health services. Children of less educated mothers with low socio-economic status and ethnic origin received less care than the others. The trend was statistically independent of the family's economic situation or level of activity faced by them suggesting a greater influence of child receiving practices rather than as a consequence of pure economic circumstance (Fergussan et al 1984). Behavioural characteristics and attitudes of mother alongside the age and health status of the child have been revealed as significant and important predictors of utilization of health services (Tessler and Mechanil 1978).

P.R. Sodani and S.D. Gupta (1988) in their study on tribal segment in Rajastan made an analysis of pattern of utilization of health care facilities with urban and rural breakup. The study proved that 50.7% of the ill persons in rural area utilized the services of traditional practitioners, while in urban areas 45.1% of the ill persons utilized the services of traditional public health facility. It is suggested that the poor equipped and low quality of public facility was the root cause for the escalation of health expenditure in both rural and urban centers.

The literature on utilization of health services has mainly looked in terms of access, in relation to geographical distance and time. Access to health care services is linked to the distance of the facility and also the time involved to reach there by the ill person (Shanon et al 1973).

To study the utilization pattern and factors determining the utilization of private and public health care services, a cross sectional study undertaken by Shenoy (1997) in both urban and rural community of Thiruvananthapuram district in Kerala state. The study was clinical and epidemiological. The study revealed that out of 4800 subjects from 1001 households consented to participate, 2237 participants had morbidity problem and out of this 1552 utilized health care services. Of the total patients utilized health care services, 67% utilized private and 33% utilized public health centers. The Study showed that for the age group 45-59 was significantly less likely to use private service as compared to adults with 14-44 years. Low SES was significantly less likely to use private service as compared to those with acute illness. The study points out the need for devising strategies to improve the accessibility and utilization of public health care services in a better manner.

The utilization of Government health services is very poor in India in general and particular in Kerala (Purohit and Siddique 1994). Based on NSS and NCAER data of 1992 he gives a picture of degree of health services utilization in India across three stage categories i.e low medium and high expenditure group. It is found that the level of government expenditure had direct influence on the availability as well as utilization of various health services in the country. The pattern of utilization shows that public institutions are utilized more for inpatient care and for outpatient care, majority of them prefer private doctors and private clinics. They revealed that the cost of hospital treatment in urban areas is higher compared to private sector hospitals. The study observed the growing popularity of indigenous non-allopathic systems and growth in private sectors involvement in expensive tertiary care.

Sreenivasa Redely (1998) highlighted the significance of accessibility, availability and quality of services in the proper utilization of maternal and child health services in Andhra Pradesh. The study reveals that utilization of antenatal services, immunization status of children, and deliveries attended by ANM (Auxiliary Nurse Midwife) increased considerably.

Sivaraju S. (1987) in his study on the differential utilization of Government hospital services in Andhrapradesh revealed that the respondents who are either partly or fully satisfied with the Govt. hospitals are relatively more in coastal Andhra Pradesh as compared to those in Rayalaseema. On the other hand in

Rayalaseema nearly one third of the respondents were not at all satisfied with the Govt. hospitals, which reveals the poor image of Govt. hospitals in the minds of the public. Better economic conditions prevailed among the people in coastal Andhra Pradesh made the people to utilize medical services in a better manner compared to other region. Cleanliness and orderliness of the clinic, time spent by the doctors in examining the patient, time spent by the patient to see the doctor, privacy provided at the clinic, facility to rest and facility offered to the accompanying person etc. was relatively better in coastal Andhra Pradesh, because of the accessibility of good infrastructural health facilities namely, optimum doctor population ratio, higher socio- economic conditions of the people as compared to their counterparts in Rayalaseema.

Pawar R.G. (1983) conducted a utilization study in five clinics of Jamnagar Medical College in India with the objective of studying factors associated with the acceptance of vaccination. The higher awareness and utilization of available immunization was observed in younger parents in both rural and urban situations. It was observed that urban children were brought at a younger age as compared to rural children. Parent's option for immunization of their children was comparatively higher in better-educated sections than in the general population of the district. The differences in social class pattern of urban and rural attendants, comparatively wider range of knowledge about vaccines was revealed among the urban acceptors. Health education about availability, and utilization of vaccine was recognized as an important weapon to boost acceptance.

Samuel et. al., (1992) in their study on utilization of health services in Karnataka, India found that the low level of economic status group had higher prevalence of sickness. It was observed that 32.2% got treatment from private sources, 41.3% from the Govt. sources and 26% from either private or the Governmental sources. It was found that for every increase of the availability of Government health facilities, there was a decrease in the proportion availing proper medical care and the reasons for choosing a particular place of treatment was due to convenience and good treatment.

The study conducted in an urban community of Meerut city in India (Garg and Singh 1985) reveal the role of elder persons in the utilization of health services. All the persons aged 50 years and above in 500 registered families constituted the study sample. A positive association between educational status of the patients and the utilization of modern medical practice was also observed. It was found that on the one hand the choice of medical care depends on factors like availability, convenience, expenditure involved and the quality of services provided, while on the other hand the belief regarding causation of diseases also plays a very important role in its determination. The education of the people about health is therefore of paramount importance in persuading the people to make proper utilization of available medical facilities more so that of the aged people, as their advice is sought in all the matters pertaining to the family health in the present social set up.

Rama V. Baru (1999) made an inter-state analysis about the structure and utilization of health services in India. It shows that in most states public sector is the major provider of curative services. Uneven spread and regional variations could be seen in the private and voluntary sectors. The study warns that if there are cut backs in the public sector, then it is likely to distort the provision of health services even further. It also noted that with the cut back of public services, the private and voluntary sectors will not immediately move into fill the gap. The private and voluntary sectors will move only into those areas where they can show profits. Since majority of the lower socio-economic groups are dependent on public provisioning, any slashing of investment in this sector will further marginalize this group. So he warns against the cutback in public provision of health services, which further deteriorates the gulf between advanced and backward areas and access among different socio- economic groups and classes.

Perception of disease is also an important factor affecting the health services utilization. Poor perception is a reflection of faulty health practices and results in health in- equality compared to better perception group in the high-class families. In his study, Stanley H. King (1962) gives the symptoms of three well-known diseases, cancer, diabetes and poliomyelitis. The analysis revealed that the number of respondents who were not able to identify even a single symptom steadily increased with decreasing education and income. Many low-income respondents perceived that cancer was a communicable disease.

Mandhakini Khandikar (1974) had conducted a study in the city of Bombay to examine the utilization pattern of maternal health services by middle-income groups and low-income groups. In addition to income she had analysed the role of age, family size, education and occupation. Within income groups she found that they too played a role in the utilization pattern of health services. The level of utilization was higher in those middle-income households, where the head of the household was engaged in white-collar job, well educated and the size of household was small.

Social class and health inequalities project the inherent inequalities, which exist not only in health but also in health care utilization services (Blexter 1976). Accordingly, the complex factors such as occupational risks, education, income living environment etc. are responsible for creating health care inequalities. To avoid health care in- equalities, he suggest for providing more doctors (women doctors) health visitors, district nurses, medical and psychiatric social workers with more responsibility.

Jatinder Bajaj (1999) in his paper attempts to study the knowledge and utilization of maternal and child health services available to woman residing in the slums of Delhi. It reveals that sanitation facilities were very worst with chocked drains and foul smell. Nearly 46% of the slum dwellers depend on private sector for their health problem. The services of NGO's are also utilized by the slum dwellers to an extent of 22% and another 22% on Government health centers and hospitals. The remaining households approach private practitioners. The study reveals low utilization of maternal and child health services provided by the public health care system. The reasons for non- utilization of these services are the lack of knowledge about these services, offered by the Government due to their illiteracy and lower accessibility of these institutions providing the services. The proportion of immunization was also very low and fell short of the achievement of the goal of universal immunization against major vaccine preventable diseases. The study points out the need for augmenting awareness among slum woman for better utilization of maternal care services provided by the Government.

Shelah S. Bloom and et. al., (2001) studied the dimensions of women autonomy and the influence of maternal health care utilizations in India. It revealed that women's freedom of movement appears to be a major determinant of maternal health care utilization among poor to middle income woman.

Rosenthal (1965) in his study found that hospital admission rate increased with the increase of age. Rodney M Coe and Albert Wessen (1965) too found in their study on the utilization of community health services that the use of health services increased with age for both sexes. The study conducted by Jerry A Solon (1966) in an outpatient Department of Beth Israel hospital at Boston showed that older age group utilized the outpatient department more than the younger age group, but the difference was not statistically significant. The difference is justified on the ground that for younger people other healthy services like school health clinic, and clinics at the place of employment were available, whereas the older people were fully dependent on Beth Israel Hospital.

Odin W. Anderson (1963) analysis of health statistics of United States showed that women utilized all sorts of health services including surgery more than men. Rodney M. Coe and Albert Wessen (1965) too found female domination over males in the health services utilization. The field data of the present study also provides a similar trend of high utilization among females especially for chronic illness as they exhibit high chronic morbidity over males.

Rajana and et. al., (1998) in their study on impact of maternal education and health services on child mortality in U.P India shows that improvement in health services education and provision of safe drinking water; all have desirable impact on child survival. The study categorically established that maternal education seems to have direct as well as indirect effects through the mothers' antenatal care as well as family formation patterns in the case of neo- natal mortality. Higher risk of death was observed for those depending on water from public sources than those having their own sources at their residence. The study proved that irrespective of socio-economic or demographic condition, mere utilization of antenatal care by pregnant woman would help in reducing neo- natal mortality to a greater extent.

Bhatnagar et. al., (1988) in their study on maternal and child health status and patterns of health status utilization in urban slums of Delhi revealed the poor health of woman and children and low level of health services utilization. The data related to utilization of maternal health care services shows very poor performance indicating the poor perception of slum dwellers about antenatal, pre-natal and postnatal health services utilization.

Financial factors were seen to be vital determinants of physician contact for the minorities, while perceived health needs seem to be the more important contributors to entry into health care (entry defined in terms of free medical care). Entry into health care found to be strongly linked to socio-economic factors. For instance a large family size cursed with low income and low education among Hispanics was a detractor from utilization than among non- Hispanics (Guendelman and Sebwalbe Joan 1986).

The significance of socio- cultural factors, behavior and beliefs in the utilization of health care services is increasingly being recognized. In the United States it was found that black children make substantially less use of health services than their white counterparts. This was due to differences in beliefs related to illness (Tangerose et. al., 1984).

Maternal use of services was identified as a powerful predictor of utilization, when the associations between maternal and ambulatory care utilization was studied. The comparison of maternal and child ambulatory care utilization patterns as measured by presence or absence of a physician visit over the course of a year as well as annual volume of use showed a close association between maternal physician utilization and child utilization. Mother's occupational and educational status along with family income and size influenced a great extent in the utilization of health care services and cause for reduction in morbidity and mortality rate (Newacbeck and Halfon 1986).

Kamal Hazari (1993) considers certain hurdles in the fuller utilization of these health care outlets. The rapid and un-organized increase in the migrant population and some attitudinal misconceptions are the limiting factors in their fuller utilization. The concept of community-based approach is the only possible way to remove such bottlenecks.

Elo Irma (1987) on the basis of data collected from Peruvian demographic and health survey made an attempt to find out the relationship between women's education and utilization of maternal health services in Peru. It was found that the formal education of woman influenced the use of maternal health services by place of residence, suggesting that much greater efforts on the part of Government are required to reach women in rural areas.

The impact of mother's education on utilization of maternal and child health services was studied with data sources from three districts of Kerala (Rajan Irudaya and Navaneethan 1994). Educated mothers use better antenatal and postnatal care, which results in better health of the mother and child. The study proved that illiterate mothers who received Tetanus injections during pregnancy was only 41%, whereas this was 82% among mothers who received 10+ years of schooling. Though the study failed to analyze the urban rural break up in the utilization of maternal and child health services and the special problems of urban mothers in Kerala, the study revealed that the education of mothers is responsible for better health status of the state compared to other states in India.

Donaldson (1976) in his study based on data from urban and inner urban areas revealed that, it is the inner urban area in which slum households are huddled together which suffers a lot due to health in equalities. The health services and health status of inner urban area is worse compared to the urban centre. The problem of un- employment, over crowding, air pollution, infant and child mortality, birth rate and mortality rate etc are also high in inner urban areas compared to urban centers. The study suggests for adopting a package measures for improving the health status and encouraging the health services utilization on the part of people in the inner urban areas. The health services and health status of inner urban area is worse compared to the urban centre. The problem of un-employment, overcrowding, air pollution, infant and child mortality, birth rate and mortality rate etc. are also high in inner urban area compared to urban centers. The study suggests for adopting a package measures for improving the health status and encouraging the health services utilization on the part of people in the inner urban areas.

Daksh Pandit and et al (1996) observed that there are socio-cultural and behavioral barriers like female illiteracy, poor economic status of women etc, which affect the maternal and child health services utilization. The study revealed that there is no dearth of health care facilities in terms of hospital beds, equipments, sophisticated treatment methods and highly specialized health manpower, still the health status of large proportion of population specially mothers and children in urban areas remain poor.

Rajna and et al (1998) in their study on impact of maternal education and health services on child mortality in U.P. India shows that improvement in health services, education and provision of safe drinking water all have desirable impact on child survival. The study categorically established that maternal education seems to have direct as well as indirect effects through the mother's antenatal care as well as family formation patterns in the case of neo- natal mortality. Higher risk of death was observed for those depending on water from public sources than those having their own sources at their residence. The study revealed that irrespective of socio-economic or bio-demographic condition, mere utilization of ante- natal care by pregnant woman would help in reducing neo-natal mortality to a greater extent.

Bhatnagar et al (1988a) in their slum study revealed the high utilization of private sources of health services by the urban dwellers in Delhi. It shows that 62% use purely private sources, 24% both Govt. and private and only 14% used Govt. sources alone indicating the sad state of affairs of the Govt. health centers and the need for improving the accessibility and utilization of Govt. health centers.

Duraiswamy (1998) examines the levels, differentials in overall and gender specific morbidity prevalence rates across the socio- economic and demographic groups in rural and urban Tamil Nadu based on the NSS data of 1986-87. The age and sex specific distribution of ills are presented and the determinants of morbidity at the individual level are analyzed. The study revealed the need for targeted health intervention to reduce the morbidity among children and elderly persons. The study also revealed that communicable diseases are concentrated in the younger age group, while aged people suffer more from non-communicable ailments. The sex wise morbidity prevalence shows that males have higher risk of being sick compared to females.

Dhanalakshmi and Moorthy (1993) in their study of socio-economic and demographic factors influencing child morbidity in two districts of Andhra Pradesh proved that without socio-economic epidemiology, bio-medical epidemiology could make a limited contribution to the reduction of morbidity. They revealed that morbidity is influenced by the size of the household, type of family, occupation of the husband and surviving children. Larger households, joint and extended families increase the level of infant and child morbidity due to more members in the families. The study empirically proved the effect of socio- economic and demographic factors on the morbidity pattern. But it neglects the environmental factors affecting morbidity.

Due to overcrowding, inadequate and poor housing, lack of adequate safe drinking water, lack of drainage, non-collection of waste water and its improper disposal etc. led to pollution of water and land in urban towns and cities to a degree much greater than in rural areas. The environmental degradation is the vital factor responsible for the emergence of both communicable and non-communicable diseases in an urban community (Shreekant V Khandewala 1996).

Adolescents and youth are exposed to many health problems including STDS, HIV and teenage pregnancies, primarily because of hypersexual activity and general ignorance. The study provides (Ramachandra Sastry 2000) the vivid picture of city slum with high incidence of promiscuous adolescent and youth sex, lack of hygiene ignorance and poverty generally have a very high incidence of sexually transmitted disease and other reproductive tract problems. There is also a high degree to morbidity due to termination pre- marital and out of wedlock pregnancies which are terminated by quacks and untrained birth attendants.

Primary urban health problems are neglected at the expense of specialty health services offered in the urban centers. Yesudian (1984) focused the poor health status of the metropolitan cities inspite of spending major chunk of funds on health services. His study based on morbidity and mortality analysis of the city of Bombay reveals that primary health care is the vital need of the city, but which is neglected for providing special health care through major hospitals including medical college hospitals and certain municipal General hospitals. The poor living in the urban slums are facing the problem of safe drinking water, the sewage problem of latrine facilities. All these worsen the prevalence of communicable diseases in the city. He observed that the health sector has failed to meet the primary health problems of the people in the urban slum.

High mortality rates associated with lower socio-economic status people are unable to utilize better health care services. Persons in lower socio- economic positions die on an average at a younger age than those in higher positions. In-equality in the face of death has been observed in almost all states in different population and using different indicators of socio- economic positions, such as social or occupational class, educational attainment, income and housing characteristics (Antonovsky 1967, Feinstein 1993, Mackenbach and others 1997). One percent increase in the schooling of woman will result in 9% of reduction in mortality rates (Jeffrey 1987).

Malati Damodaran and et al (1994) in their study about the breast feeding practice of mothers revealed that urban mothers introduced commercial milk supplements at an earlier period compared to mothers in rural which accounts for higher morbidity among the urban children. They suggested that the effect of urbanization on breast-feeding and supplementary feeding was striking in urban centers. It also revealed that attack of all child diseases was higher in urban areas compared to rural one.

Chojhacka and Adeybola (1984) in their study proved that although both medical and non-medical factors contributed to the change in morbidity pattern, the role of socio-economic factors were also found to be significant. Kaplan and Taylor (1985) have shown association between the occupation of the father and infant and child morbidity.

After reviewing the health scenario in the country Kapilalakshmi (2000) suggested that Government and the community should take steps to improve the quality of life of the people. Non-communicable diseases are a major health problem and the study empirically proves the effect of socio-economic and demographic factors on the morbidity pattern.

Conclusion

Many studies have been done in the general area of health services utilization. As is clear from the preceding detailed review, existing literature in the field of health services utilization and morbidity problems in urban India; attempts made so far suffer discerningly from the following significant limitation. None of the studies touch the core reality of health issues of the down trodden and under privileged groups in the urban slums and urban areas. The present study also take into account the perception of health needs before analyzing the utilization pattern which is also an improvement over the existing literature on health services utilization. Major studies are based either urban or urban rural comparison in health services utilization and health problems and none of the studies compares the health problems and health services utilization of urban and urban slum on the basis of their socio-economic set-up, and other variables related to health services. All these studies have a predominant bias of being macro studies. Such studies by their nature do not touch the core-reality, since it is not possible to know from the top what is going on at the inner base of the mountain of the problem. The correct approach necessarily is the slicing method that is to divide the problem into small pieces and then an intensive effort to assess them really.[6]

NOTES

1. The burden of disease is not easy to assess and information on morbidity patterns in India is extremely scarce (this is one symptom, among others, of the low priority assigned to health matters in public policy). Nevertheless, a number of recent studies throw useful light on disease patterns in India. See particularly Murray and Lopez (1996) Vaidynathan (1997) Sheriff (1999) Duraiswamy (2000) International Institute for Population Sciences (2000); also World Bank (2001a) and the studies summarized in that report.
2. World Bank (2001a), P.28 This proportion is much larger than India's share of the world population, which is about 17%.
3. See World Bank (2001a) PP 32.9 and 81-9.
4. Though literacy is not a direct measure of health status, It can indirectly contribute to the enhancement of heath status.
5. The number of identified slums increased from 705 in 1985 to 1169 in 1996 and population also increased from 2,78,674 to 3, 580121 over the same period.

6. What is intended to highlight is the fact that, it is always better to have several representative micro studies before undertaking a micro level study for making safe generalization at the national level. In any empirical exercise having a bearing on policy study remains evergreen.

REFERENCES

Anderson R and Adey L.A., (1978), Access to Medical Care in the U.S. Realised and Potential, Medical Care Vol. 16, pp.533-46.

Antia W.H., (1999), The Social Path to Kerala's Health, in Rethinking Development, Kerala's Development Experience Edited by Ommen M.A., Concept Publishing Company, New Delhi.

Antonovsky, Aaron, (1967), Social Class, Life Expectancy and Overall Mortality, Milbank Memorial Fund, Quarterly, Vol. 45, pp. 31-73.

Azurin J.C. and Alvero M., (1974), Field Evaluation of Environmental Sanitation, Measures Against Cholera, Bulletin of World Health Organisation Vol. 51 No.1 p.21.

Banerjee D., (1973), Health Behaviour of Rural Population, Impact of Rural Health Services, Economic and Political Weekly Vol. 18.

Benyoussef A. Wessen A.R., (1974), Utilization of Health Services in Developing Countries, Tunisia, Social Science and Medicine, Vol. 8, pp. 287-304.

Bhatnagar et. al., (1988a), Utilization of Health Care Facilities in an Urban Slums of Delhi. Health Population Perspective and Issues, Vol. 11 No. 4, pp. 162-170.

Bhatnagar S. Dosajh V. and Kapoor S.D., (1988), Maternal and Child Health Status and Patterns of Health Care in Urban Slums of Delhi. Health Population Perspectives and Issues, Vol. II, No.3.

Blexter M., (1976), Social Class and Health in Equalities in Co-carter and John Peel (eds) Equalities and in-equality in Health, Academic Press, London, pp.11-124.

Brink LSG and Nader P.R., (1981), Pattern of Primary Care Utilization in a Triethnic Urban Population of School Children, Medical Care, Vol. 19, pp. 591-599.

Chojhacka H. and O. Adeybola, (1984), The Determinants of Infant and Child Morbidity and Mortality in Lagus, Nigeria, Social Science and Medicine, 19 (8) pp. 799- 810.

Daksh Pandit et. al., (1996), Evaluation of MCH Services Provided by an Urban Health Centre, Health and Population Perspectives and Issues, Vol. 19 No.1. pp. 41-49.

Davids Salvekar , (1975), Economic Class Differentials, Access to Care, Comparison Among Health Care System, International Journal of Health Statistics Vol. 15, No. 3 pp. 373-396.

Dhanalakshmi N. Moorthy M.S.K., (1973), Socio-economic and Demographic Factors Influencing Child Morbidity, Indian Journal of Social Work, Vol. LIV, No.3, pp. 429-436.

Donaldson R.J., (1976), Urban and Suburban Differentials in Co Carter and John Peel (eds) Equalities and in Equalities in Health, Academic Press, London, pp. 127-140.

Duraiswamy P., (1998), Morbidity in Tamil Nadu, Levels Differentials and Determinants, Economic and Political Weekly, Vol. XXXIII, No.17.

Duraiswamy P., (2000), 'Health Status and Health Care in Rural India' Mimeo, Department of Econometrics, University of Madras, Chennai.

Ebrahim G.J., (1984), Primary Care and Urban Poor, Journal of Tropical Paediatrics, No.1, Feb. 29, (2-3).

Elo Irma T., (1987), Utilization of Maternal Health Services in Peru, the Role of Women's Education, Populations Centre, University of Pennsylvania, Philadelphia.

Fein Stein Jonathan S., (1993), The Relationship Between Socio-economic Status and Health. A Review of Literature, Milbank Memorial Fund, Quarterly, Vol. 71, pp. 279-322.

Fergussan D.M., Dineoad M.E., Horwood C.J. and Shannoi F.T., (1984), The Utilization of Pre-school Health and Education Sources, Social Science and Medicine, Vol. 19, No.11, pp. 1173-1180.

Garg B.S. and Singh J.V., (1985), Belief about Causation of Diseases and Preference of Utilization of Health Agencies by Elderly Persons in Urban Community, Health and Population Perspectives and Issues, Vol.8, No.1.

Gerald Rosenthal, (1965), Factors Affecting the Utilization of Short Term General Hospital. American Journal of Public Health and Nations Health, Vol. 55, pp. 1739.

Gesler W.M. and Meade M.S., (1988), Locational and Population Factors in Health Care Seeking Behaviour in Savannah Georgian Health Services Research, Vol. 23, pp. 443-462.

Govt. of India, (1997), Compendium of Environmental Statistics 1997, Central Statistical Organization, Dept of Statistics, Ministry of Planning and Programme Implementation, New Delhi.

Govt. of India, (2001), Census of India, Provisional Population Totals, Keralä, Series 33.

Govt. of Kerala, (1995), Malaria Persistence in the District, Records in the District Medical Office, Kannur.

Govt. of Kerala, (1997), Urban Slums in Kerala 1995-96 Town Planning Department, Trivandrum.

Govt. of Kerala, (1998), Report of the Steering Committee on Health Water Supply, Sanitation and Nutrition Ninth Five Year Plan 1997-2002 State Planning Board p. 63.

Govt. of Kerala, (1999), Malaria Persistence in Kerala, Records with the Directorate of Health Services, Thiruvananthapuram.

Guendelman Sylvia and Sebwalbe Joan, (1986), Medical Care Utilization by Hispanics Children, Medical Care, Vol. 24 No. 10 pp. 925-940.

Haynes R., (1991), In-equalities in Health and Health Service Use, Evidence from the General Household Survey, Social Science and Medicine Vol. 33, pp. 361-368.

Hazari Kamal, (1993), Contraceptive Acceptance and Immunization Status in Urban Slums in Umashankar P.K. and Misra Girish (eds) Urban Health System, Reliance Publishing House, New Delhi.

Heller Celia S., (1969), Structural Social in Equality and Social Stratification, Macmillan Company, New York.

International Institute for Population Sciences, (2000), National Family Health Survey, 1998-99 (NFHS-2); 11PS, Mumbai.

ISEC, (1999), Rapid Household Survey Phase I, Under Reproductive Child Health Project, Population Research Centre, Banglore.

Jah S.S., (1986), Structure of Urban Poverty, the Case of Urban Slums, Popular Prakashan, Bombay.

Jatindar Bajaj, (1999), Knowledge and Utilization of Maternal and child health services in Delhi slums, The Journal of Family Welfare, Vol. 45 No.1.

Jean Dreze and Amartya Sen, (2002), India, Development and Participation, Oxford University Press, New Delhi.

Jeffrey Robin, (1987), Govt. and Culture How Woman made Kerala Literate, Pacific Affairs, Vol. 6, No. 3.

Jerry A. Solon, (1966), Pattern of Medical Care Variation Among a Hospital Outpatients, American Journal of Public Health and Nations Health, Vol. 56, pp. 883.

Joseph George, Desrochers John, Mariamma Kalathil, (1983) Health Care in India, Centre for Social Action, Banglore.

Kannan K.P. et. al., (1991), Health and Development in Rural Kerala, Kerala Sasthra Sahithya Parishad, Thiruvanathapuram.

Kapilalakshmi M.C., (2000), Review of the Present Health Status of India. Emerging Health Problems and their Solutions, Health Population Perspectives and Issues, Vol. 23 No.1, pp. 1-10.

Kaplan and Taylor C., (1985), Bio-social Factors in the Epidemiology of Childhood Asthma in British National Sample, Journal of Epidemiology and Community Health, Vol. 39, pp. 152-156.

Khandiker Mandhakini, (1974), Utilization of Social and Welfare Services in Greater Bombay, Bombay, Tata Institute of Social Sciences.

Kumar M. and Kumar R., (1987), Environmental Impact of Slums on Health in R. Kumar (ed). Environmental Pollution and Health Hazards in India Ashish Publishing House, New Delhi p. 58.

Mackenbach, Johan P. and Anton E. Kust, (1997), Measuring the Magnitude of Socio-economic in-equalities in Health. An Overview of Available Measures Illustrated with 2 Examples from Europe. Social Science and Medicine, Vol. 44, No.6, pp. 757-771.

Madhava Menon, (2000), The Health Status of Kerala, Health for Millions Vol. 26 No. 2, p.11.

Malati Damodaran, Soman C.R., Paniker P.G.K., (1994), A Study of Infant Feeding and Child Rearing Practices in Thiruvanathapuram city and Rural Areas, C.D.S, Thiruvananthapuram.

Mukherjee R.K., (1971), Six Villages of Bengal, Popular Prakashan, Bombay.

Mukhopadhyay, (1997), Report of the Independent Commission on Health in India, Voluntary Health Association of India, New Delhi, p. 87.

Murray, C.J.C. and Lopez A.D. (eds), (1996), The Global Burden of Disease, M.A. Harward University Press, Cambridge.

Mutatkar R.K., (1995), Public Health Problems of Urbanization, Social Science and Medicine, Vol. 4 No.7.

Nangia Praveen, Kamla Gupta and Tiwari N.C., (1996), Emergence of Slums, A Case Study, Thane Urban Agglomeration, Indian Journal of Social Work, Vol. 57, No.4.

Nayar M.D., (2000), Needed Multi Pronged Strategy, The Hindu, 25th April.

Odin W. Anderson, (1963), The Utilization of Health Services in Howard Freeman and others (eds) Hand Book of Medical Sociology, New Jersey, Prentice Hall Inc. p. 363.

Panicker P.G.K., (1979), Resources Not the Constraint on Health Improvement. A Case Study of Kerala, EPW No.14, No.44.

Panicker P.G.K., (1985), Health Care System in Kerala and its Impact on Infant Mortality in S. Halstead et. al., (eds) Good Health at Low Cost, Rock Feller Foundation, New Delhi.

Panicker P.G.K. and Soman C.R., (1994), Health Status of Kerala. The Paradox of Economic Backwardness and Health Development, C.D.S. Trivandrum.

Paul P. Appaswamy, (1993), Health and Environment, the Interaction in Urban Areas, 23rd Inter Disciplinary Research Methodology Workshop on Health and Human Resources Development, Madras Institute of Development Studies, Madras.

Pawar R.G., (1983), Utilization of Preventive Services, A Study of Vaccine Acceptors, Indian Journal of Preventive and Social Medicine, Vol. 14, No.1 and 2.

Pawl W. Newacbeck and Halfon, (1986), The Association Between Mothers and Children, The use of Physicians Service, Medical Care, Vol. 24 No.11 pp. 30-38.

Purohit Brijesh C. and Siddique Tasleem, (1994), Utilization of Health Services in India, Economic and Political Weekly, Vol. 29, No. 17.

Rajan Irudaya and Mohana Chandran P., (1999), Estimating Infant Mortality in Kerala, Economic and Political Weekly, Vol. 34. No.20.

Rajan Irudaya and Navaneetham, (1994), Maternal and Child Health Immunization on Infant Survival in Kerala, Janasamkhya Vol. 12 No.1 and 2.

Rajna and et. al., (1998), Impact of Maternal and Child Health Services on Child Mortality in U.P. Asia Pacific Population Journal, Vol.13, No.2 pp. 27-36.

Rama V. Baru, (1999), The Structure and Utilization of Health Services. An Inter-state Analysis in Mohan Rao (ed.) Disinvesting in Health, Sage Publications, New Delhi, pp. 127-140.

Ramachandra Sastry K., (2000), Promoting Responsible Sexual Behaviour Among Youths in Banglore in Sunil Misra (ed.) Voluntary Action in Health and Population Age, Sage Publications, New Delhi, pp. 156-166.

Ramankutty V. et. al., (1993), How Socio-economic Status Affects Birth and Death Rates in Rural Kerala India, Results of a Health Study, International Journal of Health Services, Vol 23. No. 2.

Rao P.S., (1981), Study on Socio-economical and Demographic Correlation of Medical Care Utilization and Health Behaviour, Research Report, ICSSR, New Delhi.

Ratna Raj, (2001), Kerala Maintains Better Urban Health, Yojana Vol. 45, pp. 46-47.

Rodney M. Coe and Albert M. Wessen, (1965), Social Psychological Factors Influencing the Use of Community Health Resources, American's Journal of Public Health and Nations Health, Vol. 55, p. 1739.

Rossi Espagnet A., (1984), Primary Health Care in Urban Areas: Reaching the Urban Poor in Developing Countries, A State of the Art Report by UNICEF and WHO, Geneva.

Rupert Samuel G.E., Gupta J.P. and Wadha V.S., (1992), Satisfaction and Utilization of Primary Health Services Facilities in Karnataka, Population Perspectives and Issues, Vol. 15, No. 3 and 4, pp. 140-152.

Sen N. K., (1987), Commodities and Capabilities, Oxford University Press, Bombay.

Shanon G.W., Sinner J.C., Buschar R.C., (1973), Time and Distance, The Journey for Medical Care, International Journal of Health Studies vol. 3 No. 2, pp. 237-244.

Shariff Abusaleh, (1995), Health Transition in India, Differentials and Determinants of Morbidity in India by Disaggregated Analysis Working Paper No. 57, NCAER, New Delhi.

Shariff, Abusaleh, (1999), India, Human Development Report, Oxford University Press, New Delhi.

Shelah S. Bloom, David Wypij and Monica Das Gupta, (2001), Dimensions of Woman Autonomy and the Influence on Maternal Health Care Utilization in a North Indian City, Demography, Vol. 38, No.1, pp. 67-76.

Shenoy K.T., (1997), Determinants of Health Care Service Utilization in Kerala, Clinical and Epidemiological, Project of the United Nation Development Programme.

Shreekant V. Khandewala, (1996), Health Administration and the Weaker Sections in an Indian Metropolis, Devika Publications.

Sivarajan, (1987), Factors Influencing Differential Utilization of Govt. Hospitals Across Two Contrasting Regions, Hospital Administration, Vol XXIV No.13 and 4.

Sodani P.R., and Gupta S.D., (1988), Health Care Expenditure, Results from a Study in Tribal areas of Rajasthan, Margin Vol 13, No.1 pp. 66-76.

Soman C.R., Malati Damodharan, Rajasree S., Kutty V.R. and Vijaya Kumar K., (1990), High Morbidity and Low Mortality, The Experience of Urban pre-school Children in Kerala, Journal of Tropical Paediatrics Vol. 37, pp. 17-41.

Sreenivasa, Reddy, (1998), Health Care Services for Maternal and Child Health through Primary Health Centre, An Innovative Approach. Health and Population Perspectives and Issues, Vol. 21, No.1, pp. 45-51.

Stanley H. King, (1962), Perception of Illness and Medical Practice, Russel Sage Foundation, New York, pp. 125-175.

Sundar Ramamani, (1995), Household Survey of Health Care Utilization and Expenditure, the Working Paper No.53, NCAER, New Delhi.

Sundar, Ramamani, (2000), The Fertility Reduction Project in a Low Income re-settlement Colony in Sunil Misra (ed) Voluntary Action in Health and Population, Sage Publications, New Delhi, pp. 178-188.

Sureender K., (2000), Health and Family Welfare Through Community Participation. Dharavi Slum Bombay in Sunil Misra (ed) Voluntary Action in Health and Population, Sage Publications, New Delhi, pp. 167–177.

Surekha G., (1999), Health Care Utilization, Differential by Socio Economic Groups and by Sex, Unpublished M. Phil Thesis, Centre for Development Studies Trivandrum.

Tangerose Suezanne, et. al., (1984), Differences in use of Health Services by Children According to Race, Medical Care, Vol 22. No.9. pp. 848-853.

Tessler R. and Mechanil P., (1978), Factors Affecting Children's use of Physician Services in a pre-paid Group Practice, Medical Care, Vol. 16, pp. 933.

Umashankar P.K. and Misra Girish eds., (1993), Urban Health System, Reliance Publishing House, New Delhi.

Underwood C.F., and Margett S., (1987) Cited in Adair L.S. Vanderslice and Zohoori urban- rural Differences in Growth and Diarrhoeal Morbidity of Filipino Infants, Urban Ecology and Health in Third World ed. by Schell C.M. Smith M.T. and Bilsborough, Cambridge University Press, Cambridge.

Vaidyanathan, A., (1997), 'Studies on Health and Health Care: A Review of Findings', Mimeo, Madras Institute of Development Studies, Chennai.

Wan T.T.H. and Soifer S.J., (1974), Determinants of Physician Utilization. A Casual Analysis, Journal of Health and Social Behaviour Vol. 15, pp. 100–108.

WHO, (!992), Role of Health Centres in the Development of Urban Health System, WHO, Geneva.

World Bank, (1993), World Development Report 1993, Washington.

World Bank, (1998), World Resources 1998-99, Oxford University Press, New York.

World Bank, (2001a), India's Future Health Systems: Issues and Options, Draft Report, World Bank, New Delhi.

World Bank (2001b), World Development Indicators 2001, Table 27 Washington D.C., World Bank.

Yesudian C.A., (1984), Primary Health Care in Urban Areas, Problems and Issues, Indian Journal of Social Work, Vol. XLV.

Yesudian C.A.K., (1981), Differential Utilization of Health Services in a Metropolitan City, Indian Journal of Social Work Vol.12 No.4.

Appendix – 1.1 : Health Status and Human Development Indicators - A Global View

Countries	Life Expectancy	IMR 1997	MMR * Per 10,000 live births 1990	Infants with low birth weight (in %) 1997	Doctors per 10,000 people 1997	Adult literacy (in % 1997)	Population Without access: To safe water (in %)1997	Population Without access: To sanitation (in %)1997	Real GDP per capita 1997
All developing Countries	64.4	64	491	18	76	71.4	28	57	3240
Least developed countries	51.7	104	1041	22	14	50.7	41	63	992
Sub Saharan Africa	48.9	105	979	15	16	58.5	50	56	1534
Arab State	65.1	53	396	11	111	58.6	18	29	4094
East Asia	70.0	37	96	9	116	83.4	32	73	3601
East Asia (excluding China)	72.8	15	114	9	134	96.1	10	1	14300
South East Asia & the Pacific	65.9	45	449	12	19	87.9	31	41	3697
South Asia	62.7	72	551	32	44	52.2	18	64	1803
South Asia (excluding India)	63.0	75	512	29	33	48.4	15	46	2147
India	62.6	71	570	-	48	53.5	19	71	1670

Contd....

Appendix – 1.1 : (Contd...)

Countries	*Life Expectancy*	*IMR 1997*	*MMR * Per 10,000 live births 1990*	*Infants with low birth weight (in %) 1997*	*Doctors per 10,000 people 1997*	*Adult literacy (in % 1997)*	*Population Without access*		*Real GDP per capita 1997*
							To safe water (in %)1997	*To sanitation (in %)1997*	
China	69.8	38	95	-	-	82.9	33	76	3130
Latin America & Caribbean	69.5	33	191	9	136	87.2	22	29	6868
East Europe	68.6	26	62	-	356	98.7	-	-	4243
Industrialised countries	77.7	6	13	6	253	98.7	-	-	23741
World	66.7	58	437	17	122	78.0	-	-	6332

Source: Human Development Report 1999 *Maternal Mortality Rate.

2

Conceptual Framework

One of the major paradox of modern medical system is that it has sufficient resources to provide high quality medical care on an unprecedented scale, yet substantial proportion of the population is unable to receive even minimally adequate medical care. Advances in medical sciences and changes in the organization of medical practice have enabled contemporary physicians to provide the highest quality of care to the ailing persons. But at the same time, the cost of this care has markedly reduced the availability of this care to different segment of population in equal proportion. The low-income families are considerably more disease prone and have considerable need for medical attention due to their typical living environment. Such families have less ability to pay for the needed medical services. "The poor social classes are more prone to a variety of behavioral patterns, that are not conducive to promoting health. These include a greater prevalence of smoking and drinking" (Smith et al 1990).

Many diseases and most of the epidemics affect the poor sections of the population in serious proportions. Poverty, squalor and disease go together. Poverty becomes the root cause of malnutrition, disease and death. So the poor section of people requires medical care in correspondingly greater proportions.

A direct consequence of inadequate official attention to health matters is that the Indian population continues to be exposed to a high incidence of communicable diseases and readily preventable illnesses. Communicable diseases are seen to be responsible for more than half of the burden of disease in India (Murray and Lopez, 1996). Many basic illnesses that have radically declined in large parts of the developing world in recent decades (such as tetanus, measles, pneumonia, leprosy, malaria, hepatitis, tuberculosis etc.) continue to be common in India.

The burden of disease also falls very unevenly on different sections of the population. The health in-equalities are very sharp in India compared with many other countries including poor ones (World Bank 2001). Class differences in health achievements in particular are large by international standards. The same applies to gender based in-equalities in health. (Drez and Sen 2002) These features of the health situation in India relate closely to the state of health services, and going beyond that, to the persistent neglect of health matters in public policy. One symptom of this neglect is the abysmally low level of public expenditure on health – around 0.8 percent of G.D.P. Among 142 countries for which the relevant data are available, only six (Barundi, Cambodia, Georgia, Indonesia, Myanmar and Sudan) have a lower figure for public expenditure on health as a proportion of GDP (Drez and Sen 2002). The low level of public expenditure on health in India is aggravated by (1) a highly inefficient use of available resources, and (2) sharp in-equalities in access to health care based on region, class, caste and gender[1].

Critical analyses of India's health care system have been dominated by two very special diagnoses, which deserve comment, given their hold. According to one school of thought, India made the cardinal mistake of following the western model of health care instead of promoting indigenous approaches[2]. Another view holds that health care in India has been undermined by the chronic in-efficiencies of public services and that greater reliance on the private sector would be, then by far the best answer.

The concept of health cannot be seen in a narrow sense as a state of sheer absence of disease. It should be seen as a broad spectrum where health is viewed as integral well being of the individuals (Mathur and Sharma 1995). This holistic perception of health is well defined as "health is state of complete physical, mental (or emotional) and social well being of a person and not mere absence of diseases (WHO 1988) The old ways of measuring the health status which included indices like mortality rates, particularly infant mortality rates and life expectancy seems to be of re-examination today in the context of holistic perception of health. Presently health status indices include in addition to IMR, variables such as drinking water, sanitation, morbidity etc. (Berg 1973, Cemper 1984).

Health is the prime concern of an individual. Within the family the concern for health is mutually shared by the individual forming the group. The head of the family bears the responsibility for attainment and maintenance of the health of its individual members. The individual, the family, the community and the state can be seen as partners sharing the unavoidable responsibility to make available health to all.

The Issues- Socio-economic Status and Health Status

The link between socio economic status and health status is well recognized. In most cities, the poor classes have a lower level of health as suggested by most indicators such as infant mortality rate, nutritional status, maternal mortality rate, infants with low birth weight and life expectancy. The Black report from Britain brings out the poor health status among the working classes (Smith et al 1990) infant mortality rates among the blacks in the USA are several fold higher, when compared to whites from the same area. This is more a reflection of their social and economic condition than a difference due to race. Similar studies have been published from South Africa and Brazil.

In a study, Kerala Sasthra Sahitya Parishad (KSSP) on Kerala (Kutty V.R. et al 1993) State, in India revealed that Socio–economic status was found to have definite influence on birth and death rate with higher socio-economic status resulting in lower birth and death rates. This effect was independent of such confounding variables as age structure of people and religion and region. It also revealed that higher risk of mortality among the poor households could partly be explained by the material deprivation. The higher birth rates could be the result of poorer educational attainments.

There are mainly two hypothesis, which attempts to explain this phenomenon. The poverty hypothesis says simply that poor health outcomes are a result of poor living conditions. People with inadequate income have less to eat, do not live in properly constructed houses and may drink contaminated or polluted water. Finally, because of their poverty, they may also lack access to medical intervention when needed. Naturally their health condition is poor. The behavioral hypothesis posits that poor people also have a propensity to indulge more in behavior patterns which are not conducive to good health such as alcoholism, over indulgence in smoking, use of narcotic drugs etc. Domestic violence is also more common among them. Part of this may be due to the fact that the poor also tend to be poorly educated. In urban slum and other places where poor people concentrates, the behavioral hypothesis certainly takes predominance.

While this general picture holds good, it can also be seen that the affluent are more likely to be affected by certain diseases when compared to the poor. This is true of non-insulin dependent diabetes in many countries. Coronary heart disease is more common among the affluent in Kerala as has been brought out by a recent study in Kerala (Kutty VR et al 1993a) Obesity is also seen more commonly among the rich in developing countries. But in the West, coronary heart disease and obesity are again more common among the poor, because the better classes with their access to more life choices have made behavioral modifications such as regular exercise, giving up smoking and eating right kind of food which has made possible to reduce the rate of these diseases. In our study we could find similar pattern of morbidity according to the socio-economic status of households. Hence socio-economic status is an important determinant of health status and health services utilization.

Conceptual Framework

The present study is based on the hypothesis that socio-economic status plays a vital role in the health status and the extent of utilization of health services. The basic assumption of the study is that as socio- economic status improves, the morbidity prevalence of illness will be less; at the same time the utilization of health services would be high. This may be due to the fact that the better socio-economic class due to their better living environment, the chances of affecting infectious or communicable illness is very rare. So the morbidity prevalence rate will be less at the same time these group of people due to their better knowledge and awareness about various illness, they seek medical aid even for slight illness which are neglected by the low socio- economic class. Similarly even from the very beginning of the symptoms of chronic illness, the better socio economic class seek medical aid, thus the chances of utilization of health services is higher among these group. In this study the socio-economic status of the household is the edifice on which the entire health service utilization aspect is examined. The socio- economic status is based upon a composite index of education, occupation, and income as developed by Kuppuswamy (Gupta and Mahajan 1995). Accordingly households were divided into five socio-economic status: namely the upper class or SES_1, the upper middle class or SES_2 the lower middle class or SES_3, the low class or SES_4 and the very low class or SES_5.

The theoretical framework of this study involves the channeling of the basic factors affecting health services utilization and its pattern of differences among various SES groups. It also examines the awareness of people about diseases and how they meet the perceived health needs.

Factors Affecting Health Services Utilization

The socio-economic classes differ in their basic characteristics, which reflects in the extent of utilization of health services. Important factors determining health services utilization are the following.

Demographic Factors

Age, sex, and marital status are the three vital factors in the utilization pattern of health services. The health needs vary from age to age and it is the vital factor in deciding the extent of utilization of health services. The morbidity problem of children and aged will be high compared to youths. So they require more health services. The study held in Tamil Nadu (Duraiswamy 1998) clearly revealed that morbidity is high at both in the lower and upper age category and the nature of the morbidity curve is 'U' shape in character. A study held in Kerala by Ramankutty and Thankappan (1994) revealed that illness reporting is high at the extremes of age (i.e. below 5 and above 60 yeas of age). Recently geriatrics as a branch of medicine had developed to a great extent for providing curative are to the aged. Geriatrics and paediatrics now constitute the major chunk of curative health care provided by the modern health care system.

Sex

It is also an important demographic factor to be considered for determining the volume of health services utilization. Women have more health problems compared to men because it is who undertake the task of procreation. So the chance of utilization of more health services during pregnancy as antenatal, natal and postnatal care is high among them. Many studies have established the high linkage between sex and health services utilization (Rodney M Coe and Wessen Albert 1965), whereas in the utilization of health services for morbidity prevalence, it could be seen that male dominates over females.

Socio-economic Factors

Since education, occupation and income have taken as the measuring rode for dividing households according to their socio- economic status, it has a bearing on the utilization of health services.

Education

Education plays a significant influence in shaping proper perception on the part of people for better health care needs. Lower perception as a result of poor education creates a negative health situation which augment the health needs. Moreover their ignorance about health services due to low or poor education status act as a hurdle in acquiring better health services. Education acts as a double-edged sword in cutting the extent of utilization of health services. The study is supported with data related to un-utilization and under utilization of health services especially preventive health services (immunization of children) by the illiterate or less educated mothers. Many studies have established the impact of education on health services utilization that educated seek immediate treatment, whereas illiterate and poorly educated will postpone it till the illness worsens (Rodney M Coe, Wessen Albert 1965, Khandekar 1974).

Occupation

Though occupation is not directly linked to one's perception of health needs and health services utilization, it exerts a strong influence on other factors that are vital in health services utilization. People involved with particular occupation require more health services compared with others. We could observe that workers like fisherman and those related with fishing always suffer from one or other type of skin diseases like scabies and they have to undergo treatment for the same. If it worsens, their daily income will be reduced, further treatment will be retarded and their health situation worsens. Similarly many beedi workers face the morbidity of allergic asthma. They are compelled to utilize more health services to mitigate the intensity of such health problems. Above all it is the occupation, which determines one's standard of living, which on the other hand has an impact on the health status.

Income

Income as a most important measuring rode to assess one's economic status has an important bearing on the degree of utilization of health services. We assumed that higher the income, higher would be the utilization of health services. Lower income groups because of their marginal income face a hand to mouth existence. When they became sick, they prefers only a delayed treatment and majority of them start treatment only when it incapacitates them. Similarly when they start treatment for certain chronic illness, it is observed that many of the very lower sections (SES_5) could not continue treatment for long as it requires huge amount, at the same time there is less chance for quick relief. In such cases they discontinue treatment for financial reasons. Income determines the stage of treatment and also the extent of treatment. These together decide the volume of health services utilized by a particular section of the community. Many studies established the impact of income on the utilization of health services (Odin W Anderson 1963, Rodncy M Coe and Albert Wessen 1965, Khandekar 1974) There is differences of opinion regarding the influence of income on health services utilization. We from our field experience realised that economic condition of the household is an important factor in determining health status and the extent of health services utilization.

Perception of Symptom and Disease

Similar to demographic and socio-economic factors, perception factor is also vital in deciding the volume of health services utilization. Knowledge of disease varies from upper class to lower class. All of them may not provide equal seriousness for a particular illness in a same manner. For e.g. Headache, or cold, though they are quite common among the people, many of them take it as serious illness and go for treatment. At the same time, some may avoid treatment even for body pain or back pain. In the present study such perceptional difference on the part of the households in different SES categories is noted. The study by Stanley H king (1962) indicates the poor perception on the part of people lead to faulty health practice and thereby un-utilization or under utilization of health services.

The utilization of health services by the people is not influenced by any one particular factor alone. All the factors act one way or other in determining the quantum and quality of health services utilized and these factors interact with one another among different socio-economic groups to create different patterns of utilization.

Anderson and his colleagues have set out a model for health care utilization called the structural model for health care utilization (Anderson R and Newman JF 1973) In this model, three sets of determinants have been proposed, that influence health services utilization. Society and system determinants are postulated to influence individual determinants, which directly impinge on service use. Societal determinants include the current state of knowledge as well as people's attitude and beliefs about health and illness. The factors operate either directly to influence the individual determinant or indirectly through their influence on the system factors. System factors include health services resources (both volume and distribution) and organization of health services. However, it is the individual determinants that are directly related to health services utilization (Figure 2.1)

Figure 2.1 : Factors affecting health services utilization according to Anderson's model

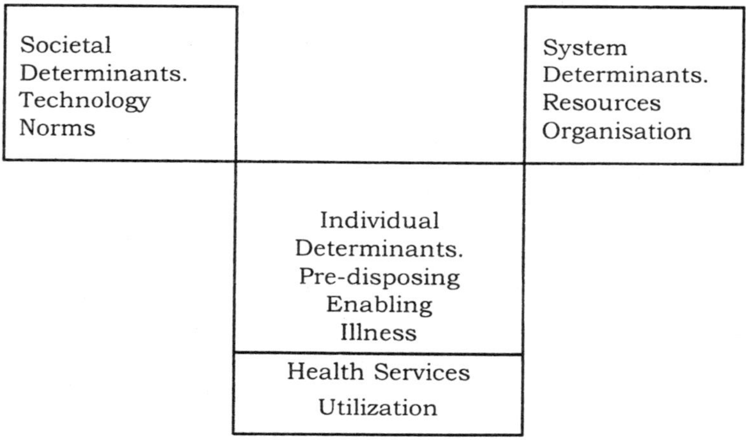

Individual determinants of health services utilization are further sub divided into three main categories, according to Anderson model (Figure 2.2) They are 1) Pre-disposing variables which are divided into demographic factors and social structure 2) Enabling factors and illness level.

Individual determinants of health services utilization

1. Pre-disposing variables which are sub divided into
   (a) Demographic factors such as age, sex and marital status and
   (b) Social structure, such as education, occupation family size religion and beliefs (e.g. values, attitudes and knowledge)

Figure 2.2 : Individual determinants of health services utilization

Pre-disposing	Enabling	Illness level
Demographic	Family	Perceived disability
Age	Income	Symptoms
Sex	Insurance	Diagnosis
	(type of accessories)	
Marital status	Community	General health
Social structure	Facilities	Evaluated health condition
Education	Costs of Service	Symptoms
Race	Region	Diagnosis
Occupation	Urban Rural	
Family size		
Ethnicity		
Religion		
Beliefs		
Values		
Attitudes		
Knowledge		

2. Enabling variables, on the other hand are the conditions, which permit the individual to health services.
   (a) Family factors such as income, health insurance type and accessibility.
   (b) Community factors such an availability, cost of service and residence.
3. Illness level is probably the most direct factor related to health service use. It includes:
   (a) Perceived disability, symptoms, and diagnosis and general health.
   (b) Evaluated health condition by health personnel (Symptoms and diagnosis)

Anderson health care utilization model depicts the various determinants that influence the utilization of health services namely societal determinants, system determinants and individual determinants. The model developed by us in figure 2.3 deals with the process of health care service utilization. The starting point for the process of health services utilization is the health status of the people of a given community. The health status generates the need for health or medical care. The need for health care influence some way the attitude of the individual (who becomes a patient) towards the heath care he enjoys or receives. Another and probably the most significant factor is the perceived value of health services, which are offered to him and are used by him. In other words the behavior of an individual towards health care partially depends upon the need for such care (e.g. its intensity, duration) but to a greater extent upon his evaluation of health services needed by him and available to him.

The patients or households socio-economic status will decide the choice of whether the free medical service or paid medical services which ultimately estimates the effective demand for health services. The need for health care plus, the socio-economic status creates an effective demand and this seems to be one of the two decisive factors contributing to the utilization of health services. Another factor is undoubtedly the supply of health services. Supply of health services available is divided into public and private and in each category all the system of medicine like allopathic, auyurveda, homoeopathy and other systems of treatment are available. In addition to this, their physical accessibility and financial feasibility is also an important element in deciding the volume of health services utilization. Physical accessibility means the distance to the health centers chosen availability of transportation facility, working time of health centers etc. Thus the degree of utilization of health services is finally dependent upon two basic factors. The supply of health

Figure 2.3 : Model of Health Service Utilization Process

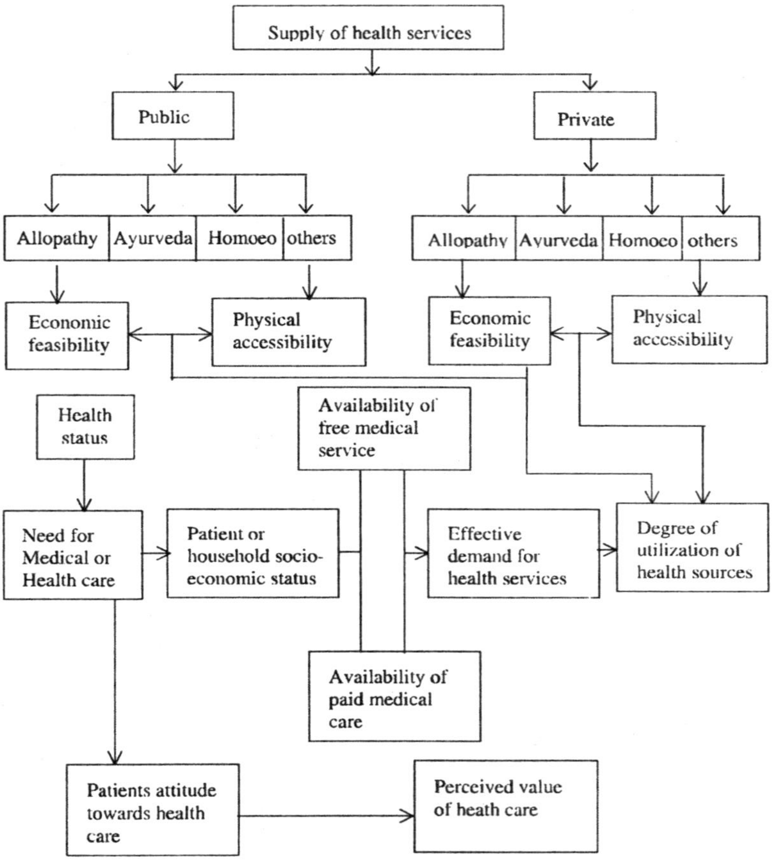

services coming from different inputs resources and the effective demand for health services whose primary source is the health condition of the people which generate their needs for health services supported economically by their financial resources.

The question regarding the factors affecting high morbidity and health services utilization is extremely significant. Once the causes for this high morbidity and factors affecting health services utilization are identified correctly, it would be easy to devise ways to control the high morbidity and augment the volume of utilization of health services. Some of the fundamental questions that need to be examined are:

1. Whether the perception of diseases, symptoms and treatment on the part of the households/ people affected the utilization of health services.
2. Is there any linkage between education, occupation and income on the one side and morbidity prevalence and utilization of health services on the other
3. Does the environment have an impact on the morbidity prevalence of the people?
4. Does the Govt. hospital meet the health needs of the area?
5. What is the extent of accessibility of doctors to serve the inpatients in Govt. hospitals and how the patients react to their tests and treatment?
6. Can health services through Govt. hospitals be re-organized to serve as many people as possible? Are there any serious deficiencies and maladies on the part of Govt. hospitals?
7. Are there any in-built constraints in rendering fair services to patients in Govt. hospitals?
8. How the urban mothers behave in the utilization of maternal and child health services.
9. What measures be developed or devised for improving the socio- economic' status of the urban poor for reducing morbidity and improving health service utilization.

Methodology

The study was conducted in two areas, an urban slum and an urban centre of Thallassery Municipal Corporation. As the urban public health infrastructure

(Govt. of Kerala 1998) is comparatively weak in northern region of Kerala compared to southern region, the study is conducted in one of the highest urban populated district (Govt. of India 1991) of Kerala, the Kannur District. Since the study focuses on urban slum, the Thallassery Municipal Corporation area is best suited for the study as it accounts for the slum density of 30,000 (Govt. of Kerala, 1997) and it is the highest slum density of northern Kerala. This density creates severe health problems arising from unhealthy living environment, as households are huddled together without any basic amenities of life.

As per the Municipal records the Municipal area is divided into 50 wards consisting of 16432 households (Govt. of Kerala 2001). In 1995 the Town planning Department had identified 10 important slum pockets in Thallassery consisting of 738 households and at the time of starting fieldwork their strength was estimated at 875 households. By considering different constraints including the time available for the research work, the size of the sample was fixed at 200 households. As the study covers both urban slum and urban area, separate samples were selected from both urban slum and urban.

For conducting the study the sample area was divided into two broad divisions. The first division consists of entire 50 words of the Municipality, which form the study area for the urban community. Eight Hundred and Seventy Five slum households scattered in 8 municipal wards form the study area for the urban slum community represent the second division. For the urban area a sample size of 120 (0.77% of population) households was selected through simple random sampling according to population proportion to size method. As there exist 15557[3] households (Urban Family Survey 2001) in 50 wards, for obtaining best representative sample all 50 wards were divided into 7 blocks on certain socio-economic aspects revealed by the urban family survey (Govt. of Kerala 2001). Since sample size is fixed at 120, these 120 households were selected from these 7 blocks by simple random sampling. Accordingly, one ward was chosen at random from each block (one ward only in respect of block I to VI and 3 wards in respect of Block VII) and sample households' proportional to the size of the households in each block was chosen. Thus, a size of 25, 13, 11,18, 31, 8 and 14 households were selected respectively from block I to block VII. The details of households selected at random are given in Appendix 2.1 and 2.2.

The urban slum households are scattered in 8 wards of the municipal area. From these eight wards slum households were listed separately in each ward and the eight slum settlements consisting of 875 households were divided into three blocks on the basis of nature of occupation as these three groups differ in this aspect. The first block consists of households with majority of whom engaged in fishing and fish related employment huddled together in the coastal belt. The second block includes with households majority of whom engaged in weaving and beedi works and settled in the midland region of the city. The third block consists of household engaged in all types of unskilled works including ragpickers, street vendors, construction workers, tamil migrant labourers, head load workers, sale workers, manual labourers etc.

As the sample size for the urban slum was fixed at eighty and all the households in these three blocks were listed ward wise and samples were taken at random. Through population proportion to size (PPS) method a sample of 58 households was selected at random from ward No.41 representing the 1st block. From the Second Block a sample size of 9 households was selected and since there is only one ward under this block, it was selected from ward No. 43. From the third block a sample size of 13 households was selected proportion to its size and it was selected at random from ward No. 36. For details of he slum households selected for the study see the Appendix 2.2.

Division of Households According to SES Category

The groupings of the households according to their socio-economic status both in the slum and urban area was done as per the SES scale developed for urban family by Kuppuswamy with modification by Gupta (Gupta and Mahajan 1995) The characteristics selected to capture socio- economic status were per capita income, education and occupation. These characteristics were given weight in descending order from 7 to 1 in the case of education, 10 to 1 in the case of occupation and 12 to 1 in the case of per capita incomes the former denoting the better off position and the latter denoting bottom position. The weights assigned to these three variables were added together and a composite index was prepared to grade 5 different classes. Though SES composite index is based upon 3 variables, a weightage is assigned for each variable according to 7-point pre-defined scale. The total of three weightages gives the SES score, which is graded to indicate 5 classes. The weightage of different items for determining the SES of urban family as per the Kuppuswamy SES scale is as follows. (Table – 2.1)

The total scores indicate SES as follows.

26-29	Upper class
16-25	Upper middle
11-15	Lower middle
5-10	Upper lower
Below 5	Lower

By considering the typical problems in the study area the researchers has made some modifications for the Kuppuswamy SES scale suggested by Gupta. The modifications made is in the percapita income slab which was replaced by a new slab as per the cut of income fixed for the poverty line by the Planning Commission.[5]

The education and occupation categories suggested by Kuppuswamy were kept same, but the different occupational categories available in the field were defined.

Table 2.1: Weightage of Different Items for Measuring the Socio-economic Status of Urban Family

	Items	*Weightage*
A.	Education of head of household	
	Professional degree/ Postgraduate and above	7
	BA/BSc/B.Com Degree	6
	Higher Secondary/ Pre degree/ Intermediate	5
	High school certificate	4
	Middle school completion	3
	Primary school completion	2
	Illiterate	1
B.	Occupation of head of household (Last occupation in case of retired)	
	Profession	10
	Semi-profession	6
	Clerk shop owner farm owner etc	5
	Skilled worker	4
	Semi- skilled worker	3
	Unskilled worker	2
	Unemployed	1
C.	Per capita income (Rupees per month)[4]	
	Rs.800 and above	12
	400-799	10
	300-399	6
	200-299	4
	120-199	3
	40-119	2
	Below 40	1

1. Un- employed means those who have no employment or activity for their livelihood. 2. Unskilled worker is defined as those workers whose work requires no intensive training or special skill. The workers who engaged in field such as beedi, hotel, construction, mason, fishing, sales, ragpicking, street vending, head load work etc. were treated as unskilled workers. 3. Semi-skilled workers are those whose work requires some type of skill

like tailors, embroidery workers, weavers etc. 4. Skilled workers are those workers whose work requires some sort of regular training and skill which reflects in the quality of work done by them, like electricians, welders, fitters, turners, plumbers and drivers of different motor vehicles. 5. Clerk, shop owner, businessmen, farm or plantation owner, government servants of class III category etc. were treated as the Vth category. 6. Semi - profession category includes school teachers, class I and class II officers in Govt. services and companies. 7. Professional category includes doctors, advocates engineers, chartered accountants or such persons with professional qualification.

Another modification carried out in the Kuppuswamy SES scale is the changes in the SES scale fixed for the Lower category of the SES scale. The researchers with their personal rapport with many slum households realized the need for changing the ceiling fixed for lower category from the SES score 5 fixed by Kupuswamy to SES score 6. Because to consider the case of a literate unskilled worker living below the poverty line as per the Kuppuswamy SES scale, his SES score will be 5 and will be included in the upper lower SES category. Many such families are living in urban slum and urban area. The researchers from their field experience realised that, if these households are included in the upper lower category then it will be a gross injustice to them. So the researcher felt the need for including such households in the lower category as their living conditions and environment is extremely worst. So the SES score of lower category was changed from 5 to 6. In addition to this the name of all SES categories was also changed and renamed it as upper class or SES_1, upper middle class or SES_2, lower middle class or SES_3 low class or SES_4 and very low class or SES_5.

In the present study for measuring SES of an urban family, the education, occupation and income of the head of the household was taken into account. The criteria of selecting a head of the household were a problem. The households' social status depends on the status of the head of the household. The eldest persons in the family cannot be treated as the head of the household, because in most cases, they were illiterate or unemployed or receivers of no income, but households social status is very high due to highest position of other members of the household. So the principal earner is taken as the head of the household. The principal earner here refers to one who contributes maximum income to the family.

The weightage of different items for determining the SES of an urban family as per the modified version of Kuppuswamy SES scale developed and used in the present study is as follows. (Table 2.2)

The score indicates SES as follows.

26- 29	Upper class or SES_1
16-25	Upper middle class or SES_2
11-15	Lower middle class or SES_3
6-10	Low class or SES_4
Upto 5	Very low class or SES_5

Rationale of SES Scale

Income occupation and education are the three major criteria in deciding the social status of households living in urban areas. Since the study focus the linkage of socio-economic status on health status, the formation of socio-economic scale is highly significant in this study. So utmost accuracy and precision was taken into account in eliciting maximum reliable information from the respondents regarding income from all sources, occupation and education.

The rationale for selecting the different SES score range for different socio- economic classes is justified. The SES score 26-29 is the highest score. To include under this class, the head of the household should be a professional with professional qualification with per capita

Table 2.2: Weightage of Different Items for Measuring the Socio-economic Status of Urban Family (Modified)

	Items	*Weightage*
A.	Education of head of household	
	Professional degree/ Post graduate & above	7
	B.A./B.Sc/B.Com Degree	6
	H.S.C/Pre- degree/ inter mediate	5
	High school certificate	4
	Middle school completed (V^{th} to VIIIth std.)	3
	Primary school or literate (upto IVth)	2
	Illiterate	1
B.	Occupation of head of household (Last occupation in case of retired)	
	Profession	10
	Semi - profession	6
	Clerk/Shop owner etc.	5
	Skilled worker	4
	Semi - skilled worker	3
	Un skilled worker	2
	Unemployed	1
C.	Per Capita Income[6] (Rupees per month)	
	1501 and above	12
	1001 to 1500	10
	801 to 1000	6
	701 to 800	4
	601 to 700	3
	478 to 600	2
	Upto 477	1

income above Rs.1000/- per month. Few such households had come across in the present study and since they top in the education, occupation and income status such households at any cost should be treated as upper class or SES_1.

Business community, semi- professional groups and certain clerical and supervisory cadre employees mostly represent the SES2 or upper middle class category. The education status of heads under this category may vary from SSLC to graduation level with the per capita income range above Rs.1000/- per month. They can never be treated as upper class at the same time they could not be bring to the level of middle class. So they are grouped under a class above the middle class called the upper middle class or SES_2 with SES score range of 16 to 25.

The SES_3 or lower middle class is represented by SES score 11-15. This group is mostly represented by skilled workers with S.S.L.C. level of education and per capita monthly income range of 601 to 801. As they do not possess the status of a middle class community, they are grouped as lower middle class. In the urban sample the proportion of this group is comparatively high.

The SES_4 or low class is with SES score in the range of 6-10. Semi-skilled and unskilled workers mostly represent it with per capita monthly income in the range of 478 to 700. They are not in the lowest ebb in their socio- economic status at the same time not at par with that of the lower middle class. So separate group called the low class or SES_4 is created. As many households are there with these characteristics in the urban and slum sample with SES score rating in the range of 6 to 10. This class called the low class is justified in the sample.

The very low class or SES_5 with SES score upto 5 is the most vulnerable and deprived groups in the sample area, as head of the households' may be either illiterate or primary level educated with unskilled or no occupation and per capita income below poverty line (Rs.477). This very low class is most common in urban slum and to a limited extent in urban area[7]. The very low class is also worth considering for the SES score developed for the study.

As per the SES scale discussed above, the households in the study sample were divided and grouped as follows in table 2.3. It is to be noted that in the urban sample the proportion of very low class is comparatively less compared to the low class and middle class. Similarly the very high class or upper class is also comparatively less. It is the upper middle and lower middle class, which dominates the population in the study area. In the case of slum, the proportion of very low or SES_5 category is around 50%, lower class category is 38.75% and slum area is void of upper class and upper middle class. Eleven percent of the slum households' belongs to SES_3 category, since they possess comparatively better education and occupation compared to the very low class in the slum. One important fact emerged from the sample data is that around 14% of the urban households and 50% of the slum households are below the poverty line as per the Planning Commission definition of poverty line for the year 1999-2000.

Table 2.3 : SES with Number of Households in the Sample

SES Class	*Urban*		*Slum*	
	No. of households	*% total*	*No. of households*	*% total*
SES_1	12	10	-	-
SES_2	40	33.3	-	-
SES_3	34	28.3	9	11.25
SES_4	20	16.7	31	38.75
SES_5	14	11.7	40	50.00
Total	120	100	80	100.00

Source : Survey Data.

Rationale for Selecting Education, Occupation and Per Capita Income for Measuring the SES Scale.

The adoption of Kupppuswamy SES scale and the inclusion of the variables like education occupation and per capita income can be justified on several grounds as it is directly linked to the health status and health care services utilization.

Education : Education and health were given very much emphasis in Kerala even from the time of princely states. Progress in education, especially female education has contributed significantly towards the health status of Kerala (Navaneetham and Irudaya Rajan 1994). Education also provides the skills for acquiring good occupation. Most of the middle class occupation is dependent on one's education level. Therefore this variable is used in the study and weights were given from 7 to 1 ranging from professional qualifications to illiterate.

Occupation : Occupation decides one's way of life to a great extent. Occupation classifies the population into professional, semi-professional, skilled workers, semi-skilled workers etc. and each of this category has its own way of life. Their dress, manners, type of school in which the children admits, the way of speech, the routine daily life etc. differ from one class to another. Similarly their health awareness also vary depending on the nature and type of occupation they carry. By considering the significance of occupation in health status and health services utilization, in the present study weights were assigned for occupation ranging from 10 to 1, 10 for the highest professional occupation and 1 for the unemployed.

Per capital income : As the utilization of health services depends on purchasing power, low purchasing power results from low income reflects in the poor health status of the people. To derive actual figure of per capita income, the total income of all members of the household was divided with number of members in the household.

NOTES

1. For detailed evidence, and further explanation, see e.g. Banerji (1996), Deolalikar and Vashishta (1996), NCAER (2000). A NCAER study reveal that three rupees of public expenditure on curative health services reach the richest 20% of the population for every rupee that reaches the poorest 20 percent
2. Even the 'national health policy' of 1983, in its valuable effort to re-focus public policy on public health and primary

health care, attributes existing biases to 'the almost wholesale adoption of health manpower development policies and the establishment of curative centres based on the western models, which are in appropriate and irrelevant to the real need of our people (Govt. of India 1985, P.35).

3. After excluding 875 slum households scattered in 8 municipal wards enumerated through fieldwork.
4. Income categories are relevant to the current prices based upon 1988-89, All India Price Index of 803 for industrial workers.
5. Poverty line here refers to the minimum amount required per person per month at 1999-2000 prices (Rs.477 for urban Kerala). Planning Commission (Govt. of India 2001) has estimated state specific poverty lines for rural and urban area. State specific urban poverty lines have been estimated using the original state specific poverty lines identified by the Lakdawala Committee and updating them to 1999-200 prices using the consumer price index for industrial workers for urban households. Thus the lowest per capita income limit was fixed at Rs.477 and other income slabs were arbitrarily fixed.
6. This classification uses percapita income derived by calculating total income of all members of the family and divided it by the number of members in the family.
7. Around 50% of the sample households are under this category.

REFERENCES

Anderson R. Newman J.F., (1973), Societal and Individual Determinants of Health Care Utilization in the U.S. Milbank Memorial Fund Q. 8, pp. 132-142.

Anderson W. Odin, (1963), The Utilization of Health Services in Howard Freeman and others (eds) Handbook of Medical Sociology, Prentice Hall Inc, New Jersy, p. 363.

Banerjee, (1996), Political Economy of Public Health in India, in Das Gupta Monica, Krishnan T.N., and Chen Lincoln C. eds. Health Poverty and Development in India, Oxford University Press, Delhi.

Berg Robert, (1973), Health Status Indexes, Hospital Research and Education Trust, Chicago.

Cemper G.E., (1984), Determinants of Health levels in Developing Countries, Research Studies Press Ltd., England.

Deolalikar, Anil and Vashishtha, Prem, (1996), The Health and Medical Sector in India : Potential Reforms and Problems, IRIS Working Paper 9 Center for Institutional Reform and the Informal Sector, University of Mary Land.

Dreze, Jean and Sen Amartya, (2002), India Development and Participation, Oxford University Press, New Delhi.

Duraiswamy, P., (1998), Morbidity in Tamil Nadu, levels Differentials and Determinants, Economic and Political Weekly XXXIII No.17.

Govt of India, (1991), Census of India 1991, Office of the Census Commissioner, Series-12, Ministry of Home Affairs, New Delhi.

Govt. of India, (1985), National Health Policy, Loksabha Secretariat, New Delhi.

Govt. of Kerala, (1997), Urban Slums in Kerala, Town Planning Department, Thiruvananthapuram.

Govt. of Kerala, (1998), List of Allopathic Medical Institutions in Kerala, Directorate of Health Services, Thiruvananthapuram.

Govt. of Kerala, (2001), Urban Family Survey, Household level Data Prepared by the Municipal Corporation, Thalassery, as Part of Urban Family Survey in Kerala.

Gupta M.C. and Mahajan B.K., (1995), A Text Book of Preventive and Social Medicine, Japee brothers, Medical Publishers, New Delhi, p. 35.

Irudaya Rajan S. and Navaneetham K., (1994), Maternal and Child Immunisation on Infant Survival in Kerala, India, Janasamkhya, Vol. 12, No. 1 and 2.

Khandekar, Mandakini, (1974), Utilization of Social and Welfare Services in Greater Bombay, Tata Institute of Social Services, Bombay, pp. 65-70.

Kutty V.R. Thankappan K.R., Kannan K.P and Aravindan K.P., (!993), How Socio-economic Status Affects Birth and Death Rates in Rural Kerala, India, Results of a Health Study, Indian Journal of Health Services, Vol. 23. No. 2.

Kutty V.R. and Thankappan K.R., (1994), Morbidity Profile in Kerala with Respect to Age Education Gender and Income,

International Congress on Kerala Studies, Abstracts, AKG Centre for Research Studies, Thiruvananthapuram 27 - 29 August.

Kutty V.R., Balachandran K.G. Jayasree A.K., and Jessy Thomas, (1993a), Prevalence of Coronary Heart Disease in Rural Population of Thiruvananthapuram District, Kerala, India, International Journal of Cardiology, Vol. 39, pp. 59-70.

Mathur Indu and Sharma Sanjay, (1995), Health Hazards, Gender and Society, Rawat Publications, New Delhi.

Murray C.J.L. and Lopez A.D. (eds), (1996), The Global Burden of disease, M.A. Harvard University Press, Cambridge.

National Council of Applied Economic Research, (2000), Who Benefits from Public Health Spending in India, Mimeo, NCAER, New Delhi.

Rodney M. Coe and Albert M. Wessen, (1965), Social Psychological Factors Influencing the Use of Community Health Resources, American Journal of Public Health and Nations Health Vol. 55, p.1024.

Smith, G.D. Bartley M., and Blane D., (1990), The Black Report on Socio-economic in-equalities in Health 10 years on, British Medical Journal 301: pp. 373- 377.

Stanley H. King, (1962), Perception of Illness and Medical Practice, Russel, Sage Foundation, New York, pp. 125-127.

WHO (1988), Managing System for Better Health Facilitator Guide, WHO, Geneva.

World Bank, (2001), India's Future Health Systems: Issues and Options, Draft Report, World Bank, New Delhi.

Appendix 2.1 : Divisions of Urban Households into 7 Blocks – Urban sample size 120

Wards with families at risk whose rates exceeds more than 11%		Wards with more than 35% of families having at least one member is in outside the state and country mainly in gulf region		Wards with families having acute problem of drinking water		Wards with families of Muslim domination		Wards with families of Hindu domination		Wards with better socio-economic status		Wards with slum house holds (Excluding slum house holds in each ward)	
Block 1		Block II		Block III		Block IV		Block V		Block VI		Block VIII	
Ward No.	No. of House-holds	Ward No.	No. of House-holds	Ward No.	No. of House-holds	Ward No.	No. of House-holds	Ward No.	No. of House-holds	Ward No.	No. of House-holds	Ward No.	No. of House-holds
6	322	10*	353	1	310	11	352	5	272	14	274	40	165
7	314	13	324	2	262	15	366	8	373	28	302	41*	162
9	323	20	362	3	314	35	317	18	362	29*	426	42	103
16	334	39	310	4	268	38	354	21	353			45	194
19	276	44	386	12*	311	47*	302	22	319			43*	216
24	300					49	256	23	301			36	273
27	336					50	324	25	313			48*	385

Contd....

Appendix 2.1 : (Contd....)

33*	329							26	365			17	333
37	354							30*	398				
46	337							31	342				
								32	339				
								34	291				
Total 10	3225	5	1735	5	1465	7	2271	12	4028	3	1002	8	1831
Ward selected is 33 sample size 25		Ward selected is 10sample size 13		Ward selected is 12 sample size 11		Ward selected is 47 sample size 18		Ward selected is 30 sample size 31		Ward selected is 29 sample size 8		Ward selected are 41,43 and 48 and sample size is 3,5 and 6 respectively Total 14	

* Wards selected at random.

Appendix 2.2 : Division of Urban Slum Households into Three Blocks – Urban Slum Sample Size 80

Wards with majority of slum households derive their income from fishing and fish based occupations		Wards with families majority of whom derive their income from beedi and manual works		Wards with majority of household engaged in unskilled works such as rag picking, street vending, construction works, head load workers etc.	
Ward No.	No of House holds	Ward No.	No of Households	Ward No.	No of Households
40	140	43*	103	17	17
41*	165			36*	95
42	255			48	25
45	75				
Total 4	635	1	103	3	137
Ward selected at random is 41 sample size 58		Ward selected at random is 43 and sample size is 9		Ward selected at random is 36 and sample size is13	

* Wards selected at random.

3

Problems and Determinants of Urban Health with Special Reference to Kerala

It has been assumed that with high concentration of health facilities and services in the cities compared with rural areas, urban health problems are less. However, for the urban poor and those living in shanty towns, the level of access to health facilities falls below the minimum equitable level, where primary health care facilities, their location, resources, quality and performance are often poor, their links to deprived communities are inadequate and their utilization is low (WHO1992). Though all varieties of health services are available in our cities, not all sections of the community are benefited by these facilities. There exist wide gap in the utilization pattern of health services and health improvement in urban area. Health improvement is influenced by three factors (Nayar 1999), a) health factors, which include medical intervention, b) health promoting factors such as housing, water supply, sanitation and hygiene. c) non-health factors which include social and economic factors. Above all the trends in urbanization that followed is also responsible for the change in health status of urban population.

Urbanization–A Global View

There has been rapid increase in the proportion of urban population in most of the countries of the world. The industrialized high-income economies witnessed a sharp rise in the urban population during the last 50 years. The world urban population was estimated as 46% in 1997. It was 74% for upper middle-income countries, 76% for high-income country and 67% for Europe and Central Asia. Out of the total urban population in the world, 59% is living in the city with population capacity of less than 7,50,000, 19% in between 7,50,000 to 3 million and 22% in cities with population beyond 3 million. Whereas it was 59%, 18% and 13% respectively for India indicating that India is at par with world rate of urbanization with regard to percentage of urban population living in three categories of cities. (World Bank 2000).

Urbanization in India

Urbanization and industrialisation so stably married in the western world were often divorced in India. (Peach 1970). The former moved at a faster pace than the latter resulting in a direct shift from agriculture to service as in other developing countries too. The growth of urban areas has produced concentration of population of unprecedented magnitude and Governments have failed to manage the resulting environmental and social service problems (Engelmen Robert 1997). The recent study of urban population growth in developing countries found that on an average each 1 percent increase in national population growth yields a 1.78% increase in urban population (Andrew Mason 1996).

The history of urbanization in the Indian sub continent goes as far back as about 2500 B.C. When a number of urban communities were flourishing in the Indus Valley like the Valleys of Tigri's, Euphrates and the Nile, the fertile Indus Valley experienced early urbanization associated with the first agricultural revolution in the world based upon invention of plough and irrigation (Raja Bella 1986). The Indus Valley civilization came to an abrupt end around 1700 BC. A kind of Dark Age seems to have started followed by the Vedic age with the advent of Aryans in Western India from Central Asia around 1400 B.C. Towns multiplied rapidly during the rule of Mauryas from 323 B.C. to 185 B.C. It was a period of political stability and economic progress. Urbanization started appearing in the Kaveri delta of South India due Partly to evolution of local civilization and partly to cultural impact of Aryans migration from the north (Sjobery 1973) A phase of stagnant urbanization followed the period of Gupta empire. It was a period when the Roman Empire also declined. With the advent of the British, trends in urbanization changed though there occurred a set back in the initial stages.

Tempo of Urbanization 1901-2001

Table 3.1 indicates the tempo of urbanization in India during 1901-2001. It reveals that: a) the proportion of urban population and the total number of urban centres has been increasing decade after decade. b) there are decadal fluctuations in the growth of the number of towns and cities. This is due to the de- classification of certain towns and the addition of new towns and cities. Further It may be noted that there is a steady rise in the total number of urban agglomerations and towns after 1961. c) As per 2001 census, a total of 285.35 million people live in urban area as against 25.85 million people in 1901. Thus during the last one century, the country's urban population has increased by little over 11 times.

Further Table 3.1 also reveals a few additional indicators of tempo urbanization. They are (i) Annual exponential growth rate of urban population. (ii) Annual percentage rates of growth in urban population to the total population and (iii) The annual growth rate of the level of urbanization. It is very important to note that the annual rate of growth has declined from 3.83% during

Table 3.1: Trend of Urbanization in India 1901-2001

Census Year	No. of UA's towns	Total Population	Urban Population	Urban Population as % of total population	Decadal growth rate of urban population (%)	Tempo of Urbanization (% per year)		
						Annual exponential growth rate	Annual gain in/ of urban population	Annual rate of gain in/ of urban population
1901	1827	238 396 327	25 851 873	10.84	-	-	-	-
1911	1815	252 093 390	25 941 633	10.29	0.35	0.03	-0.06	-0.51
1921	1949	251 321 213	28 086 167	11.18	8.27	0.79	0.09	0.86
1931	2072	278 977 238	33 455 989	11.99	19.12	1.75	0.08	0.72
1941	2250	318 660 580	44 153 297	13.86	31.97	2.77	0.19	1.56
1951	2843	361 088 090	62 443 709	17.29	41.42	3.47	0.34	2.47
1961	2365	439 234 771	78 936 603	17.97	26.41	2.34	0.07	0.41
1971	2590	548 159 652	109 113 977	19,91	38.23	3.21	0.19	1.08
1981	3378	683 329 097	159 462 547	23.34	46.14	3.83	0.34	1.72
1991	3768	844 324 222	217 177 625	25.72	36.19	3.09	0.24	1.02
2001	4378	1027 015 247	285 354 954	27.78	31.39	2.73	0.21	0.80

Source: 1. Government of India 1, census of India 1991, Series –1 paper 2 of 1991 provisional population totals: Rural urban distribution, Registrar General and Census Commissioner, India. Kerala.

2. Government of India.1 Census of India 2001, series –33 paper 2 of 2001 provisional population totals: Rural urban distribution Director of census operation, Kerala.

3. Government of India .1 (2003) Document Rural urban 2001- office of the Registrar General of India, New Delhi.

1971-81 to 3.09% during 1981-91 and to 2.73 in 1991-2001. During the decade 1971-81 the level of urbanization increased by 3.43 percentage points. During 1981-91 decade the increase has been only of 2.38 percentage points and for 1991-2001 decade the increase has been only of 2.06. As a consequence the annual rate of gain in percentage of urban population has also declined from 1.72 to 1.02 in for the decade 1981-91 and to 0.80 in 1991-2001. This indicates that the tempo of urbanization in India has slowed down during the last two decade 1981-91 and 1991-2001 compared to the previous decade (i.e. 1971-81).

Urbanization trend at the state level is given in table 3.2. It shows that among the states Mizoram, followed by Goa and Tamil Nadu accounts for the highest proportion of urban population in the last census. The four South Indian states Kerala, Karnataka, Tamil Nadu and Andhra Pradesh, has emerged as the largest urban populated states, whereas at the all India level, Mizoram has become the largest urban populated state (proportion of urban population) followed by Goa and Tamil Nadu. The states where the percentage of urban population estimated at higher than the all India level of proportion of urban population (i.e 27.78) are Punjab, Haryana, Mizoram, West Bengal, Gujarat, Maharashtra, Karnataka, Goa and Tamil Nadu. Among the states Bihar, Manipur and Kerala recorded a decrease in the percentage to urban population in the 2001 census compared to 1991. The 2001 urban population of India accounts for 27.78% as against 25.72% in 1991. Thus, a little over one fourth of the population is urbanized.

Urbanization Trends in Kerala 1901-2001

Kerala has been witnessing an increasing trend of urbanization from 1901. But the degree of urbanization (the percentage of population living in urban areas) has been very slow in the sense that it was invariably lagging behind the corresponding all India figures from 1901 to

Table 3.2 : Level of Urbanization in Major States

State	*Level of Urbanization*	
	1991	*2001*
India	25.72	27.78
Andhra Pradesh	26.84	27.08
Assam	11.08	12.72
Bihar	13.17	10.47
Gujarat	34.40	37.35
Haryana	24.79	29.00
Himachal Pradesh	8.70	9.79
Jammu &Kashmir	23.83	24.88
Karnataka	30.91	33.98
Kerala	26.44	25.97
Madhya Pradesh	23.21	26.67
Maharashtra	38.73	42.40
Orissa	13.43	14.97
Punjab	20.26	33.95
Rajasthan	22.88	23.38
Tamil Nadu	34.20	43.86
Uttar Pradesh	19.89	20.78
West Bengal	27.39	28.03
Goa	41.02	49.47
Meghalaya	18.69	19.63
Mazoram	46.20	49.50
Manipur	27.69	23.88
Nagaland	17.28	17.74
Sikkim	9.12	11.10

Source: 1. Govt. of India, Census of India 1991, series-1 paper 2 of 1991 Provisional Population totals. Rural urban distribution, Registrar General and Commissioner, India.

2. Government of India, Census of India 2001 series –33 Kerala paper 2 of 2001, provisional population totals, Director of Census operations, Kerala.

1981. It is interesting to note that there has been a tremendous growth in the degree of urbanization in Kerala in the 1980's, which exceeds the all India figures. The degree of urbanization has been on the increase in Kerala between 1901-1991 but declined slightly in 2001 as shown in table 3.3. This is mainly due to reduction in population in class III towns from 31.86% in 1981 to 19.07% in 1991 and to 14.05% in 2001. Similarly in the case of class IV cities urban population was 6.78% in 1991, it declined to 4.98% in 2001 witnessing 20.91% negative decadal growth rate.

From the table 3.3 it can be seen that there is only a slow growth in the proportion of population living in urban areas for the period 1901 to 1941, which was only 7.11% in 1901 to 10.84% in 1941. The position has picked up from 1981. It is significant to note that there is a

Table 3.3 : Urban Population in Kerala and India

Census Year	*Kerala Degree of urbani-zation*	*Decennial growth of urbani-zation (percent)*	*India degree of urbani-zation*	*Decennial growth rate of urban population (percent)*
1901	7.11	-	11	-
1911	7.34	15.44	10.4	0.35
1021	8,73	29.78	11.3	8.27
1031	9.64	34.58	12.2	19.12
1941	10.84	30.47	14.1	31.97
1951	13.48	52.72	17.6	41.42
1961	15.11	39.89	18.3	26.41
1971	16.24	35.72	19.93	35.72
1981	18.74	37.64	23.7	46.14
1991	26.39	60.97	25.75	36.19
2001	25.97	7.64	27.78	31.39

Source: 1. Government of India, Census of India series 33 Kerala Paper 2 of 2001 provisional population totals, Director of Census operations, Kerala.

phenomenal increase in the degree of urbanization in terms of decennial growth rate between 1941 and 1951 as per table 3.3. But from 1961 to 1981 there is a slight stagnancy in the decennial growth rate of urban population in Kerala. From 1901-1911 to 1921-1931 the decennial growth rate of urban population has shown a steady increase. It has shown a fluctuating trend from 1931-1941 to 1961-1971. The decennial growth rate of the urban population was the highest during 1981-91 (69.97%) and the lowest (7.64%) during 1991-2001. However, it is observed from table that the degree of urbanization in Kerala has been relatively low compared to all India figures from 1901 to 1981. The unprecedented growth that has been witnessed in Kerala in 1991 is a turning point in the trend of state's urbanization, but witnessed an abrupt decline in 2001.

Profile of Urban Growth Across Size Class Categories

Demographers and urban planners have often expressed concern over a larger proportion of urban population getting concentrated in million plus and class I cities over time (Kundu 94) Table 3.4 gives the percentage distribution of urban population by five classes of towns according to the size of population in Kerala and growth rate of urban population in each size classes from 1981-2001. The percentage decadal growth of urban population in each size class in column (5) and (6) of the table 3.4 has been worked according to the size class of the town in 1981 census in respect of the decade 1981-91 and size class of the town in 1991 in respect of the decade 1991-2001. A size class wise analysis of percentage of urban population in 2001 reveals that, it is highest in class I (68.82%) towns, followed by class III towns (14.05%). The same trend was visible in 1981 and 1991 census showing thereby more concentration of population in class III towns than in class II towns. The percentage urban population in size class I has witnessed steady increase from 1981 onwards, while in size class II and V the percentage of urban population has decreased in 1991 and again increased in 2001. In size class III there has been a steady decreasing trend since 1981 in respect of percentage of urban population.

The percentage decadal growth during 1981-91 has the highest in class IV town (128.49%) followed by class

Table 3.4 : Percentage Distribution of Urban Population by Size Class of Cities 1981-2001

Population Size	*Proportion of population in each size class to total urban population*			*Percentage decadal growth*	
	1981 (1)	*1991 (2)*	*2001 (3)*	*1981-91 (4)*	*1991-01 (5)*
Class I (100000 and above)	53.14 (8)	66.34 (14)	68.82 (14)	+100.97	+11.66
Class II (50,000-99,999)	9.52 (7)	7.22 (9)	11.33 (14)	+22.15	+68.81
Class III (20,000-49,999)	31.86 (49)	19.07 (46)	14.05 (35)	+3.64	-20.71
Class IV (10,000-19,999)	4.78 (17)	6.78 (34)	4.98 (26)	+128.49	-20.91
Class V (5000-9,999)	0.70 (4)	0.58 (6)	0.82 (9)	+32.82	+52.35
All Classes	100 (85)	100 (109)	100 (98)	100	100

Source: Government of India, Census of India 2001 series 33 Kerala Paper 2 of 2001, provisional population totals, D.C.O. Kerala. P. 101. (Figures in parenthesis indicate No. of cities).

I town (100.97%). The lowest percentage of decadal growth for 1981-91 has been observed in class III towns. During 1991-2001 the percentage decadal growth rate in all the size class other than class II and class V were less than that during 1981-91. The analysis reveals that for 1991-2001 a steady and specific growth in urbanization was witnessed in the case of Class I, class II and Class V towns and an important finding is that the process of urbanization in Kerala has been essentially a process of city ward migration.

Urbanization Trend at the District Level

The urbanization trend at the district level is revealed in table 3.5. It shows the district wise distribution of urban population in 1991 and 2001 and the corresponding Rate in 1991 and 2001. The Kannur district is identified as the prominent one (Rank one) in respect of percentage of urban population in the state and the lowest rank goes for Wynad in both 1991 and 2001 Census. Kollam and Kottayam district have been relegated to 8th and 9th Rank respectively from 7th and 8th rank with regard to percentage to urban population in 2001 census. While Kasargod district has been elevated to 7th rank in 2001 from 9th rank elevated in 1991. Only five districts (Thrissur, Malappuram, Idukki, Wynad and Kasargod) have recorded an increase in the percentage of urban population in 2001, whereas all other districts recorded a slight reduction in the proportion than the 1991 figures.

Table 3.5: District Wise Percentage of Urban Population and their Rank in 1991 and 2001 Kerala

District	*Percentage of Urban Population*			*Rank in 1991*	*Rank in 2001*
	1981	*1991*	*2001*		
Kannur	23.39	50.87	50.46	1	1
Ernakulam	39.56	48.74	47.65	2	2
Kozhikode	27.18	38.34	38.25	3	3
Thiruvananthapuram	25.26	33.88	33.78	4	4
Alappuzha	15.89	30.46	29.36	5	5
Thrissur	21.10	26.31	28.21	6	6
Kasargod	9	16.45	19.42	9	7
Kollam	13.15	18.53	18.03	7	8
Kottayam	9.37	17.55	15.35	8	9
Palakkad	10.11	15.72	13.62	10	10
Pathanamthitta	-	13.05	10.03	11	11
Malapuram	7.40	9.12	9.81	12	12
Idukki	4.59	4.72	5.07	13	13
Wynad	-	3.41	3.76	14	14
Total	18.74	26.44	25.97		

Source: Government of India, Census of India 2001 series 33 Kerala paper 2 of 2001 provisional population totals, Director of Census Operation, Kerala.

Problems of Urban Health

The lack of quality and comprehensiveness is not only the problem of urban health, but also the fact that, because of maldistribution facilities, it is not easily accessible to those who required (WHO 1992). The problem of accessibility of medical institutions and hospital beds was formerly a problem in the areas of rural health, but with trends in urbanization, this problem has spread to urban areas also. Regional variation that exist in the availability of Govt. Hospital beds in the towns and cities reflect the extent in the utilization of health services and its victims will be the slum dwellers and poor sections in the urban areas. Table 3.6 provides regional differences in the distribution of Govt. hospital beds in the urban areas of various districts in Kerala.

Table 3.6 reveals that availability and accessibility of bed is more in the urban areas of Kottayam district (No. of beds per 1000 population) followed by Trivandrum and Kozhikode. It is very worse in the case of Kollam where even a single bed is not available for 1000 population. In the case of number of beds per 10 km^2 in the urban areas, the Kozhikode district comes first followed by Trivandrum and Kottayam. The table reveals that the study district (Kannur) the urban areas suffer from the shortage of beds and its position is less than the state average of 3.1 beds per 1000 population.

Among the districts, Thrissur district lags in the proportion of doctors available to urban areas compared to population size of the urban area. It can be seen that 28.1% of the urban population of the district is covered by 21.2% of the doctors in the district. Similar is the case of Kannur District where 50.46% of the urban population is served by 47.5% of the doctors available in the district. The data revealed that the study district is facing the problem of lower doctor population ratio with respect to urban areas (Table 3.7).

Table 3.6 : District wise Distribution of Urban Hospital Beds in Kerala- 2001*

District	*No. of beds*	*No. of beds Per 1000 population*	*No. of beds in 10 Km²*
Thiruvananthapuram	5871	5.4	354
Kollam	423	0.9	80
Pathanamthitta	495	4.1	49
Alappuzha	2327	3.8	210
Kottayam	2295	7.7	317
Idukki	274	4.8	77
Ernakulam	2688	1.8	116
Thrissur	2274	2.7	203
Palakkad	875	2.5	52
Malappuram	1171	3.3	80
Kozhikode	4961	4.5	477
Wynad	43	1.5	11
Kannur	1542	1.3	76
Kasargod	401	1.7	71
Kerala	25640	3.1	160

Source: 1. Census of India 2001, Gen. Population Tables, Kerala series – 33.

2. Survey of Allopathic Medical Institutions in Kerala 2001, Director of Health Services, Thiruvananthapuram.

* No. of beds as on 31.3.2001.

For a city to tackle its health problems there must be a social contract in which the better off accept responsibility for enabling the poor to have access to essential services. A comprehensive programme of primary health care for urban areas would therefore include not only, the provision of health services, but also creation of jobs through support for new enterprises, increased efficiency of food distribution, support for community gardens and support for self built housing and sanitation as well as for public education system

Table 3.7: District wise Distribution of Doctors in the Government Health Institutions in Kerala - 1999

District	No. of doctors		Percentage of doctors available to the urban	Percentage of urban population to total population
	Rural	Urban		
Thiruvananthapuram	192	221	53.5	33.78
Kollam	148	64	30.1	18.03
Pathanamthitta	83	37	30.8	10.3
Alapuzha	157	86	35.3	29.36
Kottayam	142	86	37.7	15.35
Idukki	91	24	20.8	5.07
Ernakulam	160	159	49.8	47.65
Thrissur	222	62	21.8	28.21
Palakkad	182	55	23.2	13.62
Malappuram	202	89	30.5	9.81
Kozhikode	130	109	45.6	38.25
Wynad	94	3	3	3.76
Kannur	129	117	47.5	50.46
Kasargod	58	46	44.2	19.42
Total	1990	1158	36.78	25.97

Source: 1. Govt. Allopathic Medical Institutions in Kerala 1998.
2. Census of India 2001. Provisional Population Totals, Rural urban distribution paper 2 of 2001, Kerala.

and initiatives in other areas of everyday life including energy supply and transport.

Access of Public and Private health services

The public and private health care sectors co-exist in most cities, but vary in the coverage they provide. In Columbia the private sector provides only 15% of medical care, whereas in Bombay the proportion is almost 50%. The voluntary agencies play a very important role in cities such as Calcutta and Dakar and their services are of high quality. In Dakar health posts run by the Christian missionaries provide better health care than Government as measured by the availability of essential drugs, but they have limited population coverage. In spite of the availability of the public sector health services catering the needs, 75% of urban poor in Bombay use the private sector for minor ailments, which constitute 80% of their health problems (WHO 1992). In Lusaka, It is estimated that 10-15% of the population use mainly traditional medicine especially for mental illness. (WHO 1992). People using the public health services tend to bypass first level services (Services provided by urban primary health centres or reference health centres), which are accordingly under utilised. In Bombay it is cheaper for a slum dweller to pay a neighborhood private practitioner during the evening than to travel to public facility and wait for a whole day thereby losing a day's wage. Although public sector facilities are usually available in cities, access to them is often a problem for the urban poor and there is a real need for services to be much more consumer oriented.

The achievement of "health for all" by 2000 has been hampered by un- equal access of medical care and preventive services, inefficient health care system, rising cost and rapid growth of physician work force, Its maldistribution and the inappropriate generalist specialist mix. A major chunk of health budget is spent on training health professionals and quality of health care is yet to improve (The Hindu, 1st may 2001). Major part of public expenditure on health both at the national and state level is devoted for paying salary and allowances and very meager is spent for supplying medicines. The public is compelled to approach private agencies for their health care needs converting Govt. hospitals and health centres as scarecrow. This is a grave problem in the urban health care system in India and the field data of the present study clearly reveals that 70% of the people are not satisfied with Government hospital and all of them who used Govt. hospitals have serious complaints against it.

In Kerala, the financial crisis of the Govt. resulted in the default of crores of rupees as payment to medical companies related to the purchase of medicines supplies to Govt. hospitals. Even for subscribing bandage and life saving drugs, Govt. hospital is now in troubled situation. The major chunk of the resources of the health department is utilized for paying salary and allowances and other expenditures associated with day-to-day administration and a very meager amount was incurred for medicine purchase. The table 3.8 shows the percentage of expenditure incurred for various purposes in the health budget of Govt. of Kerala.

Table 3.8: Percentage of Expenditure on Various Expenditure Categories in the Health Budge of Government of Kerala

	Period				
Expenditure Items	1970	1980	1990	1995	1999
Pay and Allowances	43.26	52.24	62.48	66.46	67.69
Office Expenses	5.68	4.34	3.35	3.74	1.21
Medicine	33.83	31.16	25.43	23.09	17.83
Hospital Accessories	8.42	4.91	2.36	2.07	3.72
Vehicles	0.31	0.22	0.21	0.11	0.38
Constructions	6.83	5.18	2.85	2.77	3.62
Grant-in-aid	1.66	1.96	3.33	1.76	5.55
Total	100	100	100	100	100

Source: Government of Kerala, Budget documents, various years.

From the table 3.8 it is very clear that for the last 30 yeas, Government health expenditure towards medicine had reduced around 48% at the same time the salary and other expenses of the personnel in the health department has increased to 56.5% during the same period. This inadequate budget allocation for medicine supply is the crucial problem in the healthcare delivery system in Kerala and It is due to the callousness of the Government in providing value to the life of the vulnerable groups in the society.

Health Centres and Urban Health

Most health centres in urban areas are primarily concerned with basic curative and preventive services and deal with some aspects of maternal and child health. Health posts and health centres are useful in providing a primary level of care, but they are limited in their capacity and in the skills at their disposal and are usually available only during official working hours. Their services are usually not adequate to meet local health needs or the growing demands made on them by a more knowledgeable and better informed local population as a result of developments in basic health technology. On the other hand, the inpatient, outpatient and emergency services of first referral or district hospitals are often congested with patients suffering minor ailments or illnesses. Inter relationships and referral and support systems between their institutions are often very weak. If they exist at all, and there are frequently no well-defined joint activities addressing community health needs in a comprehensive way.

There has often been an assumption that, there is a high concentration of health facilities and services in the cities as compared with rural areas and there is no urban health problem. But for the poor and especially for those living in slums and shantytowns, the level of access to health facilities falls the minimum equitable level. Though the growth of medical institutions and beds availability had risen sharply in the last 50 years (as shown in table 3.9) in Kerala, their location resources, quality and performance are often poor. From the table 3.9 it is seen that for the last 5 decades the total number of medical care institutions under the Govt. have multiplied several fold. The growth rate of institutions registered a steady rise of 31% during 1950-55, 61.7% during 1955-65, and 46.3% during 1980-2000. As a whole the institutions attained the growth rate of 472% for the period 1950-2000. Similarly the whole bed capacity increased to the rate of 576% for the period 1950-2000.

Table 3.9 : Growth of Institutions and Beds (Allopathy) in Kerala 1950-2000

Year	*Govt. Hospitals*	*Govt. Dispen-saries & T.B. Clinics*	*PHCs including MCH centres*	*Grant-in -aid institu-tions*	*Others including CHCs*	*Total No. of Institu-tions*	*Total No. of beds*	*Growth rate of bed in Percent*	*Growth rate of institutions in Percent*
1950	56	135	6	33	-	230	6752	-	-
1955	58	156	6	33	4	303	9405	39.2	31
1965	101	217	157	13	2	490	18526	96.9	61.7
1970	112	261	163	15	2	553	21777	17.5	12.8
1980	145	645	173	12	6	981	31206	43.2	3.4
1985	151	543	299	16	6	1015	35740	14.5	15.3
1990	140	71	883	36	69	1199	38223	6.9	18.1
1995	147	73	940	36	67	1263	42126	10.2	5.3
2000	143	74	944	36	120	1317	45684	8.4	4.2

Source: Government of Kerala, Economic Review, State Planning Board, 2001.

Urban Poverty and Health Hazards

The rapid growth of densely populated predominantly low-income settlements in the cities of third world has come to constitute one of the most serious threats to urban health. Available data on low-income settlements reveal that (WHO 1988), three major types of pathology are emerging.

1. Infectious and gastro intestinal diseases often termed "diseases of poverty" (these have by and large disappeared from developed countries, but are today major source of morbidity and mortality in children in the developing world).
2. Chronic degenerative diseases associated with poor living and working conditions.
3. Pathogenic conditions associated with stress often precipitated by social isolation, insecurity, dissolution of primary (family) relation and cultural conflict where there is rapid urban development.

Recent case studies in squatter settlements have revealed a very high level of premature death and ill health especially among infants and children. In 1984, for instance a survey (Misra 1987) in Chheetpur squatter settlements with 500 inhabitants in the city of Allahabad, India found that 55% of the children and 45% of the adults had worm infection, while 60% had scabies. Most of the population had intakes of less then 1500 calories a day. The survey also reveals that 90% of the infants and children in the age of 4 had intakes significantly below their needs. Malaria was the most commonly identified cause of death followed by tetanus, injuries from accidents and burns, diarrhoea, and dysentery. The site of the settlement was subject to flooding in the rainy season and lack of drainage meant that stagnant pools were present for much of the year (Misra 1987).

Case study from Haitis capital suggests that health problem is more serious for the urban poor than for the rural dwellers. In the slums of Haitis capital, the Portwaprince, the infant mortality rate was found to be 200 per 1000 live births with another 100 per 1000 dying between the first and second birthdays, these were almost 3 times the equivalent rates in the countries rural areas (Rodhe J.E 1983). The infant mortality in the bustees of Delhi was found to be 221 per 1000 live births and twice as much for some of the lowest castes. (WHO 1988) In Manila, the infant mortality rate in the squatter communities was found to be 3 times the average for the rest of the city; the proportion of people with tuberculosis was also 9 times higher and diarrhoea was twice as common (Basta 1976).

Urban poor can be regarded as the interface between under development and industrialization and their disease pattern often reflects the problem of both. From the first they acquire a heavy burden of infectious disease and mal-nutrition and from the second the wide range of chronic and social diseases that is becoming typical of urban centres in developing countries. Three main groups of health hazards have synergistic impact on the poor (WHO 1988). The first includes poor education, insufficient nutrition, over crowding and under protection leading to excessive vulnerability and exposure to pathogenic agents and hence to infectious diseases and malnutrition. The second relates more specifically to manmade conditions of the urban environment including pollution, exposure to unregulated traffic stress and alienation leading to cardio vascular, neo-plastic mental diseases and accidents in the home, at work and on the road. The third group of hazards reflects the environmental neglect that is common where national or local finances are unable to meet needs in vector and environmental engineering.

It is hardly equitable to expect people in lower income groups to take responsibility for their own garbage and waste water disposal, while those in middle and upper income groups are provided with sewers and services for the regular collection of household wastes. The survey data also specifically points out this urban problem, that poor dwellings and slum areas are free from drainage and sewage, even if it is provided, it may be either open Kachcha or open pucca, which always remain chocked with breeding of mosquitoes and spreading foul smell.

Over crowding, poor ventilation, poor temperature control and environmental pollution are all associated with respiratory infection in early childhood (Pio A 1984) and are in turn common to urban slum and squatter settlements. The survey data for the present study also reveals the positive linkage between room density and prevalence of communicable illness, as there are cases of eleven persons living in one room in slum settlements (survey data).

Maternal Health: Another Threat to Urban Health

Unnecessary medical intervention without valid medical indication especially in delivery cases is another serious problem faced in the urban health care delivery system. Mukherjee et al (1995) proved that caesarean rate increased from 5% to 25% in just a matter of 2 decades (Madhukar Pai, 2000). In 1995 the caesarean rate in the USA was 21%. The rate in England was estimated to be around 12%. A recent ecological study from Latin America estimated national caesarean rates for 19 countries in the region (Delizan et al 1999). Of the 19 countries, 12 had caesarean rates above 15% ranging from around 17% to 40%. They estimated that over 8,50,000 unnecessary caesarean sections are performed each year in Latin America.

The Kerala Sastra Sahitya Parishad survey in rural Kerala highlighted the issue of hike in caesarean rates from 1987 to 1996[1] (Kannan et al 1991, Kunhikannan et al 2000). However the problem of caesarean section is too much in urban centres where the socio-economic family setup is most suited for this. A study conducted in Thiruvananthapuram, the capital city of the state of

Kerala (Thankappan 1999) showed an average caesarean rate of around 10% in Govt. hospitals as compared to a rate of around 30% in private hospitals. In most cases compulsion of hospital authorities is noted as the important reason for the acceptance of caesarean section. Caesarean births have now become a status symbol among the middle and upper class women.

The prevalence of caesarean rates is also high due to the encouragement offered by teaching hospitals in Kerala. It provides a lot of cutting chance to improve the surgical competence of medical students undergoing post graduation in obstetrics and Gynaecology. The hike in caesarean section also resulted in high post operative morbidity among the women like wound infection, complications like incisional hernia, severe blood loss requiring transfusion, anaesthetic complications like post spinal headache and problems like placenta praevia and placenta accreta in the subsequent pregnancy (Madhukar Pai 2000). The caesarean section may also create morbidity problems among the new born babies and in certain cases it leads to death.

Maternal health in urban Kerala is in danger due to the unhygienic condition of the maternity ward of the Govt. hospital. Many poor sections prefer Govt. hospital as the choice of their delivery place due to free or concession treatment. The maternity ward of the Govt. hospital is a place like hell. If we walk carelessly in the ward, new born and mothers will be within our legs. That much of rush can be seen in Govt. hospitals. The major problems faced in the maternal ward are lack of beds, indifferent attitude of authorities to wash the bed sheet and failure to provide water in the latrine. Mushroom growth of mosquitoes and unmovable fans in the hospital ward converts the ward into a hell where mothers and new borns are fighting for their survival (Malayala Manorama, 2000). The General Hospital functioning in the study area is the best replica of the above-mentioned maternal ward. The observations made as part of the study in the General Hospital revealed the actual sufferings of the patients admitted there. The General Hospital had a bed capacity of 541, but it had always more than 600 to 650 patients admitted. Many of then lay on the floor without even any mattress. As the visit was made during rainy season in most of the wards water is flowing into the room through the windows. This was due to the non-replacement of broken glass shutters of the windows. Though water was flowing into the wards, the latrine attached with certain wards had no water supply due to the damage caused to connecting pipe. The maintenance works of the hospital buildings and other accessories are very rare, so the common people have become the victim of a callousness of the Govt. hospital authorities.

Morbidity and Urban Health Care System

Health care system in India in the last 45 years has focused on increasing coverage in rural areas. There has been little or no development of organized health care services for the vast urban areas. Out of 300 plus urban local bodies in India, only about 100 have been some semblance to health care service, while the rest have only a sanitary inspector or even a lower functionary to look after the health care system (Sachar and Gill 1993). The three metropolitan cities Bombay, Calcutta and Madras show prevalence of very high level of malnutrition. It is estimated that in Bombay 63.6% males 73.1% females are malnourished and this was 75.9% and 75% for Calcutta and 67.8% and 77.8% for Madras (Gopalan 1985).

The studies done by Ebrahim (1984) and Espagnet (1984) provide the common health problems of the urban poor. Espagnet suggested that in addition to all the diseases, there are three other group of factors, which are detrimental to health and operate heavily against urban poor. First include low income, limited education, insufficient diet, over crowding and under protection. The second relates to the manmade conditions of the urban environment such as industrialization, pollution, traffic stress and alienation. The third is the result of social and psychological instability and insecurity.

Women in slum areas seek work in adverse and low economic jobs and they have little access to health and MCH (Maternal and Child Health) services. In urban slums of Delhi, the untrained dais conducted 74% of all deliveries and the proportion of women registered for antenatal check-up was only 21.4% (Bhatnagar 1985). The table 3.10 shows the interstate variations in the maternal care indicators by state. The table reveals five different maternal care indicators for births recorded by the NFHS survey 1998-99. The first indicator is a summary antenatal care indicator which shows the percentage of births whose mothers received all of the following: Three or more antenatal check-ups, (with the first check-up within the first trimester of pregnancy) two or more tetanus toxic injections and iron and folic acid tablets. The next two indicators pertain to care during delivery and show the percentage of births delivered in medical institutions and deliveries assisted by health professional. The last two indicators pertain to post natal care and show the percentage of non-institutional deliveries with postpartum check-up within two months of birth and within two days of birth. For India as a whole, mothers of only 20% births received all the required components of antenatal care. In this regard, Kerala ranks first with 65% followed by Goa with 61% to a low of only 4% in Uttar Pradesh. The states like Bihar, Rajasthan, Nagaland where only 6-9% of women received the required components of antenatal care. Kerala, followed closely by Goa also out perform all other states in terms of delivery care with over 90% deliveries taking place in medical institutions and a similarly high percentage of deliveries assisted by health professionals. Tamil Nadu with 79% of births delivered in medical institutions and 84% of deliveries assisted by health professional ranks third

Table 3.10: Maternal Care Indicators by States 1998-99

State	Percentage who received all recommended types of Antenatal care[a]	Percentage of births delivered in a medical institutions	Percentage of deliveries assisted by a health professional[b]	Percentage of non-institutional deliveries with a postpartum check-up within two months of birth[c]	Percentage of non-institutional deliveries with a postpartum check-up within two days of birth
India	20.0	33.6	42.3	16.5	2.3
Delhi	32.8	59.1	65.9	19.5	2.1
Haryana	20.8	22.4	42.0	15.7	2.5
Himachal Predesh	30.2	28.9	40.2	21.2	2.9
Jammu Kashmir	30.7	35.6	42.4	27.6	1.1
Punjab	31.7	37.5	62.6	20.3	5.7
Rajastan	8.3	21.5	35.8	6.4	0.5
Madhya Pradesh	10.9	20.1	29.7	10.0	0.5
Uttar Pradesh	4.4	15.5	22.4	7.2	1.5
Bihar	6.4	14.6	23.4	10.0	1.4
Orissa	21.4	22.6	33.4	19.2	2.2
West Bengal	19.7	40.1	44.2	31.6	7.1
Arunachal Pradesh	17.3	31.2	31.9	10.5	0.3
Assam	15.8	17.6	21.4	25.5	0.5
Manipur	18.3	34.5	53.9	27.1	1.4
Meghalaya	10.4	17.3	20.6	20.8	0.0

Contd....

Table 3.10 : (Contd...)

State	*Percentage who received all recommended types of Antenatal care*[a]	*Percentage of births delivered in a medical institutions*	*Percentage of deliveries assisted by a health professional*[b]	*Percentage of non-institutional deliveries with a postpartum check-up within two months of birth*[c]	*Percentage of non-institutional deliveries with a postpartum check-up within two days of birth*
Mizoran	13.5	57.7	67.5	20.9	0.9
Nagaland	8.9	12.1	32.8	4.3	0.0
Sikkim	15.3	31.5	35.1	38.0	0.7
Kerala	64.9	93.0	94.0	27.4	7.5
Tamil Nadu	50.8	79.3	83.8	53.0	10.1
Andhra Pradesh	35.6	49.8	65.2	44.9	1.6
Karnataka	41.5	51.1	59.1	35.3	3.6
Maharashtra	31.0	52.6	59.4	29.8	6.9
Gujarat	25.0	46.3	53.5	10.4	1.6
Goa	60.6	90.8	90.8	41.0	6.9

Source: National Family Health Survey –2, 1998-99 International Institute for Population sciences, Mumbai. P.315.

Note : Table includes only the two most recent births during the three years preceeding the survey.

(a) Three or more ANC (with the first check-up within the first trimester of pregnancy) two or more tetanus toxoid injections and IFA tablets.

(b) Doctor auxiliary nurse midwife, nurse, midwife, lady health visitor or other health professional.

(c) Based on births in the 2-35 months preceding the survey.

among the states on this delivery care indicators. By contrast in Nagaland, Bihar and Uttar Pradesh only 12-16 percent of births were delivered in medical institutions and health professionals assisted in Meghalaya, Assam, Uttar Pradesh and Bihar only 21-23 percent deliveries.

What is particularly notable however is the poor performance of almost all states in the two indicators of postpartum care, both in absolute terms as well as relative to their performance on the antenatal and delivery care indicators. There is no state other than Tamil Nadu where more than half of the non-institutional deliveries in the three years preceeding the survey were followed by a postpartum check-up within 2 months and there are only six states where this percentage was 30- 45 percent. In 19 states less than 5% of the non-institutional deliveries were followed by a postpartum check-up within 2 days, whereas in 2 states the percentage of receiving such check-up was zero.

An examination of the performance of each state on the different safe motherhood indicators reveals that the performance was below the national average in most of the states including Arunachal Pradesh, Bihar, Madhya Pradesh, Nagaland, Rajasthan, Uttar Pradesh, Assam, Meghalaya and Sikkim. The performance of Kerala was far better compared to all other states.

Social and psychological problems as a result of political, economic and social instability form another group of problems for urban poor. The protective structure of the local communities and extended family is generally replaced by nuclear family and migration into the city. Gupta identified (Gupta 1993) the major problems in the organization and functioning of health care in urban areas such as: poor coverage, fragmentation of responsibilities between different institutions with consequent lack of services in some areas and unnecessary duplication in others, increasing demand for health services and increasing costs, lack of co-ordination between different type of services mainly curative and preventive services, lack of staff with proper managerial capabilities, lack of area wide planning with maldistribution of health facilities and services.

Urban Morbidity

Communicable disease flourish where resistance levels are low, immunization is inadequate and the environmental barriers against their spread are weak. Poor nutrition makes particularly the young and the feeble more vulnerable to infection. The situation is made worse by over crowding, by the exposure of population to diseases to which they have never been exposed before and by the multiplication of animal and insects hosts because of environmental behaviour and ecological changes.

Environmental conditions favouring the spread of communicable diseases include insufficient and unsafe water supplies, poor sanitation, inadequate disposal of solid wastes, inadequate drainage of surface water, poor personal and domestic hygiene, inadequate housing and over crowding. Much of the burden of chronic disease and trauma including poisoning, burns and injuries is associated with urban environment and life styles, inadequate early detection and treatment of disease and poor health education (WHO 1993).

Recently Kerala witnessed severe shocks due to the attack to weils disease. The increase of rats both in the urban and rural areas accounts for the spread of this disease. The table 3.11 reveals the gravity of the disease in Kerala. The data shows that the problem of weils is increasing year after year in Kerala.

The morbidity prevalence of major diseases among different states in India shows a varied proportion. Table 3.12 shows the inter-state difference in the morbidity prevalence of four important diseases. The prevalence of asthma varies considerably by state from a low of 1204 per 100000 in Delhi to a high of 5995 per 100000 in

Table 3.11 Deaths Occurred Due to Weils in Five Medical Colleges in Kerala 1998-2000

Year	*Medical Colleges*	*No. of persons affected*	*No. of deaths occurred*
1998	Kottayam	610	66
	Alappuzha	58	4
	Trivandrum	572	38
	Trichur	91	8
	Calicut	64	14
	Total	1395	130
1999	Kottayam	696	57
	Alapuzha	113	2
	Trivandrum	557	50
	Trichur	76	1
	Calicut	371	-
	Total	1813	110
2000	Kottayam(upto July 31)	203	22
	Alappuzha(Upto July 31)	52	1
	Trivandrum(Upto June 30)	197	21
	Trichur(Upto August 15th)	27	1
	Calicut(Upto April 30)	39	-
	Total	574	45

Source: Vanitha, Nov. 1-14, 2000.

Meghalaya. State variations in the prevalence rate of tuberculosis are such that which ranges from 207 per 100,000 in Punjab to 1654 per 100,000 in Nagaland. Jaundice is most common in Nagaland, but it is also a substantial problem in most other northeastern states, West Bangal and Goa. Malaria was most often reported in Meghalaya, Nagaland, Arunachal Pradesh and Madhyapradesh where 10-17 percent of the populations were reported to have malaria during the three months preceeding the NFHS survey.

Table 3.12 : Morbidity Prevalence Due to Asthma, Tuberculosis, Jaundice & Malaria by Residence India – 1999

States	Urban				
	No. of persons per 100000 suffering from				
	Asthma	Tuberculosis	Medically treated tuberculosis	Jaundice during the past 12 months	Malaria during the past 3 months
India	1966	390	307	1225	2156
Delhi	1216	548	483	946	592
Haryana	1545	305	284	885	1217
Himachal Pradesh	841	200	177	575	177
Jammu Kashmir	1158	320	320	977	199
Punjab	1112	200	164	1057	949
Rajastan	2573	329	290	808	3007
Madhya Pradesh	1737	405	326	1310	5240
Uttar Pradesh	1667	490	347	1037	1441
Bihar	1430	629	558	1551	1833
Orissa	3000	819	652	1152	4571
West Bengal	2410	357	170	1892	918
Arunachal Pradesh	1451	1055	792	1451	11346
Assam	1931	583	345	2716	1910
Manipur	1900	1086	1086	1324	847
Meghalaya	2798	580	506	1306	5533
Mizoram	2112	1096	907	1837	4438
Nagaland	4343	1723	1546	6972	14447
Sikkim	3197	1151	128	2046	1535
Goa	2003	445	329	1989	1267
Gujarat	1304	279	242	1141	3378
Maharashtra	2172	342	282	1618	3551
Andhra Pradesh	3525	299	199	1456	2613
Karnataka	1442	216	190	372	280
Kerala	3901	348	301	165	47
Tamil Nadu	1318	431	366	1185	346

Source: National Family Health Survey, 1998-99.

Morbidity of communicable Diseases in Kerala : The morbidity prevalence of communicable illness was quite high in Kerala for the last few years. The table 3.13 provides morbidity due to major communicable illness in Kerala in 2001. The morbidity prevalence of communicable illness in Kerala for the last 6 years increased to a great extent from 116.2% in the case of Acute Respiratory Infection, 29.4% in the case of pneumonia, 83.8% in the case of all other diseases (un classified). The overall prevalence of communicable illness increased to 85,3% for the last 6 years. At the same time certain diseases like acute diarrhoeal diseases, whopping cough, measles, enteric fever etc. recorded a decline of 19.9%, 81.2%, 53.9% and 10.6% respectively. During the

Table 3.13 : Morbidity due to major Communicable Diseases in Kerala-2001

Diseases	*1995*		*2001*	
	Attack	*Death*	*Attack*	*Death*
Acute Diarrhoeal Diseases	700974	16	561354	19
Whooping cough	1566	-	293	-
Measles	7026	1	3234	-
Chicken Pox	-		8943	6
Acute Respiratory Infection	3189579	130	6896930	368
Pneumonia	18955	28	24530	52
Enteric Fever	8413	6	7521	6
Viral Hepatitis A	10489	11	4632	6
Viral Hepatitis B	-	-	597	6
Weils disease	-	-	2582	129
Rabies	149	9	11	11
Pulminary Tuberculosis	39241	278	27348	153
All other diseases	1,11,65090	4336	20525608	8414
Total	1,51,41,482	4815	28063583	9170

Source: Government of Kerala, 2002, Directorate of Health Services, Thiruvananthapuram.

same period the infection rate was the highest among people in the coastal areas, where the problem of overcrowding and environmental sanitation were at their worst. The prevalence of diarrhoeal disorder was also the highest in the coastal areas where over crowding, lack of facilities for excreta disposal and scarcity of drinking water provided an ideal breeding ground for the water borne disease (Panikar 1999). Faecal contamination of drinking water and food are chiefly responsible for the spread of diarrhoeal disorders. Intensive parasitism widely prevalent in Kerala is associated with the unfavourable environment (Panikar and Soman 1981).

The urban slums in India, new born are facing acute morbidity due to Pre-maturity, low birth weight, birth asphyxia, seplicemia, hyper bilirubinaemia, respiratory distress syndrome, congenital defects etc. The study held in the obstetric Department of Jawaharlal Nehru Medical College hospital, Aligarh Muslim University, Aligarh, for the period 1987 to 1990 proved that 26.92% is facing the pre- maturity morbidity, birth asphyxia 21.48% and respiratory distress syndrome 20.66% which is higher than other specialized centers of India (Manazir Ali 1993)

Table 3.14 reveals the problem of infant deaths in Kerala. The district wise rural urban data on infant deaths for the year 1995 revealed that the problem is acute in the urban areas compared to rural. Among the districts Wynad, Idukki and Kottayam have recorded a higher infant death in rural areas and all other districts the problem is very high in urban centres. The extent of infant death is 42.9% higher in urban Kerala compared to rural in the year 1995. This may be due to the larger proportion of the urban poor in the urban population, existence of slum population and the lack of sufficient nutrition among the infants in urban areas. Above all the maternity hospitals and places of delivery centres are more centred in urban areas, so the chances of infant deaths due to delivery complications is also high in urban areas.

Table 3.14 : District wise Infant Deaths in Kerala 1995

District	*Infant deaths*	
	Urban	*Rural*
Kasargod	138	36
Kannur	211	171
Wynad	23	104
Kozhikode	845	23
Malappuram	342	177
Palakkad	247	125
Thrissur	500	202
Ernakulam	429	26
Idukki	54	125
Kottayam	42	438
Alappuzha	264	36
Pathanamthitta	108	33
Kollam	181	89
Thiruvananthapuram	663	32
Total	4047	1617

Source: Economic Review, State Planning Board, 2001.

Morbidity and the Aged Population

The morbidity of the aged is an important health problem in the urban areas in India and their proportion is high in Kerala compared to other Indian states. Table 3.15 shows the growth of 60 plus age population in India since 1950. The table reveals that number of person's aged 60 plus and their percentage are increasing steadily.

Table 3.15 : Size and Proportion of Population of India in 60 Plus Age Group in Census Years 1951-2001

Census Year	*1951*	*1961*	*1971*	*1981*	*1991*	*2001*
No. of persons (millions)	21	25	33	42	55	76
Percentage of Total Population	5.7	5.7	6.1	6.5	6.6	6.7

Source: Kumudini Dandekar, the Elderly in India, p-20.
Figures for 2001 is estimated.

The matter is of grave concern as the aged population is increasing at a faster rate than that of total population growth (Table 3.16). The table 3.16 reveals that, the 60 plus age group increased at a very high rate from 22.4% in 1951-61 to 38.02% in 1991, whereas the total population increase was only 21.5 to 23.5% for the same period.

Table 3.16 : Growth Rate of Total Population and 60 Plus Population in India from 1951-1991

Period	*Percentage increase in Total population*	*Percent Increase in 60 plus population*
1951-61	21.51	22.40
1961-71	24.80	32.40
1971-81	24.75	31.60
1981-91	23.50	38.02

Source: Kumudini Dandeker, the Elderly in India.

The age wise morbidity prevalence data available for India as a whole reveals that among the 60 plus population (common for male and female) the morbidity prevalence rate is high both in rural and urban India and it is highest in urban India (Sundar 1995). The NCAER data reveals that out of every 1000 population 214.6 male and 192.2 female in rural and 219.7 male and 215.9 female in urban areas suffers from morbidity prevalence (Sundar 1995). The survey results of the present study also indicate high morbidity prevalence among the 60 plus population. The health problem of the aged is reflected more in chronic illness, as the age itself is responsible for certain diseases. The Table 3.17 shows the inter- state variations in chronic illness among old men and women in rural and urban areas. The table shows the proportion of chronically ill elderly in urban and rural areas for both sexes. Urban Kerala records the highest number of chronically ill elderly in India. In Kerala both in the rural and urban, it is the females, which dominates over the males in the chronically ill aged

Table 3.17 : Inter State Variations in Chronic Diseases Among Old Men and Women

State	*Proportion of chronically ill Per 1000*		*Proportion of chronicallyill per 1000*	
	Urban		*Slum*	
	Male	*Female*	*Male*	*Female*
Andhra Pradesh	525	568	560	573
Assam	643	505	639	607
Bihar	435	441	438	435
Gujarat	305	322	322	288
Haryana	360	324	367	375
Himachal Pradesh	332	344	371	359
Jammu Kashmir	439	442	469	585
Karnataka	354	408	372	349
Kerala	707	738	691	697
Madhya pradesh	376	426	414	393
Maharashtra	411	406	431	432
Orissa	487	554	464	517
Punjab	429	468	486	574
Rajasthan	420	382	418	364
Tamil Nadu	349	352	366	340
Uttar Pradesh	458	480	432	470
West Bengal	591	630	647	606
All India	443	455	451	448

Source: Kumudini Dandekar, Elderly in India.

persons. Among the states, it is Gujarat, which has recorded the lowest chronically ill aged both in urban and rural areas. An important reason suggested for the increase in chronically ill aged group is that, the aged in Kerala is least gainfully active compared to people in other states. In urban Kerala, 50.41% of the 60 to 64 age group and 28.66% in the 70 plus age group were gainfully active, whereas this was 68.64% and 34.93% respectively in the case of Himachal Pradesh, 58.21% and 26.74% respectively in the case of Tamil Nadu (Dandekar 1996). The proportion of the gainfully active was much lower than the all India average both for rural and urban Kerala and coupled with this the lack of exercise, fast food habit etc. also accounts for the hike in morbidity of the aged people in Kerala especially among the urban population. Another striking feature of the old age population in Kerala is that, the proportion of the aged 75 years and above is estimated at 1.96% (Registrar General 1996), which is the highest in India, at the same time the all India average was only 1.25%. Certain statistics shows that by the end of 2026, the proportion of 60 plus population in the population of Kerala will be more than 18% (Leela Gulathi, and Rajan Irudaya 1989).

Determinants of Health

Determinants of health are those indicators or factors, which have a direct bearing on improving the health status of the people. Studies conducted in this regard by different agencies and individuals (WHO 1988, Nayar 1997, Rosen 1993, World Bank 1999, NFHS 1995, Smith 1987) reveals that different factors are in operation which influence the health status of the urban community, and act as the determinants of health. The vital determinants of health which have a direct link in improving or deciding the health status of urban community is as follows:

Housing Condition

Makeshift dwellings do not provide protection against extremes of heat and cold. Chaga's disease which affect 16 to 18 million people in Latin America is transmitted by bugs that live and breed in cracks, in the walls of mud or wooden houses (WHO 1988). It was observed that in Kachcha or Semi-Pucca type of houses prevalence of respiratory diseases are high (NFHS 1995, Smith 1987). If there are less number of rooms in the houses, chances of respiratory diseases increase because of less dispersion of smoke. The field data of the present study also indicates a negative correlation between the existence of number of rooms and morbidity prevalence. A study conducted in Tamil Nadu in India proved that (Jyothi Parikh and Vijayalakshmi 2000) good ventilation, cleaner fuels, rational cooking technology can substantially reduce the level of pollution and is an important determinant of health status. Many other studies (Smith 1987, NFHS, 1995) also established the link of air pollution with respiratory diseases. The adverse housing situation is responsible for the deterioration of health status of the deprived and vulnerable groups in the urban areas. The whitely commission in 1930 documented the actual scene of the housing condition of urban slums. Houses many without plinths, windows and adequate ventilation usually consist of single small room, the only opening being a doorway often too low to enter without stooping. In order to secure some privacy old kerosene tins and gunny bags are used to form screens which further restrict the entrance of light and air in dwellings such has these human beings are born sleep, eat, live and die (Agarval 1982).

Drinking Water

Water is a primary medium for the transmission of disease, the most important of which are typhoid, cholera, hepatitis, poliomyelitis, dysentery and infection by intestinal protozoa. People supplied with piped water from communal tap 100 meters from the house they live in (those in the category of piped water supply) are unable to use as much water as those with a supply piped directly into the house (WHO 1988). The quantity of water available to a household has any important influence of health, no household is likely to make a liberal use water to wash cloths or cooking and cleaning utensils or personal hygiene, if it has to be carried a long distance with the possibility of long queues at the tap. It is observed that piped water supplies are often contaminated by sewage seeping into the network when water pressure drops in an over loaded and poorly maintained distribution system. The survey data of the present study reveals that 90% of the slum households have public tap as the source of drinking water and for that too they have to walk more than 150 meters. It also reveals that the proportion of communicable disease patients is very high among the public tap users compared to private well or private tap users. The NSS 44th round data regarding drinking water source shows that, in urban Kerala 64.24% had drinking water within the premises and all others have to walk some extent for their drinking water source.

Studies conducted in different countries show that a medium reduction of 27% in diarrhoea morbidity and 30% in diarrhoea mortality could be achieved by the provision of improved water supply and excreta disposal (Jameson etal, 1993). The Kerala study (Kannan et al 1991) also reveals the linkage of morbidity and mortality with the environmental status. The environmental status considered here includes water supply, sanitation, cooking devices, and disposal of wastewater and solid waste. It was seen that the incidence of sporadic diarrhoea cases was more among those used public taps and public wells and less among those using own wells and piped water supply at home. Victoria etal (1988) reported a 4.8 times higher likelihood of infant death from diarrhoea in families using public taps compared to infants with inhouse piped water. Similarly Pickering et al (1985) estimated death rates in Gambia twice as high for children using public tap water compared to those having a household connection.

Land

Housing sites and nearby open space contaminated with faecal matter, chemicals and other wastes pose major health hazard especially for children playing on them. Pools of standing water may become contaminated and transmit enteric disease. They also serve as ideal breeding grounds for mosquito's pests and vectors thus contributing to the spread of filariasis, malaria and other diseases. (WHO 1988).

Sanitary Facilities

By analyzing data from Ten Indian states, Nayar (Nayar 1997) established a moderate to strong negative correlation between housing amenities and health improvement, especially households with exclusive latrine and infant mortality, household with water sources in premises and infant mortality rate. The 19th century England witnessed rapid strides in production and burgeoning urban localities characterized by over crowding, congestion and unsanitary conditions. As towns spring up, the problem became one of packing as many people as possible as fast as possible, somewhere, some how and anyhow (Rosen 1993). The cholera epidemics of 1831 and 1832 in England were mainly due to the unsanitary and unlivable dangers in towns and urban area. During the 19th century in America communicable diseases like yellow fever, cholera, small pox, typhoid and typhus erupted in the form of epidemics (Rosen 1993) Urban India is a collection of stink chambers. Next to poverty sanitation is the crucial problem of urban slum dwellers. One-third of the urban dwellers does not have access to any type of latrine and another one-third is served by bucket latrines which are hardly sanitary. In the urban slum of the study area, the researchers could find that 50% of the slum households does not posses any type of latrine and resort open defecation. The morbidity analysis of the slum households revealed that lack of sanitation facilities resulted a hike in morbidity prevalence among the households.

Food Safety

Safety of foodstuffs is an important determinant of urban health status. Slum households and people in low-income areas do not have a proper storage facility for their food items. Often rats and other insects will spoil food items and also deliver their excreta in the food items. When people began to eat this, they may become the carriers of different diseases.

Air

Air pollution created by indoor fires and stoves has serious effects on the health of millions of people in the third world. Use of kerosene and firewood as a source of cooking fuel without proper ventilation culminates in the generation of certain chronic diseases. The survey data from the micro study reveals that households in the Kachcha residence suffer more of chronic diseases related air pollution than households in the semi-pucca or pucca type of residence.

Education

Schooling promotes the use of new technologies in the home for health, nutrition, learning and contraception. In this parents schooling especially the mothers is critical. Mother's education enables them to raise healthier children in four ways (World Bank 1999). 1. It imparts basic information about health and nutrition when such information is made part of the curriculum. 2. It enables mothers to monitor their children's health more accurately and to read written instructions from phamlets distributed by health workers in the labels or bottles of medicines. 3. It helps to over come some inhibiting traditional practices and for treatment of their children they resort modern methods rather than traditional remedies. 4. It increases the self-confidence of mothers to use more of public health service.

Available data from Bolivia, Mali, Uganda, Philippines and Nepal (World Bank1999) reveals that child mortality falls as mother's learn or when they move from illiterate stage to primary, secondary or higher level of education.

Environmental Determinants

Specific environmental risks and potential hazards associated with small scale economic activities in the slums were exceedingly high. Small industries unit operating in the slum are not providing any attention to the workers safety. The small industry that engaged to recover and recycle metal from old car bodies, which is then used to manufacture telephone cables is a specific example in this regard. At the final stage the shifting process produces large quantities of fine metal dust, which the workers continuously inhale. This results in severe respiratory and lung infection at a later stage. A large number of dye industries are functioning in urban and slum areas of Gujarath. Most of the dyes manufactured are Benzedrin based which is known occupational carcinogen (Ray and Rout 2000). Similarly, the textile industry is also causing severe health hazards to its working population. Chronic bronchitis, byssinosis of different grades and pulminary tuberculosis are the most prevalent diseases among the workers of textile industry. Workers engaged in cutting polishing, and finishing work of diamond are also exposed to serious health hazards of pulminary tuberculosis. Pulminary tuberculosis in Municipal sweepers was observed to be 5.35%, which is considered very high (Ray and Rout 2000).

Street level habitation of the majority of the urban poor ensures the inhalation of and continuous exposure to vehicle exhaust, fumes known to be rich in carbon Monoxide, Oxides of Nitrates and transient suspended particulates, the human health effect of which have been widely studied (Hamza, 1989, WHO 1991).

Infant Health Status Determinants

Chen and Mosley (1987) identified 5 important determinants of infant health status. They include 1) Environment, 2) Maternal factors like age of delivery, gap between birth, lactation etc 3) Nutrition 4) Accidents and injuries 5) Health care immunization and treatment.

Economic Factors as the Determinant of Health

Similar to environmental and social factors, economic factors also exert a strong pressure on the health status of urban community. The difference in population, geography, and extent of urbanization create differences in cost of access to health and other social services whose significance must be evaluated in the light of levels of individual income, Government budget and patterns of individual and social demand. Difference in human fertility are not purely biological nature, but can be analysed in terms of decisions to invest in a greater or lesser number of children according to the expected levels of associated costs and rates of return (Schultz 1980). Differences in nutrition reflect not only environmental and technological factors but also income levels, relative prices, and consumer tasks individually or socially determined. The availability and accessibility of social services- health care, education, water supply and sanitation clearly reflects economic factors.

Vulnerable Groups a Threat to Urban Health

The largest group at risk in the city is the urban poor. Poverty intensifies the risks that go with childhood, old age, being female, racial minority status, disability and occupations. The poor are usually further afflicted by limited access to health education, social and other public services. Children who have no legal status or who are separated from their families are at the highest risk. It has been estimated that there are over 20 million homeless "street" children in Latin America alone (WHO 1993). Although on the whole infant mortality in developing countries has been reduced, the rates remain high in poor urban communities. Despite the success in tackling the immunizable diseases each year 2.8 million children die from them and a further 3 million suffer chronic ill health as a result of them.

Women's health is undermined by poverty, poor education and disadvantage and discrimination in the work place. Woman may be at a disadvantage from birth onwards because of inadequate nutrition, lack of education, heavy work load, early marriage and early and frequent pregnancies; their vulnerability increases when they have no partner. Inadequate contraception, unsafe abortion, lack of sanitation and inferior health care explain why the risk of dying in childbirth is over 100 times greater among poor women from developing countries.

Conclusion

The problem of urban health and determinants of health status discussed above clearly reveals the need for proper urban planning in providing basic infrastructure and social inputs to the urban dwellers to be free from both infectious and non-infectious illness and for leading a healthy life. This include provision for safe drinking water facilities, good housing and sanitation, proper drainage, disposal of solid waste management, electricity, efficient health care services, with enough accessibility for curative care, child care centres, maternity and child health centres, adult education centres etc. Above all for the improvement of economic status of the urban poor specific income generating activities must also be created for them, so as to utilize their labour power effectively. If antibiotics are helped to save millions from dying due to typhoid, cholera and dysentery, hundreds of millions can be saved from contracting these diseases through improved water supply, hygiene, sanitation, and safe water disposal. If thousands of cancer patients are given an extended lease of life through radiation and chemotherapy, millions and millions can be saved from cancer through measures to reduce air pollution and clean up the environment, apart from modification of life styles and nutritional habits. Improvement of the urban environment by all means suitable for a healthy life is a must for alleviating the problem of urban health.

NOTES

1. The percentage of caesarean sections has gone up from 11.9% in 1987 to 21.4% in 1996. This is only a rural sample. The urban figures are likely to be higher than this, which would make the caesarean rate in the state one of the highest in the world.

REFERENCES

Agarval, A., (1982), The State of India's Environment. A Citizens Report Centre for Science and Environment, New Delhi.

Ali S. Manazir, (1993), Status of Morbidity and Mortality of New Borns Delivered to Urban Mothers, in Umashankar P.K.and Misra K. Girish, eds, Urban Health System, Reliance Publishing House, New Delhi.

Andrew Mason, (1996), Population Housing and the Economy in Denni's A. Albery ed., The Impact of Population Growth in Developing Countries, Springer, Berlin.

Basta, (1976), Nutrition and Health in Low Income Urban Areas of Third World, Ecology of Food and Nutrition pp.113-124.

Bhatnagar, S., (1985), Magnitude of Morbidity and Mortality Among Children Below 5 Years of Age in Urban Slums of Delhi, National Institute of Health and Family Welfare, Delhi.

Dandekar Kumudini, (1996), The Elderly in India, Sage Publications, New Delhi.

Dean T. Jameson et. al. eds., (1993), Disease Control Parasites in Developing Countries, Oxford University Press, pp. 100-101.

Delizan et. al., (1999), Cited in Unwanted Medical Intervention, Caesarean Sections as a Case Study, Madhukar Pai, Economic and Political Weekly Vol. XXXV, No.31, 2000, July 29 – August 4.

Ebraham G.T., (1984), Primary Care and the Urban Poor, Journal of Tropical Paediatrics No.1.

Engelman Robert, (1997), Why Population Matters, Population Action International, Washington DC.

Espagnet Ross, (1984), A Primary Health Care in Urban Areas Reaching the Urban Poor in Developing Countries. A State of the Art Report, Unpublished UNICEF/WHO Document SHS 84.4 cited in WHO's Urbanization and its Implication for Child Health, Geneva, 1988.

Gopalan C., (1985), The Mother and Child in India, Economic and Political weekly Vol. 20, No.4, p. 162.

Govt. of India, (1991), Census of India, Population of Kerala Series 12 paper 2, Director of Census Operations, Thiruvananthapuram.

Govt. of India, (2001), Census of India, Population of Kerala Series 33, Paper 2 of 2001, Provisional Population Totals, Director of Census Operations, Thiruvananthapuram.

Govt. of Kerala, (1997), Urban Slums in Kerala, Town Planning Department, Thiruvananthapuram.

Gupta, J.P., (1993), Referral Services in Urban Health Care Delivery System in Umashanker P.K. and Missra K. Girish (eds.) Urban Health System, Reliance Publishing House, New Delhi, p. 152.

Hamza, A., (1989), An Appraisal of Environmental Degradation in Bogota, Columbia, Urbanization and Environment, Vol. 1, No.1, pp. 16-21.

Jyothi Parikh and Vijayalakshmi, (2000), Bio–fuels, Pollution and Health Linkages Vol. 35, No. 47, pp. 4125- 4137.

Kannan K.P. et.al., (1991), Health and Development in Rural Kerala, Kerala Sastra Sahitya Parishad, Thiruvanantha-puram.

Kundu Amitab, (1994), Cited in Patterns Causes and Consequences of Urbanization by D. Retnaraj in Kerala's Economic Development Issues and Problems ed. B.A. Prakash, Sage publications, New Delhi, 1999.

Kunhikannan T.P., Aravindan K.P., (2000), Changes in Health Status of Kerala 1987-1997, Kerala Sastra Sahitya Parishad, Thiruvananthapuram.

Leela Gulathi and Rajan Irudaya, (1989), Ageing of Population in Kerala, Centre for Development Studies, Thiruvanantha-puram.

Malayala Manorama, (2000), July 26, Kottayam.

Misra, H.N., (1987), Popular Settlements in the City of Allahabad (India) and the Health Problems of their Inhabitants, Findings from Three Case Studies, International Institute of Development Research, Allahabad.

Mosely W.H. and Chen C.C., (1987), An Analytical Frameworks for the Study of Child Survival in Developing Countries, Population and Development Review Supplement to Vol. 10. No.4, pp. 25-45.

Mukherjee J. and Samaddar J.C., (1995), How Safe is Caesarean Section, Journal of Obstetrics and Gynaecology, Vol. 21, No. 1, pp. 17-21.

Nayar K.R., (1997), Housing Amenities and Health Improvement, Some Findings Economic and Political Weekly Vol. XXXII No. 2.

Nayar, K.R., (1999), Housing and Health Another Kerala Conandrum in Rethinking and Development, Oommen M.A. ed, Vol. 2, Concept Publishing Company, Delhi, p.44.

N.F.H.S., (1995), National Family Health Survey (Maternal and Child Health and Family Planning) India, 1992-93 International Institute of Population Science Mumbai.

Pai Madhukar, (2000), Unwanted Medical Intervention Caesarean Section as a Case Study, Economic and Political Weekly Vol. XXXV, No. 31, pp. 2755-2761.

Panikar, P.G.K., (1999), Health Transition in Kerala, C.D.S Working Paper No.10, Thiruvananthapuram, p.31.

Panikar, P.G.K. and Soman C.R., (1981), Health Status of Kerala, Paradox of Economic Backwardness and Health Development, C.D.S., pp. 72-77.

Peach, G.C.K., (1970), Urbanization in India in Beckinsale and Houston J.M. eds. Urbanization and its Problem Blackwell, Basil, p.297.

Pickering et. al., (1989), Cited in Health and Nutrition of the Urban Poor, the Case of Calcutta Slums in Dasgupta Monica, Chine Lincoln, Krishnan T.N. (eds.) Health Poverty and Development in India, Oxford University Press, Delhi, p. 190.

Pio, A., (1984), The Magnitude of the Problem of Acute Respiratory Infection in Children, Proceedings of an International Workshop, University of Adelaide, Sydney, p. 376.

Raja Bala, (1986), Trends of Urbanization in India, Rawat Publications Jaipur.

Ray, C.N., Rout P.R., (2000), Environmental Risk, Assessment of Municipal Corporation of Gujarath, Nagarlok Vol. XXXII, No. 2, pp. 11-30.

Registrar General of India, (1996), Population Projection for India and State 1996-2016, Census of India 1991, New Delhi, 1996, Table 2, pp. 27-34.

Rodhe, J.E., (1983), Why the other Half Dies : The Science and Politics of Child Mortality in the Third World, Assignment Children, pp. 61-62.

Rosen, (1993), Cited in K.R. Nayar's Housing Amenities and Health Environment, Some Findings, Economic and Political Weekly, Vol. XXXII, No. 2, pp. 1275-1279.

Sachar, R.K. and Gill P.V.S., (1993), Development and Urbanization, Its Implication for Childhood Mal Nutrition in Umashankar P.K. and Misra K. Girish, eds, Urban Health System, Reliance Publishing House, New Delhi, p. 24.

Schultz, T.P., (1980), Assessing the Causes and Consequences of the Incidence of Disease and Death, Interpretation of Relations Among Health. Household Economies and the Health Environment, WHO MIMEO.

Sjobery, O.G., (1973), The Origin and Evolution of Cities in Davis K. ed, Cities their Origin, Growth and Human Impact, L.H. Freeman and Co. Sanfransisco, p. 20.

Smith, K.R., (1987), Bio–fuels Air Pollution and Health, Plennum Press, New York.

Sundar Ramamani, (1995), Household Survey of Health Care Utilization and Expenditure, NCAER, New Delhi.

Thankappan, (1999), Caesarean Section Deliveries on the Rise in Kerala, National Medical Journal of India, Vol. 12, No.6, p. 297.

The Hindu, (2001), 1st May.

Victoria, C.G., Smith P.G. Vanghan J.P., (1988), Water Supply Sanitation and Housing in Relation to the Risk of Infant Mortality from Diarrhoea. International Journal of Epidemiology Vol. 17, pp. 651-654.

WHO, (1988), Urbanization and its Implication for Child Health, Potential for Action, Geneva.

WHO, (1991), Indoor Air Pollution from Bio- mass Fuel, Geneva.

WHO, (1992), The Role of Health Centres in the Development of Urban Health Systems, Report of the WHO Study Group on Primary Health Care in Urban Areas, Geneva.

WHO, (1993), The Urban Health Crisis : Strategies for Health for all in the Face of Rapid Urbanization, Report of the Technical Discussions at 44th World Health Assembly, World Health Organization, Geneva.

World Bank (1999), World Development Report, Oxford University Press, p.41.

World Bank, (2000), The World Development Report 1999-2000, Oxford University Press, Page to 19.

4

Profile of Study Area and General Characteristics of Sample Households

The state of Kerala, one of the advanced states in health status in India, was formed in 1956 by the integration of princely states of Travancore and Cochin and the Malabar regions of the erstwhile Madras state. It has an area of 38,863 sq K.M. The table 4.1 given in the introductory chapter provides the important human development indicators of Kerala. The study area selected is the Thallasery Municipal corporation of Kannur District in Kerala.* The specific justification for the selection of the Kannur District and Thallasery Municipal Corporation for the micro study is justified in the section on methodology in the second chapter.

In this section a brief profile of the study area especially with thrust on health aspect is noted with demographic and socio-economic characteristics of the sample households.

---

* The map of the Thallasery Municipal corporation area is given as Appendix 4.1 and 4.2 to Chapter IV to identify the wards selected for the study.

Thalasserry a Historical Background

Thalasserry was an ancient centre for trade and a principal port of Malabar. Hence it was not at all surprising that East India Company choose Thalaserry to be the first regular settlement on the Malabar cost. They made their permanent settlement in Thalasserry from 1708 onwards (Bench Mark Survey, 1993). The company obtained several privileges from Kolathiri kingdom between 1708 and 1761. Invasion of Malabar by Hyderali limited the operations of the company. The tension between the king of Mysore and East India Company continued until Tippu Sulthan formally gave Malabar to the British according to the treaty of Sreerangapatnum in 1772. Thereafter Thalassery remained under the British rule along with other places in Malabar until independence. However Thalasserry became a Municipal Township on the first November 1886 under the Act X of 1865. In 1941, adding Thali desom to it enlarged the area of municipality. After the formation of Kerala State, in 1961 including Mannayad, Kunnoth, Kavumbagam and Vayalam area to it further extended the area. Presently Thalassary has an area of 23.97 square kiliometers. As per the 2001 census, the total population of the municipality was recorded at 99386 with 46767 males and 52619 females. The total literacy rate of the area was estimated at 95.90 with female literacy of 94.52 and male literacy of 97.48. The sex ratio of the municipality was estimated at 1125 in the 2001 census.

Geography and Boundary

Thalassery a coastal town in a rocky region is the Taluk headquarters and a major urban centre in the Kannur District. It is also the judicial head quarters of the district. The town is located at 67Km north of Kozhikode and 22km South of Kannur. The town has the Arabian Sea as the Western boundary, while the east is bound by Mahe Municipality and Eranholi Panchayath and in the South the New Mahe Gram Panchayath and Mahe Municipality.

Climate

The climate in the area is more or less similar to the West coast climate, which is characterized by the uniformity of temperature. Throughout the year the fluctuation in temperature is in between 25-35 degree centigrade. The area is getting about 400 mm rainfall in a year caused by the South West monsoon starting from the end of May and extending upto 3 months.

Population

The population at the first assessment made in 1881 after the formation of Municipality was 26410. Thereafter the population in the Municipality has showed an increasing trend except during the decade 1911-21. The following table gives (Table 4.1) the decennial population growth and the growth rate from 1901 to 2001.

Table 4.1 : Growth of Population in the Thalasserry Municipality

Year	*Population*	*Change in decade*	*Percentage of population growth in decade*	*Cumulative variation*
1901	27883	-	-	-
1911	29258	1375	4.93	-
1921	27576	-1682	-5.75	-0.82
1931	30349	2773	10.06	9.24
1941	36320	5971	19.67	28.91
1951	40040	3720	10.24	39.15
1961	44763	4723	11.80	50.95
1971	68759	23996	53.61	104.56
1981	75560	6801	9.89	114.45
1991	1,03,579	28017	37.08	151.53
2001	99386	-4193	-4.04	147.48

Source: Census of India–Kerala, Various years.

An abnormal increase in population had been observed during the decades of 1961-71 and 1981-91.

This is mainly because of the expansion of the geographical area of the municipality during these periods.

Slum Population

According to Government of India's definition a slum area means any area where such dwellings predominate which by reason of dilapidation, over crowding, faulty arrangement of design of building, narrowness or faulty arrangement of street, lack of ventilation, light or sanitation facilities, inadequacy of open spaces and community facilities or any combination of these factors are detrimental to safety, health or morale (Govt. of Kerala 1997). Based on this definition, the Town Planning Department had identified 9 slum pockets in the Thalassery Municipality with 654 households in 1996. As per the recent ward division these 9 slum pockets are centred in 8 municipal wards and one typical slum, which was formerly in the nearby panchayath, was also included in the municipality in the ward division of 1998. As part of the fieldwork, the number of households in the slum pockets identified by the Town planning Dept. had been updated and is shown in Table 4.2.

Table 4.2: Ward wise Distribution of Slum Households-2001

Sl. No.	*Name of identified slum*	*No. of households*	*Representing Ward No.*
1.	Kuttimakool Sambava	17	17
2.	Kaivattom	74	42
3.	Ambalavattom	73	42
4.	Gopalpetta	165	41
5.	Mattampuram	75	45
6.	Chalil	108	42
7.	St. Peters slum	140	40
8.	Weavers street	103	43
9.	Chettam Kunnu Harijan Colony	25	48
10.	Pettipalam Colony[1]	95	36
	Total	875	8

Source: Survey Data.

Health Infrastructure of the District

The health status and health service utilization of an urban community depends to a lot on the availability and accessibility of health infrastructure. Before examining the health infrastructure of the municipality, it is better to have a picture about health infrastructure of the district. There exist a total of 106 allopathic Government medical institutions in the district with 2776 beds and 230 doctors. Table 4.3 gives the health infrastructure of the district in which the study was carried out.

From the table it is very clear that private medical institutions dominate the district. There exist a total of 211 medical institutions in the private sector. In the case of doctors by considering all the systems of medicine together there are only 350 doctors in the Government sector, at the same time 1312 doctors are there in the private sector.

Similarly there are only 3017 beds in the Government sector whereas 4099 beds are there in the private sector: When we examine the case of allopathy which is the most popular system of medicine in the state and in the district, it can be seen that there is only 10.2 doctors per one lakh population in the Govt. sector whereas there are 258 doctors per one lakh population in the private sector. As a total, there exist 36 doctors per one lakh population in the district and it is less than the national average of 48 doctors per one lakh population (Government of India 1998) and is at par with the state average of 36 (Govt. of Kerala 1996)[3]. Similarly in the bed population ratio there are 97 beds per one lakh population in the Government sector and 176 beds in the private sector and a total of 273 beds per one lakh population in the district. Though there exist more ayurvedic and homoeopathic private medical institutions in the district, the availability of bed is more in the Govt. hospital in the district, at the same time the proportion of doctors working is more in the private sector both in ayurveda and homoeopathy.

Table 4.3 : Health Institutions, Beds and Doctors (System wise) in Kannur District

Items	*Allopathy*			*Auyurveda*			*Homoeo*			*Others*			*Total*	
	a. Govt.	*b. Private*	*Total*	*a. Govt.*	*b. Pvt.*	*c. Total*	*a. Govt.*	*b. Pvt.*	*Total*	*a. Govt*	*b. Pvt.*	*Total*	*a. Govt*	*b. Pvt.*
No. of institution	106	235	341	67	233	300	49	152	187	-	16	16	211	636
No. of beds	2776[2]	3952	6728	216	122	338	25	25	50	-	0	0	3017	4099
No. of doctors	230	581	811	80	431	498	33	283	316	-	17	17	350	1312

Source: a. Government of Kerala Economic Review, State Planning Board, Thiruvananthapuram 2001.

b. Government of Kerala Survey of Private medical institutions in Kerala 1995, Directorate economics and statistics, Thiruvananthapuram.

If we examine the distribution of manpower in the allopathic system of medicine in the district, it can be seen that the inefficiency of public health system is leading to huge drain of funds from the public exchequer. The table 4.4 shows the distribution of manpower in the allopathic system of medicine.

Table 4.4 : Distribution of Manpower and Beds in the Allopathic System of Medicine -Kannur District

Institution	*Beds*	*Doctors*	*Paramedical staff*	*Technical staff*	*Ministerial*	*Total*
a. Govt.	2776	230	2143	179	324	2876
b. Pvt.	3952	581	1177	218	143	2119

Source: a. Government of Kerala, Economic Review, State Planning Board, Thiruvananchapuram, 2001.

b. Government of Kerala, Survey of Private medical institution in Kerala 1996,Directorate Economics and Statistics, Thiruvananthapuram.

The available data on manpower in the allopathic medical sector in Kannur district reveals that Govt. institution is burdened with more paramedical, technical and ministerial staff compared to the private sector, though the availability of beds and doctors is very less in Govt. institutions. Table 4.4 reveals the over domination of non- medical personnel in the Govt. allopathic medical system in the district, which is a reflection of the system in the state. Major chunk of the Government health budget is devoted for providing salary and allowances to these medical and non-medical persons in the health sector and very meager amount is devoted for purchasing drugs and medicines. Many Govt. hospitals in the district is functioning even without bandage required for wounds. In such circumstances even the most deprived sections prefer private hospitals for curative care.

Health Infrastructure

Thalassery municipality is one of the biggest municipalities in the Kannur district. It has one General hospital with 541 beds. There exist two Government dispensaries one each in allopathy and homoeopathy and one ayurvedic hospital with inpatient facility. The private sector is very influential in the study area and dominates over the Govt. hospital in providing curative care services to the people. The table 4.5 shows medical institutions and bed capacity in the study area. Though the General hospital in the region is the biggest one, it is not providing proper services to the public. Though few costly types of equipment are installed in the hospital, most of the time it was on complaint and no effort were taken for the repair and maintenance of such equipment. The blood bank is not functioning and for X-ray and ECG patients have to depend on private sources. The maintenance works of the General hospital was very rare so causing severe problem during rainy seasons.

General Characteristics of the Sample

This section attempts to provide the General features of the sample population including the education, occupation and income of the head of the household. On the basis of education, occupation and income of the head of the households' the entire sample households are divided into five different socio-economic status (SES) groups. Different health services utilization studies reveals that the education, occupation and income of the households exert a strong influence in the health services utilization (Kannan et al 1991, Yesudian 1981, IIPS 2000, Ramankutty 1989, Smith et al 1990, Ramankutty et al 1993). In the present study the head of the household is taken as one who earns and brings maximum income to the family. Since he can have great control in the decision making of the household, which involves financial commitment, he may have greater voice in this regard. Health service utilization is one such decision making issue in which the decision of the head will be significant. Since the head is taking the decision, his education, occupation and income status of the family is considered for dividing the households according to their socio-

Table 4.5: Medical Institutions in the Thalassery Municipal Region

(as on 31.3.2001)

	Hospitals						*Dispensaries*					
	Govt.			*Private*			*Govt.*			*Private*		
	No.	*Beds*	*Doctors*	*No.*	*Beds*	*Doctors*	*No.*	*Beds*	*Doctors*	*No.*	*Beds*	*Doctors*
Alopathy	1	541	42	18	965	103	1	-	1	-	-	-
Ayurvedic	1	20	3	1	-	1	-	-	-	-	-	-
Homoeo	-	-	-	1	5	2	1	-	1	5	-	5
Total	2	561	45	20	970	106	2	-	2	5	-	5

Source: Municipal records.

economic status (SES). In most cases an effort was made to consider the head of the household itself as the respondent for the study. In certain exceptional cases (as the head was out of station) another person in the family who has sufficient knowledge and control over the family was taken as the respondent.

Socio-economic status (SES) is an important determinant of health and nutritional status as well as morbidity and mortality (Mahajan and Gupta 1995). The variables that affect socio- economic status are different in case of urban and rural societies. For eg. the influence of caste on social status is very strong in rural communities, but not so much in cities. So separate scales are needed for measuring SES in rural and urban areas. The SES scale developed by Kuppuswamy for urban family is accepted in this study, as the classification is essential to understand the perception of the households in different groups about different illness and also to measure the extent of differences in the utilization of health services by these different socio-economic status groups.

Socio-economic status was found to have a definite influence on birth and death rates, with higher socio-economic status resulting in lower birth and death rates. The higher risk of mortality among the poor households can partly be explained by the material deprivation. The higher birth rates could be the result of poorer educational attainments (Ramankutty et al 1993).

The important rationale behind the classification of households in to SES groups for the analysis of health services utilization is that poor social classes are more prone to a variety of behavioural patterns that are not conducive to promoting health. These include a greater prevalence of smoking and drinking (Smith et al 1990). Apart from this, their living conditions leave much to be desired from the standpoint of health, because of poor housing and poor sanitary conditions. But equally important, these social classes are also likely to have less access to medical care, the barriers being money, travel time and waiting time (Ramankutty et al 1989).

This section considers in addition to the socio-economic status of household, the housing and civic amenities including the source of drinking water, sanitation, drainage and the type of housing etc. as all these are directly linked to health status of the people. As a whole this chapter is divided into three sections, namely: Characteristics of the head of the household, characteristics of the household members and housing and civic amenities.

Characteristics of the Head of the Household

As the study is based on the SES scale developed based on the education and occupation of head of the household and his per capita income as per the Kupuswamy model, the head of the household occupies a pivotal role in this study. So the analysis of the demographic and socio-economic particulars of the head of the household is highly significant.

Demographic Characteristics : Demographic characteristics of the head of the households provide age distribution, sex and marital status and socio-economic features provide, education, occupation and income and it is revealed in table 4.6. The sex of the head of the household reveals a different situation in urban and slum areas. Only 10.8% females have shouldered the responsibility of the head of the household in urban areas, whereas this was 30% in slum. In slum, out of this 30% female heads 25% belongs to the lowest SES category, which reveals that in slum areas as socio-economic status declines, the proportion of females shouldering the responsibility of house management increases. But this trend cannot be seen in urban areas, as in all SES classes the proportion of female heads is less than 10% except in SES_2.

Table 4.6 : Sex of the Head of the Households and SES Class

SES Class	Urban			Slum		
	Male	*Female*	*Total*	*Male*	*Female*	*Total*
SES_1	11	1	12	-	-	-
SES_2	34	6	40	-	-	-
SES_3	31	3	34	7	2	9
SES_4	18	2	20	29	2	31
SES_5	13	1	14	20	20	40
Total	107 (89.2)	13 (10.8)	120 (100)	56 (70)	24 (30)	80 (100)

Source: Survey data. Figures in Parentheses indicate percentage.

Education : Education status of the head is significant for analysis because education status of the head reflects in the perception of health of the household and also in determining the social and economic status of the households, which is the basis of the study. Table 4.7 gives the education level of the head of the household and it reveals that the proportion of the illiterate head is only 2.5% in urban areas, that too only in the very low class (SES_5), whereas the proportion of illiterate head was very high at 15% in the slum. In the urban sample 73.4% of the heads are high school and above education, whereas in the slum this was only 22.5% and this reflects in the health awareness and their perception about diseases. In the SES wise division, around 30% of SES_5 in slum and 2.4% of SES_5 in urban are illiterate and it bear the health service utilization of the entire household. From the table it is clear that as socio-economic status declines, the education status of the heads also declines. The analysis of education of the head is significant in the sense that the perception about the disease, the choice of treatment centre, and system of medical care used etc. has influenced a lot on the decision and discretion of the head. So this analysis is vital for the study.

Table 4.7 : SES Class and Education level of the Head of the Households

Education	*Urban*						*Slum*			
	SES Class						*SES Class*			
	SES_1	SES_2	SES_3	SES_4	SES_5	*Total*	SES_3	SES_4	SES_5	*Total*
Illiterate	-	-	-	-	3	3(2.5)	-	-	12	12(15)
Primary	-	1	2	9	10	22(18.3)	-	7	26	33(41.3)
Middle	-	1	3	2	1	7(5.8)	-	16	1	17(21.3)
High school	-	15	19	7	-	41(34.2)	5	6	1	12(15)
Inter/Higher Secondary	-	12	4	2	-	18(15)	3	2	-	5(6.2)
Graduate	-	11	4	-	-	15(12.5)	1	-	-	1(12)
Professional/ Post graduate	12	-	2	-	-	14(11.7)	-	-	-	-
Total	12	40	34	20	14	120(100)	9	31	40	80(100)

Source: Survey data. Figures in Parentheses indicate percentage.

Occupation : Occupation play a vital role in determining the socio-economic status of a household. It is an index to measure the standard of living of person and his family and have an important linkage in the health status and health services utilization. The occupation of the head also decides the regularity and volume of income of the family and also the chances of receiving medical benefits to them and their family members. Table 4.8 provides occupation of the head of the households and it can be seen that in urban sample 100% of the SES_1 class belongs to professional heads with doctors, engineers, advocates etc. Similarly all heads of SES_5 class belongs to unskilled workers with no stable income like masons, hotel workers, construction workers, painters, casual labourers etc. Similarly 70% of the SES_2 heads are engaged in clerical and business field and the proportion of this in the SES_3 and SES_4 was 52% and 15% respectively. In the case of slum, out of total heads of households 77.5% are engaged in unskilled work such as rag picking, hotel work, construction work, fish trading and fishing, painting, street vending, and such menial jobs with no security of work and income. Majority of the upper middle and middle class heads (SES_2 and SES_3) in urban areas are engaged in business and in these category most of them belongs to Muslim community and business is their traditional occupation. Teachers represent the semi-professional category and they are dominated in the SES_2 category. The heads with unskilled worker category is only 17.5% in urban sample and it is more in the middle class (SES_3) households.

Income : Income is also considered as another important criteria in selecting the head of the household. That who earns highest income in the family was taken as the head. Table 4.9 shows the monthly income of the head of the household with their SES class. From the table it can be seen that in the urban sample 75% of the head of households in the SES_1 group and 45% of heads in the SES_2 group is having the monthly income of above

Table 4.8 : SES Class and Occupation of Head of the Households

Occupation	*Urban*						*Slum*			
	Socio-economic class						*Socio-economic class*			
	SES_1	SES_2	SES_3	SES_4	SES_5	*Total*	SES_3	SES_4	SES_5	*Total*
Unskilled	-	-	4	7	14	25(20.8)	1	23	38	62(77.5)
Semi-skilled	-	-	-	2	-	2(1.7)	-	1	2	3(3.75)
Skilled	-	3	10	8	-	21(17.5)	4	2	-	6(7.5)
Clerk/Shop/ business	-	28	18	3	-	49(40.8)	1	5	-	6(7.5)
Semi- Professional	-	9	2	-	-	11(9.2)	3	-	-	3(3.75)
Professional	12	-	-	-	-	12(10.0)	-	-	-	-
Total	12	40	34	20	14	120(100)	9	31	40	80(100)

Source: Survey data. Figures in Parentheses indicate percentage.

Table 4.9 : SES Class and Monthly Income of Head of the Households

Monthly Income in Rupees	*Urban*						*Slum*			
	Socio-economic class						*Socio-economic class*			
	SES_1	SES_2	SES_3	SES_4	SES_5	*Total*	SES_3	SES_4	SES_5	*Total*
Upto 500	-	-	-	-	3	3(2.5)	-	1	8	9(11.3)
501 to 1000	-	-	1	3	8	12(10)	-	7	16	23(28.7)
1001 to 1500	-	-	2	7	2	11(9.2)	1	13	13	27(33.8)
1501 to 2000	-	-	5	5	1	11(9.2)	2	7	3	12(!5)
2001 to 3000	1	4	14	5	-	24(20)	5	3	-	8(10)
3001 to 5000	2	18	12	-	-	32(26.6)	1	-	-	1(2/3)
Above 5000	9	18	-	-	-	27(22.5)	-	-	-	-
Total	12	40	34	20	14	120(100)	9	31	40	80(100)

Source: Survey data. Figures in Parentheses indicate percentage.

Rs.5000. Whereas 73.8% of the heads of the households in slum possess a monthly income of less than or equal to Rs.1500. Hence income is an important criteria which decides one's capacity to pay for health services. Usually the heads income is a vital element in determining the type of health centres approached for the curative care of the members in the family. From the table 4.9 it is clear that, as SES class moves from SES_1 to SES_5 the number of heads with higher income decreases and shows a positive correlation between SES Rank and monthly income.

Characteristics of Household Members

The analysis of the characteristics of the household members including their living condition was a must for the study as it determines to a great extent the health status and health problems of people in different socio-economic groups and also the method and system of health services they preferred.

Monthly Per-capita Income

Income is an important criterion used for measuring the standard of living of households and also the health services utilization capacity. As it is generally observed, higher the income higher would be the temptation for seeking super and super specialized treatment for illness and other ailments. Table 4.10 provides the monthly per-capita income of households with socio- economic status class.

Monthly per-capita income rather than total income of the household is a best measure to judge the purchasing capacity of a household. Though a family possesses large household income, but it will be offset by the presence of more household members with joint or extended families. So monthly percapita income obtained by dividing total monthly income of a household with the number of household members will provide true purchasing capacity on the part of household.

Table 4.10: SES Class and Monthly Percapita Income

Monthly per capita income in Rupees	*Urban*						*Slum*			
	Socio-economic class						*Socio-economic class*			
	SES_1	*SES_2*	*SES_3*	*SES_4*	*SES_5*	*Total*	*SES_3*	*SES_4*	*SES_5*	*Total*
Upto 477	-	-	-	11	14	25(20.8)	-	27	40	67(83.7)
478 to 600	-	-	7	8	-	15(12.5)	2	4	-	6(7.5)
601 to 700	-	-	12	-	-	12(10)	5	-	-	5(6.3)
701 to 800	-	-	4	1	-	5(4.2)	2	-	-	2(2.5)
801 to 1000	-	4	9	-	-	13(10.8)	-	-	-	-
1001 to 1500	5	21	2	-	-	28(23.4)	-	-	-	-
Above 1500	7	15	-	-	-	22(18.3)	-	-	-	-
Total	12	40	34	20	14	120(100)	9	31	40	80(100

Source: Survey data. Figures in Parentheses indicate percentage.

From the table 4.10 it is clear that 20.8% of the households in urban area had monthly percapita income less than Rs.477, which is the cut of income for poverty line fixed by the Planning Commission for urban Kerala as per the current level of prices of 1999-2000. In the slum under study, it is very pathetic to note that 83.7% had income below the poverty line and it can be assumed that almost all households (with the exception of few) are living under the constant threat of poverty and hunger and this reflects in the health services utilization and living environment. It is to be noted here that almost all households in SES_5 category both in the slum and urban belongs to the below poverty line limit.

Smoking and Drinking Habit

The major cause of poverty of the slum households has smoking and drinking habit. From the field it is observed that many who have addicted to alcohol will go for work only few days in a week and the remaining days will be spend for its hangover. Moreover, the addiction of alcohol may also invite different chronic illness. Table 4.11 shows the number of households with smoking and drinking habit members. Illness, poverty, tension and conflict are the net result of addiction to alcohol. They destroy the physical and mental health of the user, his family and social relationship and occupational efficiency. The table revealed that both in the slum and urban as SES rank declines, households with smoking and drinking habit persons increases and there is inverse relation between socio-economic status and smoking and drinking habit. In the slum 78.8% of the households are having members with smoking and drinking habit, whereas in urban it was only 25.8% indicating prevalence of unhealthy elements in the slum. Many respondents in the slum informed us that alcohol is a sleeping tablet for them, without some alcohol they couldn't sleep in the night and their work and type of dwelling is such that it is a must for hard sleep in the night. So addiction to alcohol is something, which is forced on the slum dwellers

Table 4.11: SES Class and No. of Households with Smoking and Drinking Members

SES Class	Urban				Slum			
	Smoking Alone	*Smoking and drinking*	*No smoking No drinking*	*Total*	*Smoking alone*	*Smoking and drinking*	*No smoking No drinking*	*Total*
SES_1	-	2(16.7)	10	12	-	-	-	-
SES_2	3	7(17.5)	33	40	-	-	-	-
SES_3	11	7(20.6)	27	34	5	5(55.6)	4	9
SES_4	9	8(40)	12	20	7	24(77.4)	7	31
SES_5	12	7(50)	7	14	11	34(85)	6	40
Total	42	31(25.8)	89	120	23	63(78.8)	17	80

Source: Survey data. Figures in Parentheses indicate percentage.

by their living and working environment, which is causing some severe health problem on their part.

Housing and Civic Amenities

Adequate housing provides protection against exposures to agents and vectors of communicable diseases, as also protection against avoidable injuries, poisonings, and thermal and other exposures that may contribute to chronic diseases and malignancies (WHO 1988). Health goals have, for the most part, been looked upon as implicit by products of improved housing but have not been given enough emphasis in planning low income housing programmes in developing countries. So the analysis of housing and civic amenities is highly significant in this study.

Housing : The housing conditions differ widely in urban areas. In Kerala houses are constructed to show one's social status and pomp in the society with enough space in the backyard and front yard. The housing conditions of the urban poor and slum dwellers are very deplorable with no latrine and bathroom. Over crowding and congestion is the hallmark of city slums. The majority of the slum households with 10 members or more are cooking eating and sleeping in one and the same room. Housing conditions have a direct bearing on health especially air pollution and sanitation related diseases. It was observed in many studies that kachcha or semi-pucca type of houses, prevalence of respiratory diseases are very high (NFHS 1995, Jyothi Prakash and Vijayalakshmi 2000). So to realize the stark reality of housing problem, some analysis is done in this direction including the type of houses, number of rooms, availability of latrine, sources of drinking water and system of drainage.

Type of House : Table 4.12 provides the type of houses with SES class. In the urban sample 55.8% of the houses are pucca type and in the slum this accounts only 2.5% where 28% are Kachcha and the remaining are of semi-pucca type. A pucca house is one, which is constructed

Table 4.12 : SES Class and Type of Housing

SES Class	Urban				Slum			
	Type of House				Type of House			
	Kachcha	*Pucca*	*Semi pucca*	*Total*	*Kachcha*	*Pucca*	*Semi pucca*	*Total*
SES_1	-	11	1	12	-	-	-	-
SES_2	1	32	7	40	-	-	-	-
SES_3	-	20	14	34	-	-	9	9
SES_4	-	4	16	20	1	2	28	31
SES_5	5	-	9	14	21	-	19	40
Total	6(5)	67(55.8)	47(39.2)	120	22(27.5)	2(20.5)	56(70)	80

Source: Survey data. Figures in Parentheses indicate percentage.

with brick or stone with cement and concrete roofing. A semi- pucca house is constructed with brick or stone with cement and tiled roofing. A kachcha house is one, which is made of mud with thatched roofing. In the present study houses with no sidewalls, with just certain sheets covered in three sides and roof are also considered as kachcha. Respiratory diseases like cough, phlegm, breathlessness wheezing, blood in sputum and eye irritation will be higher among persons staying in kachcha houses compared to those staying in pucca houses (Jyothi Prakash and Vijayalakshmi 2000). The housing condition of the slum dwellers itself is responsible for high morbidity among them. There is no proper ventilation inside the room. In order to enter the house they have to stoop their heads and inside the house it is a horizon of dark. As the fieldwork was conducted in May-June, we have got the chance to see the deplorable picture of the housing situation in the slum. It was actually a hell, in the sense that, there is only one room inside the house. Since it is rainy small kids had defecated in one side of the room, just near to it another kid is eating 'Kanji' with insects and bees fully covered on the plate. As the thatched roof had spoiled due to extreme heat during the summer, water is falling through the holes in the roof to inside the room and thus the only living, eating and sleeping room available is spoiled. This was the condition of many slum dwellers during the rainy season. If they escape from any infectious diseases, it is just because of their good luck, such a bizarrious condition was there in the slums.

Number of Rooms : The number of rooms in the house is very important information as far as the indoor air pollution is concerned. It is being observed, if there are less number of rooms in the houses, chances of respiratory diseases increase because of less dispersion of smoke (Jyothi Prakash and Vijayalakshmi 2000). The number of rooms available to the household indicates the extent of over crowding and congestion. The Table 4.13 shows the SES class with number of rooms available

Table 4.13 : SES Class with Number of Rooms in the House

No. of rooms	*Urban*						*Slum*			
	Socio-economic class						*Socio-economic class*			
	SES_1	SES_2	SES_3	SES_4	SES_5	*Total*	SES_3	SES_4	SES_5	*Total*
1 room	-	-	-	2	5	7(5.8)	-	2	25	27(33.7)
2 rooms	-	-	5	9	7	21(17.5)	6	20	12	38(47.5)
3 to 5 rooms	7	26	26	9	2	70(58.3)	3	9	3	15(18.8)
6 to 8 rooms	4	11	3	-	-	18(15.0)	-	-	-	-
Above 8 rooms	1	3	-	-	-	4(3.4)	-	-	-	-
Total	12	40	34	20	14	120(100)	9	31	40	80(100)

Source: Survey data. Figures in Parentheses indicate percentage.

in the house. The number of rooms in a house means, number of rooms available for sleeping including kitchen. Since most of the slum dwellers have only one room where kitchen and bedroom are one and the same. Most of the upper class and upper middle class (SES_1 and SES_2) lived in houses of 3 to 5 rooms. In the urban sample a total of 58.3% of households had 3 to 5 rooms in their houses. It is observed that 41.6% of the SES_1 and 35% of SES_2 households have more than 6 rooms in their houses, whereas 62.5% of SES_5 households in the slum and 35.7% SES_5 in urban lived in one room houses. From this it is very clear that urban poor has became the victim of overcrowding's and congestion, where people of two generation are living together by cooking eating and breeding in the same room. The higher room density account for hike in morbidity.

Latrine Facilities : Table 4.14 shows the availability of latrine in the study sample households. It can be seen that as a whole for the slum 57.5% had no latrine and 56.2% had no bathroom. But if we go through a class

Table 4.14 : SES Class and Availability Latrine and Bathroom

SES class	*Urban*					
	Latrine	*No latrine*	*Total*	*Bath-room*	*No bath-room*	*Total*
SES_1	12(100)	-	12	12(100)	-	12(100)
SES_2	40(100)	-	40	40(100)	-	40(100)
SES_3	34(100)	-	34	34(100)	-	34(100)
SES_4	19(95)	1(5)	20	19(95)	1(5)	20(100)
SES_5	9(64.3)	5(35.7)	14	8(57.1)	6(42.8)	14(100)
Total	114(95)	6(5)	120	113(94.2)	7(5.8)	120(100)
	SLUM					
SES_3	8(88.9)	1(11.1)	9(100)	8(88.9)	1(11.1)	9(100)
SES_4	22(71)	9(29)	31(!00)	21(67.7)	10(32.3)	31(100)
SES_5	4(!0)	36(90)	40(100)	6(15)	34(85)	40(100)
Total	34(42.5)	46(57.5)	80(100)	35(43.7)	45(56.2)	80(100)

Source: Survey data. Figures in Parentheses indicate percentage.

wise analysis, it is shocking that in the slum 90% of the SES_5 had no latrine and 85% had no bathroom. Similarly in the SES_4 class 29% had no latrine and 32.3% had no bathroom facilities. Whereas for the urban as a whole only 5% had no latrine facility and 58% had no bathroom. The class wise analysis here also reveals that households in the lower SES scale (SES_5) had no latrine facility for 35.7% and they have to share the dirty community latrine provided by the municipality, which is responsible for the spread of many communicable diseases.

The more pitiable condition is that, as the slum dwellers have no community or public latrine near to their residence, they have no other resort other than open space. During the fieldwork, many women in the slum settlement informed us that, they actually fast in the daytime to avoid defecation in open space during daytime. The women's were the actual victim of lack of latrine facilities in the slum areas, as they cannot use open space like railway track and seashore during daytime. They have to wait till dusk for open defecation. From the table it can be observed that households in the lower socio-economic status alone had suffered the lack of latrine and bathroom facilities and this caused for the spread of many infectious diseases in slum dwellings.

Source of Drinking Water : Drinking water is an important civic amenities required for healthful living. The problem is more serious in urban areas as it is difficult to collect drinking water from neighbor's well, which is possible only in the rural set up. It is well known that many communicable diseases are waterborne type, so the availability and accessibility of clean drinking water is a fundamental health problem in the study area. Many households have to walk more than one kilometer for collecting their drinking water and sometimes they may have to wait for long in the queue. Table 4.15 shows SES class with source of drinking water. It revealed the extent of dependence on public tap by the urban slum households.

Table 4.15 : SES Class and Source of Drinking Water

SES class	*Urban*				*Slum*			
	Source of drinking water				*Source of drinking water*			
	Private well/ private tap	*Community well*	*Public tap*	*Total*	*Private well/ private tap*	*Community well*	*Public tap*	*Total*
SES_1	12(100)	-	-	12	-	-	-	-
SES_2	39(97.5)	-	1(2.5)	40	-	-	-	-
SES_3	29(85.3)	-	5(14.7)	34	1(11.1)	-	8(88.9)	9(100)
SES_4	11(55)	-	9(45)	20	4(12.9)	3(9.7)	24(77.4)	31(100)
SES_5	5(35.7)	2(14.3)	7(50)	14	-	1(2.5)	39(97.5)	40(100)
Total	96(80)	2(1.7)	22(18.3)	120	5(6.3)	4(5)	71(88.7)	80(100)

Source: Survey data. Figures in Parentheses indicate percentage.

The households in the lower socio-economic status fully depend on the public tap for the drinking water, which is always interrupted in supply. According to the users the muddy water delivered through the public tap is not at all good to drink. In many places the public water supply's pipe passes through dirty places and drainage areas and since the pipe was laid down years before, through the small holes in the pipe dirty water and waste in the drainage may enter the pipe and thereby the pipe water is polluted. Drinking of this polluted water will bring many water borne infectious diseases. The chances of this event are quite usual in the water supply delivered to urban especially in the slum areas. All of the slum dwellers raise this problem and informed us their grievances. Many women respondent in the slum informed that it is better not to supply water through public taps because the women had to wait for hours near the tap and they fight each other when water comes, which sometimes leads to disruption of harmony in the slum settlements. Many complained that water supplied is unchlorinated and muddy water is pumped directly from the river.

From the table 4.15 it is visible that as socio- economic status declines, dependence on public tap is increasing. In the slum under study 98% of the SES_5 and 77% of SES_4 depends on public tap for the drinking water.

Drainage : Proper drainage in the city area is a must for healthy environment. The problem of lack of proper drainage causes serious havoc in the slum causing water stagnation, accumulation of garbage and filth. In many cases even if drainage system is there, it is not maintained properly and most of them are open kachcha and open pucca and only very few is having covered by pucca type. Table 4.16 shows SES class and availability of drainage. In the urban sample of the 120 households, 37.5% did not have any drainage system. Similarly in the slum 59% households did not have any drainage system. From the table it can be seen that 68% of the

Table 4.16 : SES Class and Type of Drainage

Type of drainage	Urban						Slum			
	Socio-economic class						Socio-economic class			
	SES_1	SES_2	SES_3	SES_4	SES_5	Total	SES_3	SES_4	SES_5	Total
Open kachcha	-	1	2	1	5	9(12)	-	4	6	10(30.3)
Open pucca	7	20	15	7	2	51(68)	2	8	10	20(60.6)
Covered pucca	4	11	-	-	-	15(20)	3	-	-	3(9.1)
Totals	11	32	17	8	7	75(100)	5	12	16	33(100)

Source: Survey data. Figures in Parentheses indicate percentage.

urban and 60.6% of the slum, drainage is open pucca type. Similarly, 10.3% in slum and 12% in urban belongs to open kachcha. The most effective drainage system that is the covered pucca type is only negligible proportion to the total drainage system and it is provided in places where households of better socio- economic status are staying. The open pucca and open kachcha drainage is causing serious health problems to the urban dwellers especially the slum households, as most of the time, the drainage remains chocked with foul smell and over flows. The maintenance of the drainage by the municipal authorities was very rare and it act as a breeding ground for mosquitoes, spreading many communicable diseases specially filariasis. During the fieldwork the researchers observed that these drainage act as nasty pools in the street quite impossible to walk along side. Around 82% of the urban dwellers and 91% of the slum dwellers are not satisfied with the drainage system offered by the municipality, and they complained that the maintenance work is very poor.

Disposal of Solid Waste : Disposal of solid waste also influence the healthy environment of the street and dwellings. It can be seen that the proportion of households that burns this solid waste is negligible in the slum areas, they simply throw out this in their premises or put in the seashore. If it is deposited within their premises for sometimes, definitely insects and worms began to emerge there causing the spread of certain diseases. Table 4.17 gives the method of solid waste management followed by households.

From the table it is revealed that as households socio-economic status rises, they resort to better and safer methods of waste disposal i.e. burns or deposit in bins. It is interesting to note that 64.2% of the urban dwellers disposed their waste by burning, whereas none of the slum dwellers resort of this method. They simply thrown out the waste (41.3%)or put it in the seashore causing serious environmental problem in the slum area.

Table 4.17 : SES with Methods of Solid Waste Management

Slum	*Slum*				
	Method of solid waste management				
	Simply Thrownout	*Burns*	*Deposit in bins*	*Throwing in seashore*	*Total*
SES_3	-	-	-	9	9
SES_4	11	-	8	12	31
SES_5	22	-	1	17	40
Total	33 (41.3)	-	9 (11.2)	38 (47.5)	80 (100)
URBAN					
SES_1	-	11	1	-	12
SES_2	2	31	7	-	40
SES_3	7	25	2	-	34
SES_4	8	8	1	3	20
SES_5	12	2	-	-	14
Total	29 (24.1)	77 (64.2)	11 (9.2)	3 (2.5)	120 (100)

Source: Survey data. Figures in Parentheses indicate percentage.

Access to Mass Media : The access to mass media including news papers, television, radio etc. is highly significant in creating health awareness and creating better perception about health, diseases, and utilization of health services. We made an attempt to see the extent of access to mass media by the households both in the slum and urban areas.

The table 4.18 clearly reveals that 69.2% of the urban sample has access to newspapers, similarly 75% owns television and 8.3% possess radio set. Whereas in the slum only 7.5% is subscribing newspapers, 13.8% had television and 48.8% possess radio. The access to mass media is weak in the slum compared to urban and it reflects in the poor perception about diseases among the slum dwellers. As socio-economic status rises, the access to mass media also rises indicating a positive relation

Table 4.18: SES Class and Access to Mass Media

SES	*Urban*									*Slum*								
	Access to mass media									*Access to mass media*								
	News Paper			*Television*			*Radio*			*News Paper*			*Television*			*Radio*		
Class	*No.*	*Yes*	*Total*	*No*	*Yes*	*Total*	*No*	*Yes*	*Total*	*No*	*Yes*	*Total*	*No*	*Yes*	*Total*	*No*	*Yes*	*Total*
SES_1	-	12	12	-	12	12	12	-	12	5	-	-	-	-	-	-	-	-
SES_2	1	39	40	-	40	40	39	1	40	-	-	-	-	-	-	-	-	-
SES_3	5	29	34	5	29	34	32	2	34	5	4	9	5	4	9	1	8	9
SES_4	19	1	20	11	9	20	16	4	20	29	2	31	24	7	31	18	13	31
SES_5	12	2	14	14	-	14	11	3	14	40	-	40	40	-	40	22	18	40
Total	37	83	120	30	90	120	110	10	14	74	6	80	69	11	80	41	39	80
	(30.8)	(69.2)	(100)	(25)	(75)	(100)	(91.7)	(8.3)	(100)	(92.5)	(7.5)	(100)	(86.2)	(13.2)	(100)	(51.2)	(48.8)	(100)

Source: Survey data. Figures in Parentheses indicate percentage.

between the two. From the class wise analysis it can be seen that, the accessibility of the urban poor or the very low class (SES_5) to mass media was very weak as 85.8% is not subscribing any news papers, 100% does not possess a T.V. set and only 8.3% of them own a radio. In the slum none of them in the very low class have access to either T.V. sets or newspapers. It is their socio-economic status which act as a hurdle in their access to mass media's which is significant in imparting knowledge about environment, sanitation, better housing and good health.

NOTES

1. Pettipalam Colony part of the Komman Vayalam ward was formerly in the Kodiyeri Panchayath. It is included in the Thalassery Municipality in 1998 and now it is a typical slum under the municipality.
2. Beds include 580 beds offered in the Pariyaram Medical College, which is now transferred to Co-operative sector.
3. See the Survey of Pvt. Medical institution in Kerala 1996 and Economic Review 1996.

REFERENCES

Benchmark Survey, (1993), Report on UBSP, Benchmark Survey of Thalassery Municipality 1993, Loyola College of Social Science, Thiurvananthapuram.

Govt. of India, (1998), Indian Population Some Salient Facts and Figures, Central Statistical Organization, Ministry of Planning and Programme implementation, New Delhi.

Govt. of Kerala, (1996), Survey of Private Medical Institutions in Kerala, Dept. of Economics and Statistics, Thiruvananthapuram.

Govt. of Kerala, (1997), Urban Slums in Kerala 1995-1996, Town Planning Department, Thiruvanathapuram.

I.I.P.S., (1995), National Family Health Survey–1992-93 International Institute of Population Science, Mumbai.

I.I.P.S., (2000), National Family Health Survey–1998-99 International Institute of Population Science, Mumbai.

Jyothi Prakash and Vijayalakshmi, (2000), Bio-fuels Pollution and Health Linkages, A Survey of Rural Tamil Nadu,

Economic and Political Weekly, Vol. 35, No. 47, pp. 4125-4137.

Kannan K.P. et. al., (1991), Health and Development in Rural Kerala, K.S.S.P., Thiruvananthapuram.

Mahajan B.K. and Gupta M., (1995), Text Book of Preventive and Social Medicine, Japee Brothers Medical Publishers, New Delhi.

Ramankutty V., (1989), Rational Medial Care in Kerala, Price and Non-price Mechanisms, Economic and Political Weekly Sept. 2-9, pp. 1991-1992.

Ramankutty V. Thankappan K.R. Kannan K.P. and Aravindan K.P., (1993), How Socio-economic Status Affects Birth and Death Rates in Rural Kerala, India : Results of a Health Study, International Journal of Health Services Vol. 23, No.2, p. 373.

Smith G.D. Bartley M. and Blane D., (1990), The Black Report on Socio-economic in Equalities, in Health 10 Years on, British Medical Journal No. 371.

WHO, (1988), Urbanization and Implication for Child Health: Potential for Action, Geneva.

Yesudian, (1981), Differential Utilization of Health Services in a Metropolitan City, Indian Journal of Social Work. Vol. 12, No. 4.

Appendix 4.1 : Map of Kerala

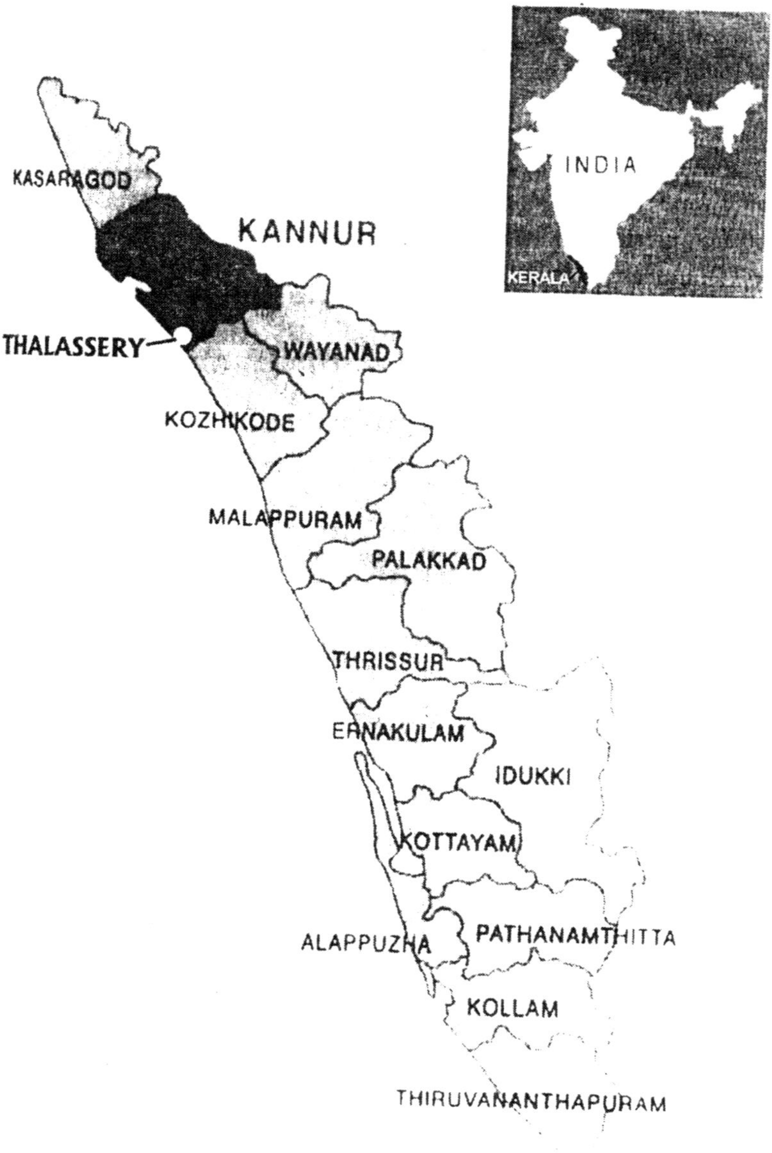

Appendix 4.2 : Map of Thalassery Municipal Corporation

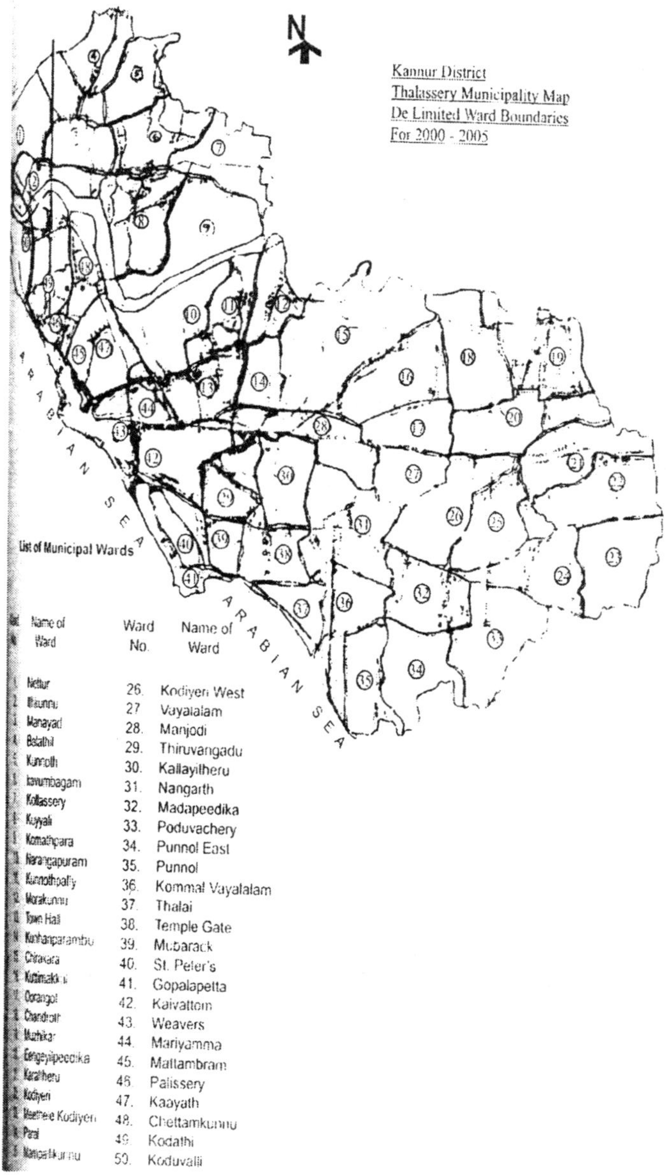

5

Morbidity Pattern and Socio-economic Status

Recently new terms such as epidemiological transition, health transitions etc. have come in vogue to describe the changes in disease profile, following the onset of demographic transition. Kerala being one of the regions in the third world, where the demographic and epidemiological transition is well underway (Kutty VR and Thankappan KR 1994). One of the major paradoxes of modern medical system is that, it has ability and resources to provide high quality medical care on an unprecedented scale, yet substantial proportion of population is unable to receive even minimally adequate medical care. Advances in medical sciences and changes in the organization of medical practice have enabled contemporary physicians to provide highest quality of medical care to the ailing persons. But at the same time the cost of this care have markedly reduced the availability of this care to different segments of population in equal proportions. The low-income families which are considerably more disease prone and which have considerable need for medical attention due to the nature of the environment in which they live, such families have less ability to pay for needed medical services. Many disease and most of the epidemics affect the poor sections of the population in very serious proportions. Poverty, squalor and disease go together. Poverty becomes the root cause of malnutrition, disease and death. This section of the population, because of its huge size requires medical care in greater proportions (Omprakash Sharma 2000).

Life expectancy at birth, mortality and morbidity rates are important indictors of health status of a population. In India the life expectancy has increased from 23 years in 1901 to 62.6 in 1997, and infant morbidity has declined from 215 per thousand in 1901 to 71 in 1997 (Human Development Report 1999). The death rates have declined from 44 per 1000 in 1901 to 10 in 1992 and 8.9 in 1996 (Registrar General of India 1998). However, there are no realistic and comparable estimates of morbidity over a period of time. The life expectancy at birth is an important indicator of quality of the people. The estimates of morbidity in general and the disease specific incidence rates in particular would serve as valuable information to the health planners and administrators for appropriate and timely measures to monitor, control and eradicate the diseases. It will also enable the administrators to allocate resources for health facilities such as hospitals, physicians' medicines, etc. and provide basic infrastructure such as sanitation, drinking water and the like. Recently morbidity estimates have been used to assess the burden of diseases (Duraiswamy 1998).

Morbidity refers to the incidence of illness or we may say that, it refers to the "disease load". A condition of low morbidity logically follows that the health status is better. However, this logic need not necessarily be true. Low morbidity can occur from actual reduction in incidence of illness. But it can also occur due to under reporting or due to lack of disease consciousness. There is considerable disagreement among researchers on how to define and measure morbidity since it is highly subjective based on perception and reporting[1]. In certain cases morbidity may be the reflection of poverty itself.

One of every three persons in India is officially poor and in urban Kerala also 30.62% are estimated as below poverty line in early 1990s (Kirit S Parikh 1999).

In general morbidity studies rely on two types of data, namely the general household level data based on lay reporting and utilization of medical services obtained from hospital or health institutions or health insurance records. In a country like India and a state like Kerala, the utilization information is incomplete since not all people seek medical service in the event of illness or injury. Moreover, public and private institutions provide the medical services and illness particulars treated in private institutions are difficult to obtain.

The data for this micro study is based on household survey conducted in the month of May-June. Different morbidity related studies revealed that Kerala accounts for high morbidity among the Indian states, though it is having better health status (Kannan et al 1991, Shariff et al 1999, Sundar 1992). But none of the above mentioned studies concentrated on urban areas and relate it with the morbidity problems of the urban slums. In the present micro study, the morbidity problem is linked with socio-economic status and morbidity is provided into three categories, namely diseases due to infection, or infectious disease, chronic diseases and other diseases. The recall period or reference period adopted for collecting the morbidity data was one month prior to the survey and it was common for all the three categories of illness (Infectious, chronic and other diseases). The study is based on lay reporting of illness and not on clinical examination.[2]

The type of disease, its degree of severity and use of health services influence not only the length of recall period, but also by the socio economic background of the area and persons involved. Hence the decision of defining a recall period of appropriate length is trivial and cannot be universalized (Gumber and Berman 1997). Since sample size is limited, to include both infectious and chronic diseases and to get maximum number of cases for analysis, in the present study a longer reference period of one month was considered. Many of the health surveys conducted in India have adopted self-perceived approach to collect data on morbidity due to various logical reasons, the most important being the cost. Belcher et al. (1976) estimated that the medical examination surveys turned out to be 8 times costlier than the self-perceived approach. The present study also adopted the self-perceived morbidity approach to collect the data on illness during the reference period of one month.

In this chapter, the morbidity pattern and its linkage with socio- economic and demographic characteristics like education, income, occupation, housing, sanitation, drinking water, age, household density etc are fully examined for urban and slum separately. Morbidity obtained from the field is compared with NSS and NCAER data for different time periods.

Diseases Due to Infection

Many infectious diseases are prevalent in India and major chunk of health resources of the nation is devoted either for curing infectious disease or for the prevention of it. The perception of health care need for the communicable illness depends on the seriousness of the disease and also on the socio-economic status of the households. The socio- economic status of the household is more significant in the sense that as social and economic status rises, even for minor ailment people my have a tendency for medical care, whereas lower and poor sections will neglect such minor ailments.

Regarding the disease due to infection, data had been collected to see the households where individuals suffered from infectious diseases for the last one-month prior to the date of survey. If any one of the house members had affected more than one disease, the disease, which affected in the last was recorded. The NCAER data presented by Shariff (1995) reveals that in urban Kerala

29.5% of the disease are infectious and 42.3% are non-infectious and 28.2% belongs to fevers. Compared to rural (where infectious diseases are only 16.8%) the proportion of infectious diseases is more in the urban Kerala, though it is lesser than the all India average of 34.4%. The table 5.1 reveals the morbidity pattern of different infectious diseases in the slum and urban areas. It can be seen that 57 out of 770 in the urban sample, 118 persons out of 672 in the slum suffered from infectious illness for the period under reference. Diseases due to infection like mumps, malaria and leprosy are totally absent in the disease profile of urban areas, at the same time morbidity pattern of chronic infectious diseases like tuberculosis, filariasis is very high in the slum dwellings. Morbidity rate of filariasis is 7.44 and tuberculosis is 11.9 for every 1000 persons in the slum, whereas it is only 3.9 in the case of tuberculosis and filariasis in the urban areas. Out of total diseases, fever accounts for 26.3% in slum and 35% in urban areas. This may be due to the peculiarity of the season in which the survey was conducted. As the survey was conducted in May-June, the starting of monsoon, fevers of short duration was there in both urban and slum and diarrhoea morbidity was high in slum.[3] When we consider the overall morbidity prevalence of infectious diseases, the slum is far ahead with 175.6 per 1000 population. The living environment of the slum areas was very deplorable which itself is responsible for hike in morbidity. The diseases like diarrhoea, dysentery, and acute respiratory infection scabies etc is highly linked to the drinking water sanitation and housing condition of the slum dwellers. Compared to urban area, the incidence of diarrhoea, dysentery, childhood infection, filariasis and tuberculosis accounts for high morbidity in the slum. The persistence of diarrhoeal and dysenteric disorders among adult populations highlights the poor quality of the environment. The NCAER data for urban Kerala reveals that (Shariff 1995) 57.7% of the diseases in urban areas are infectious in character (including fevers). In the

Table 5.1: Morbidity Pattern of Diseases Due to Infection

Diseases	*Urban*			*Slum*		
	Frequency	*Morbidity Rate per 1000*	*Percentage to total illness*	*Frequency*	*Morbidity Rate per 1000*	*Percentage to total illness*
Typhoid	2	2.6	3.5	3	4.46	2.5
Jaundice	6	7.79	10.5	3	4.46	2.5
Chickenpox	4	5.19	7	7	10.42	5.9
Mums	-	-	-	4	5.95	3.5
Malaria	-	-	-	2	2.98	1.7
Tuberculosis	3	3.9	5.3	8	11.90	6.8
Filariasis	3	3.9	5.3	5	7.44	4
Leprosy	-	-	-	4	5.95	3.4
Dysentery	3	3.9	5.3	7	10.42	5.9
Fever	20	25.97	35.1	31	46.13	26.3
Diarrhoea	2	2.6	3.5	17	25.30	14.5
Acute Respiratory infection	2	2.6	3.5	11	16.37	9.3
Others	12	15.58	21	16	23.81	13.6
Total	57	74.03	100	118	175.60	100

Source : Survey data.

present study 58.4% of the diseases in slum are infectious in character, whereas in the urban sample proportion of infectious disease in the total disease load was only 33.7%. If we add the urban and slum sample together it can be seen that the proportion of infectious disease is 47.16. It can be observed that the problem in the slum is somewhat similar to the national level data of infectious diseases, whereas urban sample shows more of chronic or non-infectious diseases. Since morbidity rates is sensitive to seasonal factors, this raises the issue of reliability of rates reported from the present study based on a single time point of one month. Hence, the rates and pattern of illness captured by this study pertains to only a specific period of the year namely the end of the hot summer and beginning of monsoon month of May-June in which the chances of communicable disease is not so higher.

Morbidity Pattern of Chronic Illness

Chronic diseases or non-infectious diseases are such diseases, which require treatment for longer period and more utilization of health services. Usually in the urban areas chronic diseases are found more in the better off sections as it is considered as the diseases of the rich and old. Major chronic diseases affecting the urban community in general are cancer, diabetes, heart disease, mental illness, Asthma, epilepsy, blood pressure etc. In the urban sample 88 persons out of 770 and in slum 62 persons of out of 672 suffered from chronic illness. The table 5.2 provides the morbidity pattern of chronic diseases. It reveals that the incidence of chronic diseases is high among the urban areas. There is 114.29 chronic diseases per 1000 persons in urban areas, whereas this was only 92.26 per 1000 persons in slum. Among chronic diseases in urban areas diabetes accounts for 22.73%, then asthma, blood pressure and heart diseases. Whereas in the slum, the highest chronic disease belongs to asthma (65%) followed by blood pressure diabetes and heart disease. The proportion of epilepsy is also high in slum, 5.95 per 1000 persons or 6.45% of total disease compared

Table 5.2 : Morbidity Pattern of Chronic Illness

Diseases	*Slum*			*Urban*		
	Frequency	*Morbidity Rate per 1000*	*Percentage to total illness*	*Frequency*	*Morbidity Rate per 1000*	*Percentage to total illness*
Diabetes	8	11.90	12.90	20	25.97	22.73
Heart disease	6	8.93	9.68	12	15.58	13.64
Cancer	2	2.98	3.23	1	1.30	1.14
Cerebral	-	-	-	2	2.60	2.27
Mental	-	-	-	5	6.49	5.68
Asthma	19	28.27	30.65	15	19.48	17.05
Epilepsy	4	5.95	6.45	3	3.90	3.41
Kidney	1	1.49	1.61	-	-	-
Ulcer	2	2.98	3.23	1	1.30	1.14
Blood Pressure	9	13.39	24.52	15	19.48	17.05
Arthritis	2	2.98	3.23	3	3.90	3.41
Other Chronic diseases	9	13.39	14.52	11	14.29	12.25
Total	62	92.96	100	88	114.29	100

Source : Survey data.

to 3.9 pr 1000 persons or 3.41% of the total disease in the urban. Other chronic disease accounts for 14.29 per 1000 persons in urban areas. The living condition and consumption pattern of the urban dwellers is responsible for this high morbidity. Compared to slum dwellers, lack of exercise, mental tension and fast food habit creates many chronic diseases among the urban dwellers. The NCAER data reveal that non-infectious disease accounts for total 42.3% of the disease of the urban areas in Kerala, whereas this micro study shows that urban non-infectious disease accounts for 66.3%, if we add slum and urban sample together then its proportion will be 52.8%.

Morbidity Pattern of other Illness

For the present study the morbidity is classified into three categories, the third category is other diseases, which include different surgeries undergone, like cataract, appendicitis, etc. and it also covers accidental injuries and illness. Table 5.3 shows morbidity of other illness. Among the other diseases accidental injuries is an important cause of morbidity in urban areas, but it is not so grave in the slum. This may be due to the fact that better of sections in the urban areas possess own vehicle and most of them travel far and wide related to their nature of work. So the chances of accidental injuries are higher among this group. Among other diseases, the others, the last item of diseases include rat bite, dog bite, tooth ache, ear ache, cuts and wounds, injury due to fall, eye disease etc. Morbidity pattern of other disease is different in both slum and urban areas, even though overall morbidity of other diseases is more or less the same.

Socio-economic Status and Morbidity Prevalence

In this section, disease and socio-economic status of the households is linked to examine which type of diseases are affected more by the urban poor and weaker sections and which type of diseases are dominated among the affluent and well to do sections in the urban areas.

Table 5.3 : Morbidity Pattern of other Illness

Diseases	*Slum*			*Urban*		
	Frequency	*Morbidity Rate per 1000*	*Percentage to total illness*	*Frequency*	*Morbidity Rate per 1000*	*Percentage to total illness*
Cataract Surgery	2	2.98	9.09	4	5.19	16.67
Insect bite	2	2.98	9.09	3	3.90	12.50
Eye diseases	3	4.46	13.64	1	1.30	4.17
Appendicitis Surgery	2	2.98	9.09	2	2.60	8.33
Accidental Injuries	-	-	-	4	5.19	16.67
Stone in bladder	1	1.49	4.54	2	2.60	8.33
Others	12	17.88	54.55	8	10.39	33.33
Total	22	32.74	100	24	31.77	100

Source : Survey data.

Socio-economic status and Infectious Illness

The data from the present study reveals that higher the socio- economic status, lower will be the incidence of infectious diseases and lower the socio-economic status higher will be incidence of infectious diseases.

From the table 5.4 it can be seen that as socio-economic status falls from SES_1 to SES_5, both in the case of urban and slum, the morbidity prevalence of infectious illness rises. It shows an inverse relation between socio-economic status of households' and morbidity prevalence of infectious illness. In the urban sample, for the SES_1 morbidity prevalence is 32.84 per 1000, for SES_2 it is 35.85 and finally for the SES_5 the most vulnerable section it is 133.33. For the urban slum though the trend is same, increase in the rate is much higher from 89.55 for SES_1 to 236.67 for SES_5 indicating a higher incidence of diseases due to infection. If we take disease wise analysis, it can be seen that incidence of tuberculosis, filariasis, leprosy etc is very dominant in the lower socio-economic status households. In the slum for every 1000 persons, 25.30 suffer from diarrhoea, 46.13 from fever, 10.42 from dysentery and 16.37 from childhood infection whereas for the urban it was 2.6, 25.97, 13.33 and 2.60 respectively showing a considerable reduction compared to slum areas. The slums actually represent a heap of various infectious illnesses and its load is very high among the poor sections of the community.

Socio-economic Status and Chronic Illness

The linkage between socio- economic status and chronic illness is explained in Table 5.5. The most popular chronic illness among the urban community is diabetes, followed by asthma, blood pressure and heart disease. In the slum, the morbidity rate due to asthma is very high followed by blood pressure and diabetes. The trends in morbidity reveals that as socio-economic status falls from SES_1 to SES_5, the morbidity prevalence of chronic illness also falls indicating that chronic illness dominates

Table 5.4 : Socio-economic Status and Morbidity Prevalence of Infectious Illness (Per 1000 persons)

Diseases	*Urban*						*Slum*			
	SES_1	SES_2	SES_3	SES_4	SES_5	*Total*	SES_3	SES_4	SES_5	*Total*
Typhoid	-	3.58	-	8.26	-	2.6	-	3.28	6.67	4.46
Jaundice	-		4.93	16.33	40	7.79	-	-	10.00	4.46
Chickenpox	32.61	3.58	-	-	-	5.19	14.93	9.84	10.00	10.42
Mumps	-	-	-	-	-	-	-	13.11	-	5.95
Malaria	-	-	-	-	-	-	-	3.78	3.33	2.98
Tuberculosis	-	-	4.93	16.53	-	3.90	14.93	-	23.33	11.90
Filariasis	-	-	14.78	-	-	3.90	-	6.56	10.00	7.44
Leprosy	-	-	-	-	-	-	-	-	13.33	5.95
Dysentery	-	-	4.93	8.26	-	13.33	14.93	9.84	10.00	10.42
Diarrhoea	-	3.58	4.93	-	-	2.60	-	9.84	46.67	25.30
Fever	-	3.58	44.33	41.32	66.67	25.97	29.85	42.62	53.33	46.13
ARI*		3.58	-	8.26	-	2.10	14.93	13.11	20.00	16.37
Others	-	-	14.79	24.79	13.33	15.58	-	22.95	30.00	23.81
Total	32.61	35.84	93.60	123.60	133.33	74.03	89.55	134.43	236.67	175.60

Source : Survey data.
ARI* Acute Respiratory Infections.

Table 5.5 : Socio-economic Status and Morbidity Prevalence of Chronic Illness (per 1000 persons)

Diseases	*Urban*						*Slum*			
	Socio-economic class						*Socio-economic class*			
	SES_1	SES_2	SES_3	SES_4	SES_5	*Total*	SES_3	SES_4	SES_5	*Total*
Diabetes	21.74	25.09	44.33	8.26	13.33	25.97	29.85	6.56	13.33	11.90
Heart Disease	-	17.92	19.70	8.26	26.67	15.58	14.93	-	16.67	8.93
Cancer	-	3.58	-	-	-	1.30	-	-	6.67	2.98
Cerebral	-	-	-	8.26	13.33	2.60	-	-	-	-
Mental	10.87	3.58	4.93	8.26	13.33	19.48	-	-	-	-
Asthma	29.74	14.34	29.56	16.53	13.33	3.90	29.85	16.39	40.00	28.27
Epilepsy	-	-	-	16.53	13.33	3.90	-	9.84	3.33	5.95
Kidney	-	-	-	-	-	-	-	-	3.33	1.49
Ulcer	-	3.58	-	-	-	1.30	-	3.28	3.33	2.98
Blood Pressure	10.87	32.26	4.93	24.79	13.33	19.48	-	19.67	10.00	13.39
Arthritis	10.87	3.58	4.93	-	-	3.90	14.93	3.28	-	2.98
Other chronic diseases	43.48	14.58	4.93	16.52	-	14.29	-	19.68	10.00	13.39
Total	119.57	118.28	113.30	107.44	106.67	114.29	89.55	78.69	106.67	92.26

Source : Survey data.

among the affluent and better off sections. If we examine the trend of morbidity prevalence of chronic illness in the slum sample, it can be seen that, though it is declining in SES_3 to SES_4 but it is slightly higher in SES_5 indicating that there are certain chronic illness, which are diseases of poverty like asthma and diseases of affluence like hypertension. The diseases like tuberculosis, filariasis, leprosy, though chronic in character, in the present study, they are included under diseases due to infection or infectious diseases category, since it is infectious in nature and want to project the infectious illness in the slum. This accounts for the reduction in the morbidity prevalence rates of chronic diseases compared to infectious illness in the urban and slum areas. The SES_5 class is more affected by asthma and its morbidity rate is 40 per 1000 population, whereas in the urban sample its morbidity rate is 13.38 per 1000 population. Another trend that can be noticed in the morbidity prevalence of chronic illness is that heart disease, blood pressure and diabetes together accounts for 61.03 per 1000 persons in the urban areas, whereas this was only 34.22 in the urban slum which support the idea that most of the chronic diseases are diseases of affluence (Sundar 1995).

Socio-economic Status and other Illness

Table 5.6 shows the socio economic status of the households and morbidity prevalence of other illness. As socio economic status comes down from SES_1 to SES_5, a definite trend of increasing the morbidity prevalence of other illness can be noticed from the data presented in Table 5.6. There is an inverse relation between SES scale and morbidity prevalence of other illness. Though overall morbidity of slum and urban area is quite similar, in the slum area the low class (SES_4) and very low class (SES_5) again reflects the morbidity of poor living conditions and malnutrition, cataract, tooth ache, ear ache etc. The morbidity of other illness in urban sample is dominated by accidents and its morbidity is high among upper class and upper middle class (i.e. SES_1 and SES_2). As most of

Table 5.6 : Socio-economic Status and Morbidity Prevalence of other Illness (per 1000 persons)

Disease	*Urban*						*Slum*			
	Socio-economic class						*Socio-economic class*			
	SES_1	SES_2	SES_3	SES_4	SES_5	*Total*	SES_3	SES_4	SES_5	*Total*
Cataract surgery	-	-	-	16.53	26.67	5.19	-	3.28	3.33	2.98
Insect bite	-	-	9.85	-	-	3.90	-	6.56	-	2.98
Eye disease	-	-	-	-	13.33	1.30	-	-	10.00	4.46
Appendicitis surgery	-	3.58	-	-	13.33	2.60	-	3.28	3.33	2.98
Accidental wounds	10.87	7.17	-	8.26	-	5.19	-	-	-	-
Stone in Bladder	-	3.58	4.93	-	-	2.60	-	3.28	-	1.49
Others	10.87	7.17	14.78	16.53	-	10.39	14.93	9.84	26.67	17.86
Total	21.74	25.09	29.56	41.32	53.33	31.17	14.93	26.23	43.33	32.74

Source : Survey data.

them possess vehicle and undertake lot of journey related to their work, they are succumbed more to such injuries, whereas no such incidence is reported form the slum areas.

The sample data reveals the close linkage between socio-economic status and morbidity prevalence.[4] Table 5.7 shows socio- economic status and overall morbidity position of urban and slum households under study and it also revealed the impact of socio-economic status on the morbidity pattern of urban households'. It can be seen that as socio-economic status comes down from SES_1 to SES_5 (i.e. from upper class to very low class) the overall morbidity prevalence rate is steadily increasing from 173.91 for SES_1 to 219.48 for SES_5, indicating that socio-economic status and morbidity prevalence rate is inversely related. Many studies (Kannan et al 1991, Sundar 1995, Charles 1998) revealed this type of morbidity prevalence rate among households. The data on slum also shows the same line, where the hike in morbidity is much greater compared to urban sample. The overall morbidity prevalence rate is 300.6 per 1000 population in slum with 219.48 for the urban. If we make disease wise analysis, it can be seen that morbidity prevalence rate of infectious illness is 74 per 1000 in urban, whereas it is more than double (175.6 per 1000 persons) in the case of slum indicating deplorability of living environment and basic facilities. Similarly, in the case of chronic illness in urban and slum different trends are exhibited. In the case of urban, as socio-economic status comes down from upper class to very low class (i.e. SES_1 to SES_5) the rate of chronic diseases is declining from 119.57 to 114.29 per thousand persons.

With the increase in income status of households, the prevalence rate of serious illness and acute illness comes down and the prevalence of chronic illness increases. In other words, with the rise economic status, the diseases of poverty and malnutrition are replaced by the diseases normally prevalent among the affluent in

Table 5.7: SES Class with Morbidity Prevalence of all Three Type of Illness

SES Class	Urban				Slum			
	Morbidity prevalence rate per1000 persons				*Morbidity prevalence rate per1000 persons*			
	Infectious illness	*Chronic illness*	*Other illness*	*Overall illnesses*	*Infectious illness*	*Chronic illness*	*Other illness*	*Overall illnesses*
SES_1	32.61	119.57	21.74	173.91	-	-	-	-
SES_2	35.84	118.28	25.09	179.21	-	-	-	-
SES_3	93.60	113.30	29.56	236.45	89.55	89.55	14.93	194.03
SES_4	123.97	107.44	41.32	272.73	134.43	78.69	26.23	239.34
SES_5	133.33	106.67	53.33	293.33	236.67	106.67	43.33	386.67
Total	74.03	114.29	31.17	219.48	175.60	92.26	32.74	300.60

Source : Survey data.

the western world (Sundar 1995) in the case of slum as revealed by table 5.7, though the morbidity prevalence of chronic illness is declining in the beginning, later it shows a similar trend with that of the lower classes of the urban sample. This may be due to the fact that chronic illnesses are mixture of poverty related disease like asthma and disease of affluence like hypertension and diabetes. In the case of other illness also as socio-economic status comes down from SES_1 to SES_5 morbidity prevalence of illness rises both in the urban and slum under study. The figures from 5.1 to 5.8 show the graphical representation of morbidity prevalence rate of different illness and the socio- economic status.

Fig. 5.1 : Socio-economic Status and Morbidity Prevalence Rate of Infectious Illness-Urban

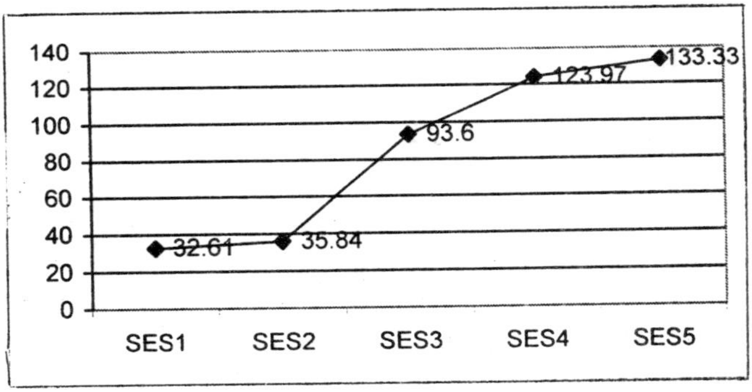

Fig. 5.2 : Socio-economic Status and Morbidity Prevalence Rate of Chronic Illness-Urban

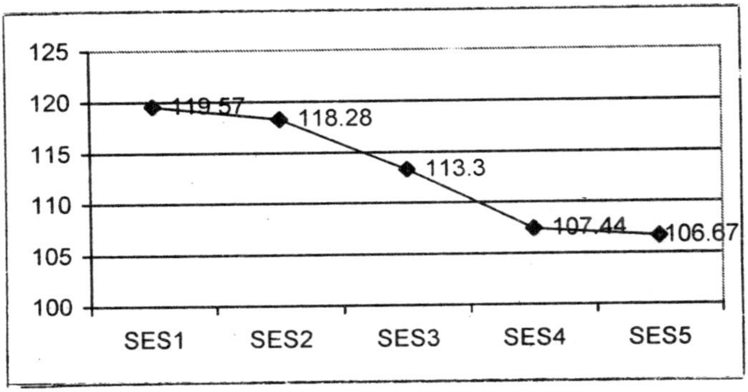

Fig. 5.3 : Socio-economic Status and Morbidity Prevalence Rate of other Illness-Urban

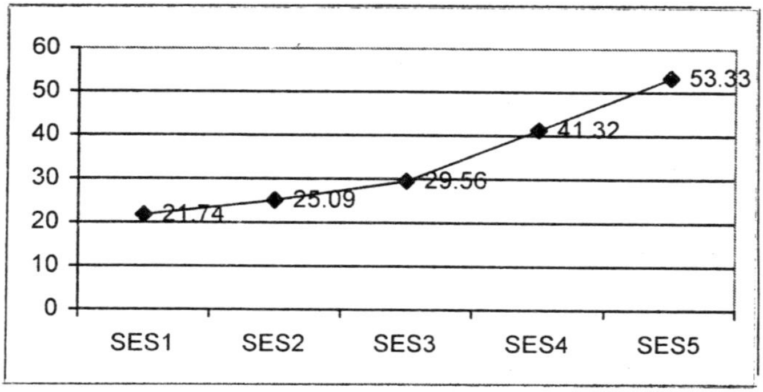

Fig. 5.4: Socio-economic Status and Morbidity Prevalence Rate of Overall Illnesses-Urban

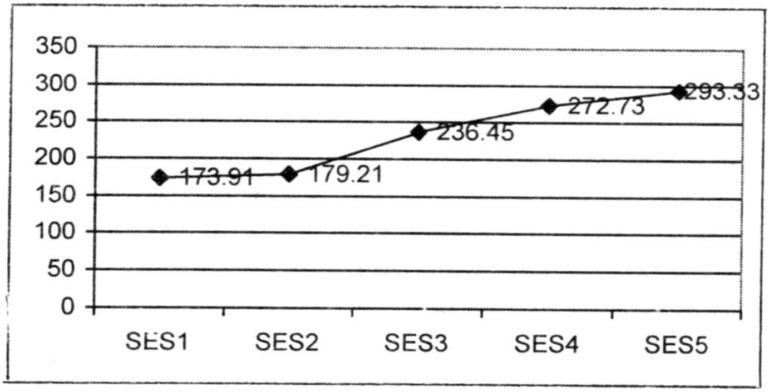

Fig. 5.5: Socio-economic Status and Morbidity Prevalence Rate of Infectious Illness-Slum

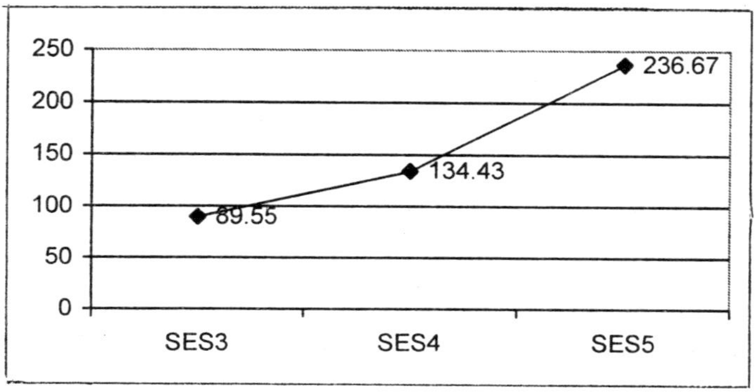

Fig. 5.6: Socio-economic Status and Morbidity Prevalence Rate of Chronic Illness-Slum

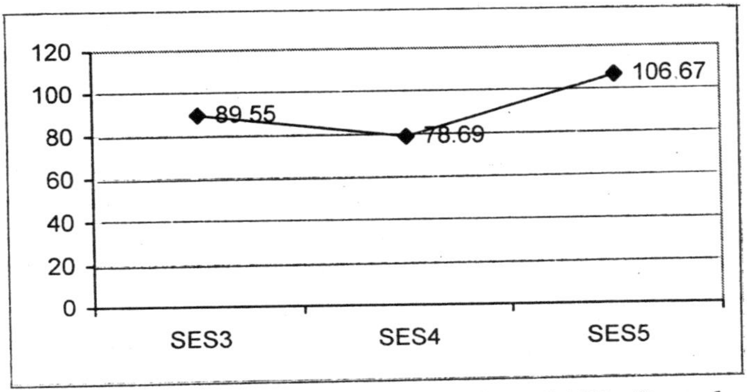

Fig. 5.7 : Socio-economic Status and Morbidity Prevalence Rate of other Illness- Slum

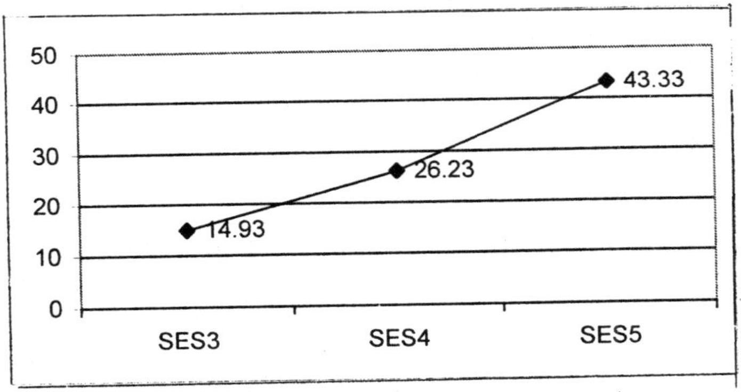

Fig. 5.8 : Socio-economic Status and Morbidity Prevalence Rate of Overall Illnesses - Slum

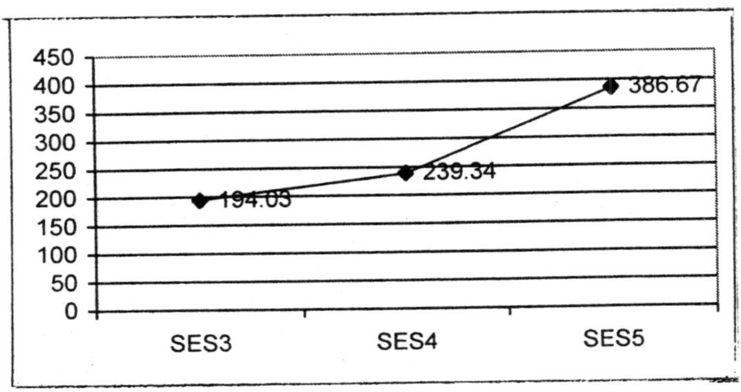

The field data from this micro study reveals that morbidity prevalence rate of illness is very high in both urban and slum in Kerala. When we compare the present morbidity data with the national level data (Shariff 1995), it can be seen that this rate is much higher. The NCAER 1993 survey is one of the rare attempts made to present morbidity prevalence at state and at the national level. The survey has estimated a morbidity prevalence rate of 104 for the rural and 101 for the urban areas for all India with 30 days recall period. (Table 5.8)

Data across Indian states for the year 1993 showed that reported illness was higher in Kerala than in any other Indian states (revealed by Table 5.8). For urban and rural morbidity prevalence rate (sex wise) considered, it is seen that for male urban morbidity Kerala exceeds all other states with 185 per 1000 and almost double of the all India average. In the case of female urban morbidity of Himachal Pradesh exceed all other states with 204 per 1000 (Shariff 1995). As regards rural male and female morbidity prevalence also, Kerala ranks first in India. Kerala a much-talked state about health, (low birth rate, low death rate and good health at low cost) records the highest morbidity rate. Punjab an economically advanced state also records high level of morbidity. The only so called backward state which has recorded high morbidity rate is Orissa. The Kerala Sasthra Sahitya Parishad study of 1991 (Kannan et al 1991) observed, on the one hand the incidence of poverty and environment related diseases has not been controlled and on the other the incidence of chronic de-generative diseases has increased. Closely related to their proportion is the statement that, the remarkable reduction in mortality was due to medical intervention, preventing death than by an effective reduction in the incidence of preventable and infectious illness.

Infectious and parasitic diseases constitute a major share of the total illness of the population (Soman C.R 1993). On the basis of inpatients statistics from SAT

Table 5.8: Morbidity Prevalence Rate per 1000 Persons According to Sex and place of Residence for Selected States

States	*All*			*Rural*			*Urban*		
	All	*Male*	*Female*	*All*	*Male*	*Female*	*All*	*Male*	*Female*
Andhra Pradesh	127	124	130	121	111	129	137	143	132
Assam	83	79	86	85	81	84	65	65	64
Bihar	99	98	99	98	98	98	102	98	106
Gujarath	78	84	72	75	78	72	84	94	74
Harayana	77	79	77	74	71	76	87	98	77
Himachal Pradesh	149	169	130	146	166	127	178	204	156
Karnataka	109	107	111	116	110	122	93	101	87
Kerala	181	177	185	183	181	185	175	166	185
Madhya Pradesh	112	114	110	110	114	107	117	113	121
Maharashtra	70	71	70	66	67	65	78	79	77
Orissa	175	204	150	177	209	149	163	172	156
Punjab	134	127	140	129	106	150	145	175	119
Rajasthan	119	128	111	109	116	103	150	166	137
Tamil Nadu	77	77	77	78	79	78	75	74	75
Uttar Pradesh	101	101	101	107	106	107	79	82	77
West Bengal	80	88	88	80	87	75	81	88	73
All India	103	105	101	104	105	102	101	106	96

Source : Shariff (1995) Health Transition in India, NCAER 1995.

hospital, Trivandrum, he indicates that in 1989, the five major causes for admission of children into hospitals were acute respiratory illness, acute diarrhoeal diseases, measles, bronchial asthma and congenital heart diseases.

The results of our study for the urban area of Thalassery have been more striking. The overall morbidity prevalence of infectious, chronic and other illness is 219.48. This may be due to the influence of time (as the survey was done in May-June). A 20% to 30% increase may occur for diarrhoeal disease during monsoon months (Kannan et al. 1991).

There is no need of wondering for high morbidity in the slum, as the area is actually a hell for the dwellers. During the monsoon period water will flow into their houses, they could never use warm clothes, never eat hot food as the house may be draining during rainy season. Diseases may occur one after another in their surrounding due to their deplorable living condition.

Another possible reason for the hike in morbidity in the urban areas may be due to the improvement of literacy. With increasing levels of literacy and extension of medical services, it is conceivable that even the minor ailments are reported as illness. This could be more so in the case of children. It is quite possible that this perception factor is the major reason for the hike in morbidity in the sample area in particular and Kerala in general. The 1990's saw acceleration in the literacy and education levels in Kerala. The reach of health care facilities widened considerably and there has been further medicalisation of the Kerala society. So the hike in morbidity from the NCAER 1993 data can be justified in this ground.

Though Kerala has only 3% of India's population, it consumes 10-12% of the drugs and medicines produced in the country. Over 750 crores worth of medicines are sold out every year in the state. Government alone spends 50 crores for purchasing medicines a year and still hospitals do not have adequate supplies (Madhava Menon 2000).

The high morbidity in the sample area can also be linked to the high density observed i.e the urban density was estimated at 3968 per square kilometer and in the slum it was 30,000 per square kilometer. Kumar and Vaidyanathan (1988) correlate morbidity with density and according to them Kerala having the maximum density and thus have the maximum morbidity. But this cannot be universally accepted for all states and regions, as exceptional states are there like Bihar, and West Bengal.

Morbidity and Education Status

Education as a socio-economic status indicator has great influence in the occurrence of illness and utilization of health services. Table 5.9 gives the morbidity prevalence and educational status of infectious, chronic and other illness patients.

From the table it can be seen that morbidity prevalence among persons with education level above high school is 38.46% in the urban sample, whereas in the slum this accounts for 16.34%, that is less than half of the urban. In the urban sample, of the total 57 communicable disease patients, 40% of them are having primary education and 1.75% is illiterate. In the case of slum, the primary level educated patients are 21.1% and illiterate constitute 16.1% indicating that morbidity prevalence of infectious illness is high among illiterate and those with primary and below primary education. In the urban sample, the proportion of primary educated patients increased because of more school going children in the sample. Another thing that is visible from the education status of the patients is that 54.5% of the urban chronic patients and 83.9% of the slum chronic are in the group of either illiterate or less than middle school level of education. Morbidity studies in Tamil Nadu revealed that education is inversely related to morbidity (Duraiswamy 1998). The present study reveals that there are exceptions for certain

Table 5.9 : Morbidity Prevalence and Educational Status

Education status	Urban				Slum			
	Type of illness				Type of illness			
	Infectious illness	Chronic illness	Other illness	Total	Infectious illness	Chronic illness	Other illness	Total
Children not enrolled	12	2	-	14 (8.28)	45	2	1	48 (23.8)
Illiterate	1	4	-	5 (2.96)	19	21	1	41 (20.3)
Primary	23	31	10	64(37.87)	25	22	10	57 (28.2)
Middle	7	13	1	21(12.43)	12	9	2	23 (11.4)
High school	11	28	7	46(27.22)	14	8	7	29 (14.4)
Higher secondary	2	7	3	12(7.10)	3	-	1	4 (1.9)
Graduate	1	2	2	5(2.96)	-	-	-	-
Professional / post graduate	-	1	1	2(1.18)	-	-	-	-
Total	57 (33.73)	88 (52.07)	24 (14.20)	169 (100)	118 (58.42)	62 (30.64)	22 (10.89)	202 (100)

Source : Survey data. Figures in parentheses indicate percentage.

diseases, in general the overall morbidity declines with rise in educational status, especially at the post high school level indicates that, the higher the educational level achieved, the lower seems to be the illness prevalence. Jeffry's (1987) study revealed that one-percent increase in the schooling of woman would result in nine percent of reduction in mortality rate.

Morbidity and Occupational Status

Occupation has an important role in increasing the chances of having a particular disease. It is seen that, scabies most often affects the fisherman staying near to coastal areas. Similarly, people working in coalmines and chemical factories may face diseases related to respiratory system. In this study occupational status has been divided as unskilled, semi- skilled, skilled, clerk/ shop owner/ business, semi- professional and professional. Table 5.10 shows morbidity prevalence and occupational status of the people. From the table it can be seen that in the slum among the employed categories, morbidity is high in the unskilled group with negligible proportion in the other categories of employment. Whereas in the urban sample though overall morbidity is somewhat equal in the unskilled and clerical business categories, morbidity of infectious illness is high in the unskilled categories (15.8%) compared to clerk/ business categories (7%). The proportion of unskilled workers with illness is somewhat near in the slum and urban indicating that since their work is floating in nature and may have to contact with many people in different locations, the chances of catching different infectious illness are high. Then another thing to be noted is that, the unemployed categories face the severe threat of chronic diseases and their proportion is also somewhat same in the slum and urban, 60% for the urban and 62.9% for the slum. Among the chronic disease patients, majority of them are woman and lack any sort of exercise and also they are not doing any work of serious nature. It is causing severe health problem among them. Students and children not enrolled

Table 5.10 : Morbidity Prevalence and Occupational Status

Occupation	*Urban*				*Slum*			
	Infectious illness	*Chronic illness*	*Other illness*	*Total*	*Infectious illness*	*Chronic illness*	*Other illness*	*Total*
Unemployed	15 (26.3)	53	6 (25)	74 (43.8)	41 (34.8)	39 (62.9)	7 (31.8)	87 (43.1)
Unskilled	9 (15.8)	10	7 (29.2)	26 (15.4)	21 (17.8)	21 (33.9)	10 (45.5)	52 (25.7)
Semi-skilled	-	-	-	-	1 (0.8)	1 (1.6)	1 (4.6)	3 (1.5)
Skilled	1 (1.8)	3 (3.4)	1 (4.2)	5 (3)	1 (0.8)	-	2 (9.1)	3 (1.5)
Clerk/shop/business	4 (7)	15 (17)	8 (33.3)	27 (16)	-	-	-	1 (0.5)
Semi-professional	-	4 (4.6)	-	4 (2.4)	1 (0.8)	-	-	1 (0.5)
Professional	-	1 (1.1)	-	1 (0.6)	-	-	-	-
Students and children not enrolled	28	2 (2.3)	2 (8.3)	32 (18.9)	53 (44.9)	-	2 (9.1)	55 (27.2)
Total	57 (100)	88 (100)	24 (100)	169 (100)	118 (100)	62 (100)	22 (100)	202 (100)

Source : Survey data. Figures in parentheses indicate percentage.

suffer mainly from infectious illness. In the case of other illness also the unskilled workers accounts for more patients as their nature of work creates the chances of injury and wounds. The occupational analysis of the patients reveals that as occupation moves from blue collar (unskilled and skilled) to white collar (clerical, semi professional and professional) morbidity is steadily declining. The higher the occupational status, the lower seems to be the illness prevalence.

Age and Morbidity

Age is a vital demographic factor affecting the morbidity. By examining the morbidity data on Kerala, Ramankutty and Tankappan (1994) opines that illness reporting is at the extremes of age. i.e below 5 years and above 60 years. Similarly Duraiswamy (1998) while analyzing morbidity trends to Tamil Nadu, both for rural and urban also reported high morbidity among children and elderly persons. It also indicates that infectious illness is concentrated in the younger age group, while the aged people suffer more from non- communicable ailments. Table 5.11 shows morbidity and age of the sample population. Form the table it is revealed that illness reporting is highest (overall illness) in age group 36 to 55, both in the urban and slum. Infectious illness is concentrated in the younger age group, while the aged people suffer more from non-infectious illness. The disease load of communicable disease is very high among the children in the urban slum as the environment is conducive for the spread of all infectious diseases and their mode of living add fuel for the spread of infectious illness (i.e. malnutrition, low intake of food etc.) The share of elderly persons with 60 years of age and above is 8.8% in Kerala.* This itself indicates the chances of higher morbidity among the population of Kerala. The share of elderly is high in Kerala when compared to other Indian states (Registrar General 1996). The trend of domination

* As per the census data of 1991.

Table 5.11: Morbidity and age of household members

Age group	*Urban*				*Slum*			
	Infectious illness	*Chronic illness*	*Other illness*	*Total*	*Infectious illness*	*Chronic illness*	*Other illness*	*Total*
Upto 3	6	1	0	7	37	1	1	39
	(10.5)	(1.1)		(4.1)	(31.4)	(1.6)	(4.5)	(19.3)
4-15	22	2	2	26	32	2	2	36
	(38.6)	(2.3)	(8.3)	(15.4)	(27.1)	(3.2)	(9)	(17.8)
16-35	11	7	9	27	19	6	9	34
	(19.3)	(8)	(37.5)	(16)	(16.1)	(9.7)	(40.9)	(16.8)
36-55	12	29	5	46	19	27	8	54
	(21.1)	(33)	(20.8)	(27.2)	(16.8)	(43.5)	(36.4)	(26.7)
56-65	5	30	4	39	8	16	2	26
	(8.8)	(34)	(16.7)	(23.1)	(4.8)	(25.8)	(9.2)	(6.5)
Above 65	1	19	4	24	3	10	0	13
	(1.7)	(21.6)	(16.7)	(14.2)	(2.5)	(16.2)		(6.5)
Total	57 (100)	88 (100)	24 (100)	169 (100)	118 (100)	62 (100)	22 (100)	202 (100)

Source : Survey data. Figures in parentheses indicate percentage.

of chronic illness among the aged group and domination of infectious illness among the younger age group is common for both urban and urban slum. As we go higher in the age group, it can be seen that infectious illness declines and chronic illness rises and it is more pronounced in urban sample compared to slum. The study revealed the targeted health intervention to reduce morbidity among the children and elderly.

Morbidity and Sex

The table 5.12 provides the socio-economic status and morbidity prevalence rate of infectious, chronic and other diseases sex wise. The gender specific difference in morbidity is an interesting issue to be examined about the sample population. Overall morbidity prevalence rate show a different picture about the urban and slum. In the slum overall morbidity prevalence rate is higher among males (334 per 1000 persons) compared to females (267 persons per 1000) whereas in the urban sample female morbidity is higher over males, it is 223 per 1000 for females and 216 per 1000 for males. Then in the case of disease wise analysis, it is seen that in chronic disease females dominates over males both in the urban and slum areas. In urban it is 87 per 1000 for males but 141 for females. In slum it is 75 for males per 1000, but 109 for females, though overall chronic illness prevalence rate is 114 and 92 for urban and slum respectively. It can be assumed that this high chronic morbidity rate among the females is due to the food habit and mode of living of the people. Over eating with lack of proper exercise and hard work results in certain diseases like diabetes, heart attack, blood pressure joint ailments respiratory diseases and certain type of cancers (Soman C.R. 2000). The problem of cholesterol is also high among the aged persons in the urban areas of Kerala (Soman C.R. 2000). As most of the women are not working and stay inside the house with fatty foods, this might have caused for certain chronic diseases. In the case of diseases due to infection both in the urban and slum, males' accounts

Table 5.12 : SES with Morbidity Prevalence and Sex (Morbidity Prevalence Rate per 1000 Persons)

SES	*Infectious illness*			*Chronic illness*			*Other illness*			*Overall illness*		
Class	*Male*	*Female*	*Total*	*Male*	*Female*	*Total*	*Male*	*Female*	*Total*	*Male*	*Female*	*Total*
Urban												
SES_1	-	68	32	83	159	120	42	-	22	125	227	173
SES_2	36	35	35	58	176	118	36	14	25	131	225	179
SES_3	92	95	94	122	105	113	61	-	30	276	200	236
SES_4	143	103	124	79	138	107	38	52	41	254	293	273
SES_5	205	73	133	118	98	107	118	-	53	441	170	293
Total	79	69	74	87	141	114	50	13	31	216	223	219
Slum												
SES_3	114	63	90	57	125	90	24	-	29	200	188	194
SES_4	166	106	134	55	100	79	34	19	26	255	225	239
SES_5	270	203	237	99	115	107	72	14	43	440	331	386
Total	208	144	176	75	109	92	51	15	33	334	267	301

Source : Survey data.

for higher proportion of being sick compared to females. In the slum for all SES classes taken together the morbidity prevalence of infectious illness is 208 per 1000 for males, whereas it is only 144 for females. Similarly in the urban it is 79 per 1000 for males and 69 for females. The socio-economic status wise analysis of morbidity revealed that, in the case of slum as SES status declines, the morbidity prevalence rate of infectious illness rises both for males and females, but the same trend cannot be seen in the case of chronic and other illness, though overall morbidity prevalence rate is higher in lower socio-economic status groups. In the urban sample rise in morbidity rates with fall in socio-economic status is clearly visible only in the case of infectious illness for males, though overall morbidity prevalence rate rise with fall in socio-economic status.

Morbidity and Crowding

The problem of density also affects morbidity prevalence (Kumar and Vaidyanathan 1988). Over crowding is an important cause of high morbidity among the children in the coastal areas of Kerala (Panicker 1999). This aspect was tested with the sample household to see the extent of room density of the patients in urban and the urban slum and it is shown in table 5.13. From the table it can be seen that the problem of crowding is so grave in the urban slum where 51.5% of the total patients belongs to the room density of 5 or more than 5 persons per room. In the urban area only 13.1% of the total patients have the room density of 5 or more than 5 persons per room. In the case of infectious disease persons in the slum, 81.4% belongs to the room density of 4 persons per room. The problem of overcrowding is acute in the case of slum dwellers as houses of kachcha or semi-pucca type are huddled together without any space in the frontyard or backyard. Whereas this problem is not acute in urban areas where houses are not huddled, even if the number of rooms are limited in the low and very low socio- economic status houses, all of them have

Table 5.13 : Morbidity Prevalence and Extent of Crowding

Room	*Urban*				*Slum*			
	Illness Frequencies				*Illness Frequencies*			
	Infectious illness	*Chronic illness*	*Other illness*	*Total*	*Infectious illness*	*Chronic illness*	*Other illness*	*Total*
Less than or equal to1 person per room	24	36	8	68 (40.2)	2	2	0	4 (2)
2 persons per room	19	17	8	44 (26)	10	6	0	16 (7.9)
3 persons per room	6	18	4	28 (16.6)	10	10	4	24 (11.9)
4 persons per room	2	3	2	7 (4.1)	33	11	10	54 (26.7)
5 persons per room	2	7	0	9 (5.3)	15	12	5	32 (15.8)
6 persons per room	0	2	0	2 (1.2)	26	8	1	35 (17.4)
7 and above per room	4	5	2	11 (6.6)	22	13	2	37 (18.3)
Total	57	88	24	169 (100)	118	62	22	202 (100)

Source : Survey data. Figures in parentheses indicate percentage.

atleast some space in their premises. In the slum setup the chances of spreading the communicable illness is also very high in most cases as there is only one room, which is used for cooking, eating and sleeping.

Morbidity Prevalence and Type of Drinking Water

Drinking water is an important determinant of health status of a people. This determinant is highly significant in the case of urban health, as most of them may not have private well in their premises. Water supply directly affects in the contamination of the household environment and facilitate incidence of various diseases such as diarrhoea: Safe drinking water reduce incidence of diarrhoea (Pradeep Kumar Panda 1997). Most of the communicable or infectious disease is water borne in nature. So the linkage of morbidity and drinking water source is significant for analysis. Morbidity related to water and airborne infections still dominate the health picture and that a very high proportion of morbidity in Kerala can be traced to the lack of protected water supply. Table 5.14 shows the morbidity prevalence and drinking water source available to the patients. From the table it can be seen that 88% of the infectious illness patients in the slum does not have private well or private source of drinking water. They are using public tap provided by the municipality, which is always subject to serious

Table 5.14 : Morbidity Prevalence and Source of Drinking Water

Source of drinking water	*Urban*	*Slum*
	Infectious illness	*Infectious illness*
Private well/ private source (open well)	42(73)	14(11.9)
Public tap	15(26.3)	99(83.9)
Community well	1(1.75)	5(4.2)
Total	57(100)	118(100)

Source : Survey data. Figures in parentheses indicate percentage.

complaints from the slum dwellers due to its poor quality. In the urban sample 73% of the infectious illness patients have private well or private source of drinking water.

The morbidity analysis of the slum area revealed that most of the infectious illness of the slum are water borne in nature, at the same time in urban areas such water borne diseases are less indicating the impact of drinking water on the infectious illness. It is said that almost 80% of the diseases that occur in the world are water borne and water related (Murugan 1994). The cholera epidemics of 1831 and 1832 in England were mainly due to the unsanitary and unlivable 'dangeons' in towns and urban areas. Studies conducted in different countries show that a median reduction of 22% in diarrhoea morbidity and 30% in diarrhoea mortality could be achieved by the provision of improved water supply and excreta disposal (Nayar 1997). Recent study on Kerala showed that mortality has a definite association with environmental status (Kannan et al 1991).

The N.S.S. data also shows that in Kerala for the availability of drinking water 378 out of 1000 households depends on tap water, and 567 out of 1000 households not own private well in Kerala. The N.S.S. 44th round (Nayar, 1999) revealed that 54.26% of the urban Kerala use piped water and 45.19% use well water. The proportion of people not accessible to safe drinking water at the all India level is estimated at 19% (Human Development Report 1999). The high morbidity in the urban Kerala is one way or other linked to a great extent on the accessibility and availability of safe drinking water.

Morbidity Prevalence (Infectious Illness) and Accessibility of Drainage and Latrine

Table 5.15 shows the availability and accessibility of drainage and latrine facility to infectious illness patients in the sample area. From the table 5.15 it can be seen that 64.4% of the infectious diseases persons in slum belongs to the category of no latrine. And in urban sample their proportion was only 3.6%. Similarly for drainage also it can be seen that 67.8% infectious illness patients in slum does not have no drainage and 32.2% slum patients and 84.2% urban patients have access to drainage. But the fact is that the available drainage is so worse that it is better to have no drainage, because most of them are open kachcha and open pucca without proper maintenance. So it always remains chocked giving enough chances for breeding mosquitoes, other worms and virus. The available data on latrine and drainage facility in Kerala and in India as a whole reveals that drainage and latrine exerts a strong impact on morbidity prevalence. The non-accessibility of sanitation for the population for India as a whole is estimated at 71%, which is higher than the average fixed for the low human development country at 63% (U.N.D.P, 1999).

Table 5.15 : Morbidity Prevalence and Drainage and Latrine Facility

	Latrine facility			*Drainage facility*		
	Within the premises			*Drainage*	*No Drainage*	*Total*
	Latrine	*No latrine*	*Total*			
Slum	42(35.6)	76(64.4)	118(100)	38(32.2)	80(67.8)	118
Urban	55(96.4)	2(3.6)	57(100)	48(84.2)	9(15.8)	57

Source : Survey data. Figures in parentheses indicate percentage.

The N.S.S. 44th round survey (Nayar, 1999) revealed that 18.67% had no latrine facility at all in urban Kerala and 15.39% shared with other households. As the households with no latrine facility resort to open defecation or service latrine which itself is responsible for spread of many communicable or infectious illness in urban areas. The very high proportion of morbidity in Kerala can be traced to the lack of proper toilet facilities within the premises of the households (Kabir and Krishnan 2000). Unsafe drinking water and non-availability of sanitation facilities create disorders of the digestive system that can lead to chronic indigestion and thus malnutrition and it is called "nutrition leakage" (Mahadevia 2000). This may also cause for hike in morbidity in the urban and slum areas.

Type of Housing and Morbidity Pattern

Health means not only absence of disease, but is a state of well being physically, mentally, socially, environmentally and spiritually. The health status of an individual is evidently the consequence of the inter play and integration of two major ecological consideration - The internal and external environment. The residential environment is very crucial not only for the physical development but also responsible for psycho- social behavior (Vijayanthimala 2000).

Housing is an important determinant of urban health status. The type of housing can influence the morbidity pattern of infectious illness to a greater extent. The field experience and informal talk with the respondents revealed that most of the kachcha houses are unhygienic in type and susceptible easily to communicable illness of children. Table 5.16 shows morbidity prevalence and type of housing. The table revealed that 99% of morbidity cases in the slum originated from kachcha and semi-pucca of houses. Similarly if we take a disease wise analysis 35.5% of the infectious illness patients and 21% of chronic patients in the slum belongs to kachcha type of houses. As houses are huddled together, the impact of kachcha type housing on morbidity is more visible in the slum compared to urban areas. The use of firewood as the cooking fuel in Kachcha type houses causes respiratory illness among women. In such houses there is no chance for the quick delivery of smoke to outside and thereby cause morbidity related to indoor air pollution. The Bhore committee considered the problem of housing and its implication for public health. The Bhore committee recommended that in India long-term policy comprehensive in scope and modern in outlook was

Table 5.16 : Morbidity Prevalence and Type of Housing

Type of house	*Urban*				*Slum*			
	Infectious illness	*Chronic illness*	*Other illness*	*Total*	*Infectious illness*	*Chronic illness*	*Other illness*	*Total*
Kachcha	4	5	-	9	42	13	5	60)
				(5.3)				(29.7
Semi- Pucca	16	38	13	67	76	47	17	140
				(39.6)				(69.3)
Pucca	37	45	11	93	0	2	0	2
				(55.1)				(1)
Total	57	88	24	169	118	62	22	202
				(100)				(100)

Source : Survey data. Figures in parentheses indicate percentage.

essential for a satisfactory solution of the housing problem (Nayar 1997).

Conclusion

Research on morbidity is rather scanty. Yet it is very important and useful indicator of the health status of the people. The concept morbidity has more than one meaning. It is complex, multi- dimensional and difficult to define and measure because it has strong cultural character, which permits it's meaning to change over time and space. The morbidity data of the present study reveals that, it is higher than the NCAER morbidity prevalence rate fixed for the urban Kerala. The differentials in morbidity prevalence (both overall and gender specific) rates across socio-economic and demographic groups are analysed. The overall morbidity prevalence rate is 219.2 per thousand for urban and 300 per thousand for slum. The prevalence rate of illness is high among children below 15 and those exceed 55 both in the slum and urban areas. Those in the age group of 36 to 55 also accounts for high morbidity both in the slum and urban areas. It is also revealed that morbidity prevalence is inversely related to education and household size. The linkage of morbidity and occupation reveals that among employed groups unskilled workers accounts for higher morbidity of infectious illness, whereas chronic diseases is dominated among business class and white-collar workers. Among the unemployed groups also the morbidity of chronic illness is high both in the slum and urban sample under study. It is also revealed that infectious illness are also high among those households who had no sanitation, safe drinking water, and good drainage system. Among the infections illness, chickenpox, Tuberculosis, diarrhoea, dysentery etc are important source of sickness. Whereas in chronic illness diabetic, heart ailments, asthma, blood pressure etc. are major ailments. In the case of other illness, surgeries undergone for cataract, appendicitis, accidental wounds and injuries, insects bite etc is major ailments. The SES wise analysis of morbidity prevalence revealed that, as socio-economic status falls, the overall morbidity prevalence rate rises, though the prevalence of chronic illness is somewhat same for all socio-economic classes. The analysis of morbidity pattern also revealed the need for targeted health intervention in certain specific age group to reduce morbidity prevalence. The high rate of morbidity in urban Kerala is a manifestation of its economic backwardness and the poverty of masses. It may be recalled that nearly 28.3% of the urban sample and 88.75% of the slum sample households belongs to the low class and very low class, most of them representing poverty ridden families.

NOTES

1. As Johansson (1991) points out, the concept of morbidity has more than one meaning and it is complex, multi-dimensional, difficult to define and measure because it has strong cultural character which permit their meaning to change over time and space.
2. Though filariasis, leprosy and tuberculosis are chronic in character, since they are communicable in nature, in the present study they are included under the category of infectious diseases. As these diseases are more in the slum and we would like to highlight the problem of high infections diseases in the slum compared to chronic illness the inclusion of these three diseases in the infectious category is justified.
3. To avoid the occurrence of certain diseases linked to climate like fevers in one particular sample area alone, the survey was arranged in such a way that one week survey in the slum was followed by one week survey in the urban, again one week survey in the slum followed by another one week in the urban till the entire sample of 120 households in the urban and 80 households in the slums are completed.
4. Morbidity prevalence rate is defined as the ratio between the number of spells of ailment suffered at any time during the reference period and the population exposed to the risk. It measures the frequency of illness prevailing during the reference period. Whereas the morbidity rate gives the proportion of persons reporting ailment suffered at any time during the reference period.

REFERENCES

Belcher D.W. et. al., (1976), Cited in Sodani P.R. and Gupta S.D Health care Expenditure, Results from a Study in Tribal Areas of Rajasthan, Margin, Vol. 31, No.1, 1998 p.70.

Charles C.C., (1997), Health Status and Health care System Among Fisher Folk : A Micro level Analysis, Unpublished M.Phil Thesis Submitted to Jawarhalal Nehru University, Centre for Development Studies, Thiruvananthapuram.

Duraiswamy P., (1998), Morbidity in Tamil Nadu : Level, Differentials and Determinants, Economic and Political Weekly, Vol. XXXIII, No. 17, pp. 982-990.

Gumber Anil and Berman Peter, (1997), Measurement and Pattern of Morbidity and the Utilization of Health Services, Some Emerging Issues from Recent Health Interview Surveys in India, Journal of Health and Population in Developing Countries, Vol.1, (1) Fall pp. 16-43.

Jeffry Robin, (1987), Government and Culture, How Woman made Kerala Literate, Pacific Affairs Vol. 60, No. 3.

Johansson S.R., (1991), The Health Transition : The Cultural Inflation of Morbidity During the Decline of Mortality, Health Transition Review Vol.1, No.1, pp. 39-68.

Kabir M. and Krishnan T.N., (1991), Social Intermediation and Health Transition, Lessons from Kerala Paper Prepared for a Seminar on Human Development in India Jointly Sponsored by the NCAER and Harvard University Centre for Population and Development Studies, held in New Delhi from 2 to 4 January 1992, Thiruvananthapuram, December.

Kannan K.P. Thankappan K.R. Kutty V.R., Aravindan K.P., (1991), Health and Development in Rural Kerala. A Study of the Linkage between Socio-economic Status and Health Status, Kerala Sastra Sahitya Parishad, Thiruvananthapuram.

Kirit S. Parikh, (1999), India Development Report 1999-2000, Indira Gandhi Development Research Institute, Oxford University Press, New Delhi, p.51.

Kumar B.G. and Vaidyanathan, (1988) Morbidity in India some Problems of Measurement, Interpretation and Analysis Paper Presented at the Sixth Annual Conference of Indian Society of Medical Statistics, Hyderabad Oct 27-29.

Kutty V.R. and Thankappan K.R., (1994), Morbidity Profile in Kerala with Respect to Age, Education, Gender and Income, International Congress on Kerala Studies, Abstracts, AKG Centre for Research Studies, Thiruvanthapuram 27 to 29 August, p. 9.

Madhava Menon, (2000), The Health Status of Kerala, Health for Millions Vol. 26, and No. 2, p.13.

Mahadevia Darshini, (2000), Health for all in Gujarath, Is it Achievable, Economic and Political Weekly, Vol. XXXV No. 35 and 36, p. 3204.

Murugan, G., (1994), Investment in Rural Water Supply and its Impact on Water Borne Diseases of Kerala, International Congress on Kerala Studies, A.K.G. Centre for Research Studies Vol. 5, Thiruvananthapuram.

Nayar, K.R., (1997), Housing Amenities and Health Improvement some Findings, Economic and Political Weekly Vol. XXXII No. 2, p. 1276.

Nayar, K.R., (1999), Housing and Health, Another Kerala Conundrun in Rethinking Development ed. By Oommen. M.A, Concept Publishing Company Delhi.

Panda, Pradeep Kumar, (1997), The Effects of Safe Drinking Water and Sanitation on Diarrhoeal Diseases Among Children in Rural Orissa, Working Paper No. 278, C.D.S. Thiruvananthapuram, p.14.

Panicker P.G.K., (1999), Health Transition in Kerala, Kerala Research Programme on local Development, C.D.S Thiruvananthapuram, p.11.

Registrar General, (1996), Population Projection for India and State 1996-2016. Census of India 1991, New Delhi, Table 2 pp. 27.34.

Registrar General, (1998), Sample Registration Bulletin Vol.32 No.1, New Delhi.

Shariff Abusaleh, (1995), Household Survey of Healthcare Utilization and Expenditure, NCAER Working Paper, No. 57, New Delhi.

Shariff Abusaleh, Gumber Anil, Duggal Ravi and Alam Moneer, (1999), Health Care Financing and Insurance Perspectives for the Ninth Plan- 1997-2002 Margin Vol. 31, No. 2, p.40.

Sharma Omprakash, (2000), Rural Health and Medical Care in India, Manak Publications, New Delhi.

Soman, C.R., (1993), Health and Fertility Transition, Lessons from Kerala, K.S. Sajeevani Lecture, Madras, April.

Soman C.R., (2000), Mode of Living and Diseases in Janakeeya Arogyam. By a Group of Writers, Kerala Sastra Sahitya Parishadh, Thiruvananthapuram, pp.75-92.

Sundar Ramamani, (1992), Household Survey of Medical Care, Margin, Vol. 24, No. 2, pp. 169.175.

Sundar Ramamani, (1995), Household Survey of Healthcare Utilization and Expenditure NCAER, Working Paper No.53, New Delhi.

U.N.D.P., (1999), Human Development Report 1999, Oxford University Press, New Delhi.

Vijayanthimala, (2000), Women and Health, The Role of Internal Environment, Environment and People Vol. 7, No. 6, p. 30.

6

Treatment Process and Utilization of Curative Health Services

The extent of utilization of health services is influenced by many factors like the perception of symptoms and diseases, the stage of illness at which treatment is sought, the type of treatment sought and the capacity to seek treatment. There is wide difference among people in choosing various system of treatment. Some may prefer allopathic system for curing certain disease, some others may prefer homoeopathic and some others ayurvedic system. In Kerala 36% of people prefer homoeopathy for treating chicken pox, and 32% prefer modern medicine. In the case of jaundice 47% choose modern medicine and 32% for ayurveda. For paralysis 56% choose for ayurveda and 39% for modern medicine (Kannan etal. 1991). It appears that over a period of time people have made their own judgments regarding the relative effectiveness of various systems of treatment for specific type of diseases.

Perception of symptoms and diseases needing treatment also varies from one section of the community to the other. Certain symptoms and diseases which are seen to be important enough to seek treatment by one section of the population may not seem important to another section of population. For eg. continuous cough may be a symptom of inception of tuberculosis. The field data of the present study revealed that socially and economically advanced sections (households with professionals and employees working in the organized sector) are very alert about cough and they seek immediate treatment. Whereas the socially and economically weaker sections (Households with poor occupational background) including the fisherman, manual labourers, rag pickers, street vendors, tamil migrant labourers neglect such symptoms and will not go for immediate treatment. This chapter has been divided into perception of people for treatment, choice of health centre for curing infectious, chronic and other illness. In Kerala as most of them are literate, the perception factor has little role in the curative health services. But due to differences in the socio-economic status, a disparity always exist among different socio-economic classes in the pattern of utilization of preventive and curative health care services.

Perception of Need for Treatment

As the seriousness of the treatment for different diseases depends on one's perception about the diseases, whether it is grave or not, or need immediate treatment or whether the treatment can postpone etc. In order to analyse the perception factor of households, the respondents were asked about certain diseases (as shown in table 6.1) and symptoms to examine, whether they will go for treatment or not, if they were the victims of such illness and symptoms.

From the table 6.1 it is clear that a majority of the households in SES_1 SES_2 and SES_3 in urban sample considers treatment as essential for almost all diseases and symptoms. Entire household in SES_1 takes treatment for body pain, back pain, chest pain, stomach pain and diarrhoea, whereas this was only 7.1%, 14.2%, 71.4%,

Table 6.1: SES Class and Percentage of Households Seeking Treatment for Different Illness and Symptoms

Diseases	*Urban*						*Slum*			
	Socio-economic class						*Socio-economic class*			
	SES_1	*SES_2*	*SES_3*	*SES_4*	*SES_5*	*Total*	*SES_3*	*SES_4*	*SES_5*	*Total*
Head ache	4.6	42.5	58	2.2	0	20.8	11	0	0	1.3
Body pain	100	38.3	44.1	2.2	7.1	54.1	80	3.2	0	6.3
Back pain	100	95	64.7	2.5	14.2	65.8	77.7	22.5	0	20
Chest pain	100	100	100	95	71.4	95.8	100	96.7	65	81.3
Stomach pain	100	92.3	94	40	40	79.1	77.7	58	37.5	50
Diarrhoea	100	100	100	95	64.2	95	100	96.7	62.5	80
Cough	91.6	95	64.7	10	25.7	64.1	55.5	32.2	12.5	28.8
Cold	33.3	7.5	2.9	0	0	6.6	0	0	0	0
Tooth ache	75	7.5	44.1	0	0	45	55.5	9.6	2.5	11.3

Source : Survey Data.

79.1% and 64.2% for SES_5 class in the urban sample. Percentage of households preferring treatment for various symptoms and diseases vary from 95.8% in the case of chest pain to 6.6% in the case of cold in the urban sample and 81.3% for chest pain to 1.3% for head ache in the slum. In the slum area for cold no one prefers treatment and for headache only 1.3% of households prefer treatment. The data revealed that as socio-economic status declines, the percentage of households seeking treatment for all nine diseases/symptoms declines. It is seen that people in the lower SES class go for treatment only in the case of illness of serious nature and in such cases too, they wait and see the severity of illness.

Reasons for Not Seeking Treatment

As perception of the households about diseases differs from one SES group to another, the reason for no treatment also varies across the SES group. Many households in the low socio economic class avoid treatment as far as possible. Table 6.2 gives the reasons for no treatment expressed by the respondents.

The reasons for no treatment in urban and slum differ widely. Most of the diseases seeking no treatment in urban sample are not serious in nature, whereas in slum diseases of serious nature are not properly treated.

Around 40% of the slum respondent opines that they avoid treatment due to reasons related to their socio-economic status. It can be seen that only 23.7% of non-treatment cases consider this symptom or diseases as minor ailments and others have pointed out that medical aid is costly (40%) and could not afford them for treatment and for some others it is not only costly but also creates a loss of day's wage (6.3%) if they go for treatment. In the urban sample 60% avoid treatment since it is minor ailments and only a total of 28% had suggested loss of day's wage and financial problem for treatment.

Table 6.2 : SES class and Reasons for Not Seeking Treatment

Reasons for not seeking Treatment in respect of certain symptoms & diseases	Urban						Slum			
	Socio-economic class						Socio-economic class			
	SES_1	SES_2	SES_3	SES_4	SES_5	*Total*	SES_3	SES_4	SES_5	*Total*
1. Medical aid is costly	-	-	-	11	6	17 (14.2)	-	13	19	32 (40)
2. Minor ailments not serious	12	33	24	2	1	72 (60)	9	7	3	19 (23.7)
3. Will miss a day's wage if go for treatment	-	-	3	7	2	12 (10)	-	4	1	5 (6.3)
4. Home Medicine	-	7	7	-	-	14 (11.7)	-	2	-	2 (2.5)
5. Medical aid is costly + will miss a day's wage if go for treatment	-	-	-	-	5	5 (4.1)	-	5	17	22 (27.5)
Total	12	40	34	20	14	120	9	31	40	80

Source : Survey Data. Figures in parentheses indicate percentage.

Stage of Illness Seeking Treatment

Health status of population influenced on utilization of health services, but the full effect of utilization depends on the stage in which treatment was sought. The data from the present study reveals wide disparity in the perception of people for attending treatment even when they realized that medical aid is the only resort. Table 6.3 gives the stage of illness for seeking treatment by households in different SES classes.

From the table it can be seen that almost all households in SES_1 and SES_2 would go for treatment for all the symptoms and diseases. In the urban sample a total of 57.5% go for treatment immediately and another 30.8% wait and see the severity and only 11.7% would wait for the illness to affect the day-to-day work. In slum only 11.2% would take immediate treatment and 44% attend for treatment when it affects the day-to-day work or when it incapacitates them. The analysis revealed that as socio-economic status declines their perception for immediate treatment of diseases also declines.

The analysis of data also revealed that percapita income[1] (PCI) of the household is an important determinant in deciding the stage of seeking treatment for illness. Table 6.4 shows the relationship between PCI of household and stage of illness seeking treatment.

From the table it can be seen that as percapita income of households increases, the stage of seeking treatment for illness is immediate and the percentage of households ready to wait and see the severity of illness for attending treatment is steadily declining. Though there exist 71 households in urban sample with percapita income below Rs.1001 per month, immediate treatment is performed only by 29.6%. It can also be seen that those with very low percapita income thinks about treatment only when it affects their day-to-day work. In the urban sample 95.2% with percapita income above Rs.750 per month will opt for immediate treatment, whereas no such families

Table 6.3 : SES Class and Stage of Illness Seeking Treatment

Stage of illness seeking treatment	*Urban*						*Slum*			
	Socio-economic class						*Socio-economic class*			
	SES_1	SES_2	SES_3	SES_4	SES_5	*Total*	SES_3	SES_4	SES_5	*Total*
Immediately	12	40	17	-	-	69 (57.5)	8	1	0	9 (11.2)
Wait & see	-	-	17	16	4	37 (30.8)	1	23	12	36 (45)
Affects day to day Work	-	-	-	4	10	14 (11.7)	0	7	28	35 (43.8)
Total	12	40	34	20	14	120	9	31	40	80

Source : Survey Data. Figures in parentheses indicate percentage.

Table 6.4 : Percapita Income of Households and Stage of Illness Seeking Treatment

PCI Slab (Amount in rupees)	Urban: Stage of illness seeking treatment				Slum: Stage of illness seeking treatment			
	Immediate	*Wait & see*	*Affects work*	*Total*	*Immediate*	*Wait & see*	*Affects work*	*Total*
Below 100	-	-	-	-	-	-	2 (100)	2
100-250	-	3 (42.8)	4 (57.2)	7	-	9 (28.1)	23 (71.9)	32
251-500	3 (10.7)	15 (53.6)	10 (35.7)	28	2 (5.3)	26 (68.4)	10 (26.3)	38
501-750	7 (30.4)	16 (69.6)	-	23	7 (87.5)	1 (12.5)	-	8
751-1000	11 (84.6)	2 (15.4)	-	13	-	-	-	-
1001-1500	26 (96.3)	1 (3.7)	-	27	-	-	-	-
Above 1500	22 (100)	-	-	22	-	-	-	-
Total	69 (57.5)	37 (30.8)	14 (11.7)	120	9 (11.3)	36 (45)	35 (43.7)	80

Source : Survey data. Figures in parentheses indicate percentage.

exist in the slum area under study as percapita income of the slum households are very low.

Causes of Disease

Knowledge about causes of disease is an important factor, which makes them conscious about the prevention, and also proper treatment through health services utilization. Table 6.5 provides the reasons for diseases suggested by respondents. From the table 6.5 it can be seen that in urban area major chunk of the households are fully conscious of the influence of living environment in causing diseases, whereas in the slum majority of them think that poverty is the root cause of all diseases supplemented by climatic factors and nature of occupation etc. The slum households are not fully conscious of the

Table 6.5 : SES Class and General Cause of Disease

Socio-economic class	*Urban*					
	Causes of diseases					
	Germs	*Unhealthy environment*	*Poverty*	*Changing climate*	*Others*	*Total*
SES_1	-	12	-	-	-	12
SES_2	10	30	-	-	-	40
SES_3	7	21	2	-	4	34
SES_4	2	4	7	-	7	20
SES_5	2	-	7	2	3	14
Total	21 (17.5)	67 (55.8)	16 (13.3)	2 (1.7)	14 (11.7)	120
	Slum					
SES_3	-	8	-	1	-	9
SES_4	2	13	8	4	4	31
SES_5	-	7	24	5	4	40
Total	2 (2.5)	28 (35)	32 (40)	10 (12.5)	8 (10)	80

Source : Survey Data. Figures in parentheses indicate percentage.

influence of their living environment in deteriorating their health status and causing health hazards for them.

Awareness on the Seriousness of the Illness

The level of knowledge of the households about different type of illness like diseases due to infection, chronic diseases etc. is highly significant in the utilization of health services by them. The respondents were asked to identify the diseases due to infection and chronic diseases from a list of 10 diseases. They include tuberculosis, cancer, epilepsy heart disease, malaria, hepatitis, polio, diabetes, cancer, asthma and dysentery. Those who had correctly identified 8 to 10 diseases were seems to have good knowledge of diseases, those who able to identify 5 to 7 infectious and chronic diseases from the list were considered to have average knowledge about diseases and those who were able to identify only less than 5 diseases had low identification capacity about diseases. Table 6.6 shows the identification capacity of different diseases by the households, and it shows that in the urban all of them had good or average identification capacity about diseases, and in the slum only 6.3% had good knowledge and 41.2% had low knowledge about diseases reflecting the poor education status and poor access to mass media. The knowledge and identification capacity of diseases influence greatly in the utilization pattern of health services. The individual should know about his illness, then only he can perceive proper health care at the early stage.

Health Check-up

It is often considered unusual to visit a doctor when a person is maintaining normal health. The major goal of health check-up is to detect the hidden symptoms, which in the future may cause illness. Health check-up enabled the people to know the chances of illness in advance. So that they can adopt preventive measures and abnormal cost in curative care can be eliminated. Health check-up

Table 6.6 : SES Class with Identification Capacity of Chronic and Infectious Diseases

Sex	Urban				Slum			
	Identification capacity				*Identification capacity*			
Class	*Good*	*Average*	*Low*	*Total*	*Good*	*Average*	*Low*	*Total*
SES_1	12	-		12				
SES_2	36	4		40				
SES_3	15	19		34	4	5	-	9
SES_4	1	19		20	1	22	8	31
SES_5	1	13		14	0	15	25	40
Total	65	55		120	5	42	33	80
	(54.2)	(45.8)			(6.3)	(52.5)	(41.2)	(100)

Source : Survey data. Figures in parentheses indicate percentage.

involves blood test urine test, stool test, X-ray etc. Thus health check-up can be treated as an effective preventive measure and the urban community in India is not prevention oriented as that of the western urban communities.

As revealed by the table 6.7 only 26.7% of urban households (of this 60% belongs to SES_1 and SES_2) had gone for voluntary health check-up. This practice is not at all popular among the slum households and majority of them opines that there is no need for health check-up (see table 6.8). From the available data it was realized that only in the case of well-educated households with good financial status and those household with members in the gulf countries utilized this health services. Since medical check-up is insisted for emigration clearance, they are compelled to undergo health check-up. Similarly table 6.8 shows the attitude of the households towards health check-up and reason suggested by them for avoiding health check-up. Of the total 120 households in

Table 6.7 : SES Class and Households Gone for Voluntary health check-up

Sex class	*Urban*			*Slum*		
	Gone for health check-up	*Not gone for health check-up*	*Total*	*Gone for health check-up*	*Not gone for health check-up*	*Total*
SES_1	10 (83.3)	2 (16.7)	12			
SES_2	21 (52.5)	19 (47.5)	40			
SES_3	1 (2.9)	33 (97.1)	34		9	9
SES_4		20	20		31	31
SES_5		14	14		40	40
Total	32 (26.7)	88 (73.3)	120 (100)		80	80 (100)

Source : Survey Data. Figures in parentheses indicate percentage.

Table 6.8 : SES Class and Reasons for Not Going for Health Check-up

Reasons	Urban						Slum			
	SES_1	SES_2	SES_3	SES_4	SES_5	*Total*	SES_3	SES_4	SES_5	*Total*
No need of medical check-up	1	9	25	12	12	59 (67)	7	24	35	66 (82.5)
Financial constrains	-	1	6	6	2	15 (17)	2	7	5	14 (17.5)
No time	1	4	-	-	-	5 (5.7)	-	-	-	-
Nobody to take upto such centres		5	2	2	-	9 (10.3)	-	-	-	-
Total	2	19	33	20	14	88	9	31	40	80

Source : Survey data. Figures in parentheses indicate percentage.

the urban, only 26.7% households had undergone for voluntary health check-up and the remaining 73.3% opines that there is no need for this. Those supported health check-up form only 24.2% households and most of them avoids this due to financial constraints, lack of time and in the case of aged people, none is there to take up them to such centres having this facilities. In the slum only 17.5% households support the idea of health check-up, they too avoid this due to lack of money on their part and 82.5% of them think that there is no need for such check-up. This indicates their poor affordability and low awareness about better health care practice.

Choice of Treatment Centre

Since man is a social animal and once he establish a relation or confidence in one health centre or doctor, he may prefer to continue the treatment under the same doctor / centre unless referred to other institutions or doctors. To know the treatment process of households, we have made an attempt to examine how many households prefer one health centre for their health needs and if so which type of health centre they prefer. The available data indicates that both in the slum and urban households members have a tendency to prefer one health centre. In the urban area 72.5% and in the slum 60% prefer one health centre for their health care needs.

Type of Health Centre

As most of the households prefer one health centre for their health care needs, the next attempt is to see which type of health centre they prefer. As the health problems of the upper class and upper middle class differ from the lower class and very low class and also their resources and accessibility to health centre varies considerably, both these classes may set different criteria to select a health centre of their choice. Table 6.9 reveals the type of health centre preferred by households in different socio-economic classes. Private clinics and private hospitals was the choice of most of the upper class

Table 6.9 : SES Class and Type of Health Centre used by the Households

Reasons	*Urban*						*Slum*			
	Socio-economic class						*Socio-economic class*			
	SES_1	*SES_2*	*SES_3*	*SES_4*	*SES_5*	*Total*	*SES_3*	*SES_4*	*SES_5*	*Total*
Govt. Hospital	-	-	1	7	6	14 (16.1)	0	11	24	35 (72.9)
Private Hospital	5	9	11	2	-	27 (31)	4	2	0	6 (12.5)
Private Clinic	7	23	9	-	-	39 (44.8)	0	0	0	0
Govt. Dispensary	0	0	1	-	-	1 (1.2)	1	1	3	5 (10.4)
Others	0	2	3	1	-	6 (6.9)	1	1	0	2 (4.2)
Total	12	34	25	10	6	87 (100)	6	15	27	48 (100)

Source : Survey data. Figures in parentheses indicate percentage.

and upper middle class. Govt. hospital and Govt. dispensary was the choice of low class and very low class (SES_4 and SES_5). Though the study area is served by one Govt. general hospital with 541-bed capacity, only the downtrodden section is utilizing the services provided by the hospital. In the slum 83% of the households having the choice of one hospital are attached with Govt. hospital and Govt. health centres. As their financial background is weak, first they move only to this hospital and later they consider alternative source of health care.

Distance of Health Centre

Distance is an important factor connected to the accessibility of health centres and its utilization by the masses. From the present study it can be seen that 77% of the urban households and 58% of the slum households who choose one particular health centre for health care is within the distance of 2.5km and it is shown in table 6.10. A majority of households in both urban and slum selected a health centre within one km. from their residence. There is one General hospital within the study area. Most of the low and very low class households who had selected the Govt. hospitals and Govt. dispensaries for health care needs were within the distance of 2.5km.

Table 6.10: SES class and distance to the health centre

Sex class	*Urban*			*Slum*		
	Upto 2.5km	*Above 2.5km*	*Total*	*Upto 2.5 km*	*Above 2.5km*	*Total*
SES_1	10	2	12	-	-	-
SES_2	29	5	34	-	-	-
SES_3	22	3	25	2	4	6
SES_4	5	5	10	12	3	15
SES_5	1	5	6	14	13	27
Total	67 (77)	20 (23)	87 (100)	28 (58.3)	20 (41.7)	48 (100)

Source : Survey data. Figures in parentheses indicate percentage.

The problem of distance is not a criteria for the upper class and upper middle class households because transportation cost is not at all a problem for them, as they prefer good treatment.

Reasons for the Choice of Health Centre

As the factors influencing the selection of a particular health centre for the health care needs varies from households to households, some reasons are there which prompt them to go for a particular health centre.

From the table it can be seen that upper class and upper middle class respondents prefer private clinics and private hospitals for specialized and good treatment. In most cases they may have personal contact with the doctors or since they being hold responsible positions and status in the society they may utilize their social position to establish a contact with the doctors they prefer. The better off sections always chase behind good medical care. In the case of poor people they may not have such access, the only criteria they prefer may be the chance of free or concession treatment. In certain cases, though they have no money and are poor, they may prefer private hospital for good treatment especially when the bread earner falls sick, because if he continues sick for long, the poverty of the households will be cumulated and poverty ridden illness will be affected by others also. The table clearly shows that 89% of the very low class (SES_5) in slum and 100% of the very low class in urban consider free or concession treatment as the force behind the selection of one particular hospital for treatment. Similarly 70% of the low class in urban and 66.7% of the low class in slum prefer one particular hospital for free treatment. Similarly a small percentage both in slum and urban prefer one centre due to proximity or nearness of health centres.

Treatment of Diseases

For the treatment procedures households in different SES categories adopt different methods like allopathy,

Table 6.11: The Reasons for the Choice of Particular Hospital/Health centre

Reasons	Urban						Slum			
	SES_1	SES_2	SES_3	SES_4	SES_5	Total	SES_3	SES_4	SES_5	Total
Nearness	1	4	3	-	-	8	-	2	3	5
	(8.3)	(11.8)	(12)			(9.2)		(13.3)	(11)	(10.4)
Highly specialized treatment	5	7	1	-	-	13	-	-	-	-
	(41.7)	(20.6)	(4)			(14.9)				
Free or concession treatment	-	-	-	7	6	13	1	10	24	35
				(70)	(100)	(149)	(16.7)	(66.7)	(89)	(72.9)
Good treatment	3	5	14	3	-	25	5	3	-	8
	(25)	(14.7)	(56)	(30)		(28.7)	(83.3)	(20)		(16.7)
Doctor is known	3	18	7		-	28	-	-	-	-
	(25)	(52.9)	(28)			(32.2)				
Total	12	34	25	10	6	87	6	15	27	48

Source : Survey data. Figures in parentheses indicate percentage.

homoeopathy and ayurveda and also prefer different agencies like private, public and voluntary etc. Adoption of agency depends on the economic status of the patients and in the private agency cost of treatment may be higher compared to Government. So in this section the agencies and method of treatment adopted by the patients in three categories of illness is discussed.

Diseases due to Infection

As explained in the morbidity section, there are 118 infectious disease patients in the slum and 57 in the urban area during the reference period of the study. Table 6.12 provides the agency of treatment utilized by the infectious disease patients. Free or concession treatment was the inspiring force on the part of low class (SES_4) and very low class (SES_5) households to prefer Govt. hospitals/ health centres for treatment. It can be seen that 60% of the SES_5 in urban and 69% of the SES_5 in slum used Govt. hospital for treatment of diseases due to infection. Whereas 100% of the upper class (SES_1) 90% of the upper middle class (SES_2) and 68.4% of the lower middle class (SES_3) utilized private health centre for treatment of diseases due to infection. The overcrowded conditions in the hospital, long waiting time and lack of personal care provided by the Govt. hospital force the socio-economically advantaged classes to opt for private health centres. Though the consultation and medicine availability was poor in Govt. hospitals or health centres, many consider that they can atleast save doctors consultation fee of Rs.25 or 30. But this does not mean that all poor classes approached Govt. hospital for treatment. Many low class and very low class households utilized private hospitals for quality care and to avoid long queue in the out patient counter of Govt. hospitals. One important fact emerged from the analysis is that, as socio-economic status comes down the tendency of preferring more and more of Govt. health centres increases and the preference for private health centres declines.

Table 6.12 : SES Class and type of Health Centre Utilized for Treating Diseases due to Infection

Sex class	Urban				Slum			
	Agency of Treatment				Agency of Treatment			
	Govt.	Private	Voluntary	Total	Govt.	Private	Voluntary	Total
SES_1	-	3 (100)	-	3	-	-	-	-
SES_2	1 (10)	9 (90)	-	10	-	-	-	-
SES_3	6 (31.6)	13 (68.4)	-	19	1 (16.7)	5 (83.3)	0	6 (100)
SES_4	8 (53.3)	7 (46.7)	-	15	21 (51.2)	19 (46.3)	1 (2.5)	41 (100)
SES_5	7 (70)	3 (30)	-	10	49 (69)	21 (29.6)	1 (1.4)	71 (100)
Total	22 (38.6)	35 (61.4)	-	57 (100)	71 (60.2)	45 (38.1)	2 (1.7)	118 (100)

Source : Survey data. Figures in parentheses indicate percentage.

Length of Stay and Type of Hospital : It means the number of days a patient spends in a hospital for obtaining treatment. Table 6.13 gives the length of stay of patients with diseases due to infection.

Table 6.13 : Type of Health Centre and Length of Stay of Patients with Diseases due to Infection

Type of health centre	Urban				Slum			
	O.P.	I.P. short	I.P. long	Total	O.P.	I.P. short	I.P. long	Total
Public	15 (31.3)	5 (71.4)	1 (50)	21 (36.8)	62 (57.9)	9 (81.8)	-	7 (60.2)
Private	33 (68.7)	2 (28.6)	1 (50)	36 (63.2)	45 (42.1)	2 (18.2)	-	47 (39.8)
Total	48 (100)	7 (100)	2 (100)	57 (100)	107 (100)	11 (100)	-	118 (100)

Source : Survey data. Figures in parentheses indicate percentage.

Patients who spends 7 or less than 7 days is called short stay and those who spends more then 7 days is called long stay. As the data reveals that public health centres are utilized more for inpatient care and less for outpatient care. This trend is quite common both in the urban and slum areas as poor section are not able to pay heavy rent and high service charge levied by private health centres. Our results are similar to NCAER findings; NCAER study shows that (Sundar 1995) at the all India level, public health centre is used by 34%, private by 60% and others including charitable, faith healers etc. by 6%. The NCAER data for urban Kerala shows that for non-hospitalized illness 42.4% used public health centres and 52.2% private and the remaining by others includes medical shop, home remedy etc. In the present study only two classification is made where public accounts for 31.3% and 68.7% by private health centres. In the case of slum it is above the NCAER data (Sundar 1995) for urban Kerala and all India average as there is high dependence on public health centres that 57.9% for public and 42.1% on private. The N.S.S.O's (42nd round) survey too found that the dependence on private health providers for the non-hospitalised cases was as high as 69% for the country as a whole (Sundar 1995).

Method of Treatment: India has number of indigenous systems of medicine. In the pre-colonial era, the ayurveda was the most prominent system of medicine. During the colonial period, there was a transition from the traditional to the modern imported systems of medicine. The transition was originally confined to the urban areas and the rural population continued to depend on the traditional systems of medicine, which included tribal and folk medicine, unani and ayurveda. Over the years, the allopathy system of medicine has turned out to be the most dominant among the various systems. However, in recent years, there has been a revival of interest among people not only in sidha, ayurveda and in homoeopathy but also in other systems like naturopathy and acupuncture. The present study along with type of health centres used also collected information on the systems of treatment sought by people for treating their ailments. The field data very well depict the dominance of allopathic treatment over other systems of medicine.

Table 6.14 gives the method of treatment adopted by the patients of diseases due to infection. The data clearly reveals that allopathic system is the most popular system of treatment used by the urban and slum households. It can be seen that 86% of the patients with diseases due to infection in urban areas and 90% of the same category in slum utilized allopathic system, as they assume that for quick relief allopathic system is the only remedy. The NCAER study (Sundar 1995) reveals that 91% outpatient care of all illness in urban Kerala used allopathic system, 4.8% homoeo and 2.8% by ayurveda and 1.4% by other systems. None of them in the slum prefers ayurvedic treatment for diseases due to infection, though they prefer homoeopathy to very limited extent.

Opinion About Health Services : 21 households from the urban and 71 households from the slum have used Govt. hospitals for treatment of diseases due to infection. Most of them used allopathic system and used private health centres. All those who used Govt. health centres were dissatisfied and raised many complaints like lack of medicine, careless treatment, rough behaviour of doctors, discharge from the hospital before recovering from illness etc. Patients with the Govt. hospital were dissatisfied and nobody raised any complaint about private hospital though all of them know that the charge was higher.

Chronic Diseases

Chronic diseases are such illness for which treatment is required for longer period. As revealed in the chapter on morbidity, there were a total of 88 chronic patients in urban and 62 patients in slum, during the reference period of the study. Table 6.15 gives the type of health centres used by the chronic patients.

Table 6.14 : SES and Method of Treatment for Diseases due to Infection

Sex	*Urban*				*Slum*			
	Systems of treatment				*Systems of treatment*			
Class	*Allopathy*	*Homoeopathy*	*Ayurveda*	*Total*	*Allopathy*	*Homoeopathy*	*Ayurveda*	*Total*
SES_1	-	3 (100)	-	3	-	-	-	-
SES_2	8 (80)	1 (10)	1 (10)	10	-	-	-	-
SES_3	17 (89.5)	2 (10.5)	-	19	5 (83.3)	1 (16.7)	-	6 (100)
SES_4	15 (100)	-	-	15	33 (80.5)	8 (19.5)	-	41 (100)
SES_5	9 (90)	-	1 (10)	10	67 (94.4)	4 (5.6)	-	71 (100)
Total	49 (86)	6 (10.5)	2 (3.5)	57 (100)	105 (89.8)	13 (10.2)	-	118 (100)

Source : Survey data. Figures in parentheses indicate percentage.

Table 6.15 : SES with Type of Health Centres Used by the Chronic Patients

Sex class	Urban				Slum			
	Type of health centre				Type of health centre			
	Govt.	Private	Voluntary	Total	Govt.	Private	Voluntary	Total
SES_1	-	11 (100)	-	11	-	-	-	-
SES_2	1 (3)	29 (87.9)	3 (9.1)	33 (100)	-	-	-	-
SES_3	3 (13)	20 (87)	-	23 (100)	1 (16.7)	5 (83.3)	-	6
SES_4	4 (30.8)	9 (69.2)	-	13 (100)	15 (62.5)	9 (37.5)	-	24
SES_5	4 (50)	4 (50)	-	8 (100)	19 (59.4)	13 (40.6)	-	32
Total	12 (13.6)	73 (83)	3 (3.4)	88 (100)	35 (56.5)	27 (43.5)	-	62

Source : Survey data. Figures in parentheses indicate percentage.

Compared to diseases due to infection, for chronic illness most of the patients prefer private health centres for the treatment. As these diseases require intensive treatment and medicines, Govt. health centres and hospitals could not provide this. It can be seen that 83% of the urban patients and 43.5% of the slum patients utilized the private health centres for the curative care of chronic illness. If we make an SES wise analysis, it can be seen that patients in SES_4 and SES_5 in the slum households and patients in SES_5 in the urban households where 50% and above utilized Govt. health centres. The fact is that even people who are living with a hand to mouth existence are compelled to go to private hospitals for treatment due to the callousness of the Govt. doctors and lack of medicine availability in Govt. hospitals. Chronic diseases require regular medicines, antibiotics and injections, but most of the Govt. hospitals lack even the paracetamol required for the fever patients. The informal talk with the respondents realized that, most of the chronic patients with illness like asthma, diabetes, blood pressure, pain in joints, epilepsy etc. required medicines daily. Govt. hospitals in the study area are not supplying medicines for such illness. So even with an empty stomach, the poor people are compelled to go to private medical care centres for saving their life and in certain cases they may even stop treatment due to financial constraints.

System of Treatment for Chronic Illness : Methods of treatment for chronic illness is similar to that of diseases due to infection, as most of them prefer allopathic system. Table 6.16 gives the system of treatment followed by the chronic patients. In the case of urban chronic patients it is interesting to note that both SES_4 and SES_5, 100% of them utilize allopathic system. Only the better off section

Table 6.16 : SES Class and Method of Treatment for Chronic Illness

Sex class	*Urban*				*Slum*			
	Method of treatment				*Method of treatment*			
	Govt.	*Private*	*Volun-tary*	*Total*	*Govt.*	*Private*	*Volun-tary*	*Total*
SES_1	8 (72.7)	-	3 (27.3)	11	-	-	-	-
SES_2	28 (84.8)	1 (3.1)	4 (12.1)	33	-	-	-	-
SES_3	20 (87)	1 (4.3)	2 (8.7)	23	5 (83.3)	1 (16.7)	-	6
SES_4	13 (100)	-	-	13	17 (70.8)	2 (8.4)	5 (20.8)	24
SES_5	8 (100)	-	-	8	30 (93.8)	2 (6.2)	-	32
Total	77 (87.5)	2 (2.3)	9 (10.2)	88	52 (83.8)	5 (8.1)	5 (8.1)	62

Source : Survey data. Figures in parentheses indicate percentage.

i.e. SES_1 SES_2 and SES_3 is shown interest for other methods like Ayurveda and Homoeopathy. When enquired about the reasons for opting ayurveda, many opines that it is free from side effects and did not cause any tiredness on their part, though it required treatment for longer period. At same time to get quick relief, chronic patients in the lower socio-economic profile prefers allopathy.

Stay of Chronic Patients in the Hospital : Seventeen percent patients in the urban sample and nineteen percent patients in the slum stayed in the hospital during the period under reference. Table 6.17 provides chronic patients and length of stay of chronic patients. Many chronic illness like heart disease, asthma, cancer etc. need inpatient care. In most unavoidable cases even the deprived sections in the slum and urban area utilized the inpatient care. While under going fieldwork, the informal talk with the respondent, we came to know that one cancer patient in the slum was admitted in the medical college hospital. As she required continuous treatment of radiation and chemotherapy, due to financial constraints she was compelled to stop treatment. Such instances are there in the slum especially among the most deprived sections.

Table 6.17 : Type of Health Centre and Length of Stay of Chronic Patients

Type of health centre	*Urban*				*Slum*			
	O.P.	*I.P. short stay*	*I.P. long stay*	*Total*	*O.P.*	*I.P. short stay*	*I.P. long stay*	*Total*
Public	8 (10.9)	2 (20)	2 (40)	12 (13.6)	25 (50)	6 (85.7)	4 (80)	35 (56.5)
Private	65 (89.1)	8 (80)	3 (60)	76 (86.4)	25 (50)	1 (14.3)	1 (20)	27 (43.5)
Total	73 (100)	10 (100)	5 (100)	88 (100)	50 (100)	7 (100)	5 (100)	62 (100)

Source : Survey data. Figures in parentheses indicate percentage.

One thing, which is very visible, is that utilization of public health centre is very high in the case of inpatient care. For treatment as inpatient requires huge amount and it is not affordable on the part of lower and upper lower socio-economic status group households. So they preferred public health centres for inpatient care. From the data revealed by table 6.17 it can be seen that 85.7% of short stay and 80% of the long stay chronic patients in the slum area is in the public health centres. Among the urban respondents this was only 20% and 40% respectively indicating the better financial status of urban dwellers. In the case of slum 50% of outpatient care depended on public health centres, whereas this was only 11% in the urban areas. The low class and very low class patients better utilized the inpatient services of the public health centres for the treatment of chronic diseases, as they could not think of the highly paid private hospitals.

Opinion About Health Services : Of the total chronic patients who used health services, only 13.6% had used Govt. health services in the urban sample whereas in the slum 56.4% patients had Government health centres for treatment. All the patients who used public health centres were dissatisfied and opined that their services are very poor and raised many complaints like lack of equipment, lack of medicine bribery, no testing facility etc. No complaint was raised about private health services except, the cost.

Other Illness

Other illness includes those diseases, which are neither due to infection, nor chronic in nature, but they are wide range of illness, which may not be related to one another. They include surgeries undergone by the patients within the reference period, injuries and wounds occurred from the work place, insect bite/rat bite etc. Our data revealed differences in utilization pattern across various SES groups. The injury includes minor injuries due to knife, injury due to fall from the construction site etc. Similarly surgery includes cataract and appendicitis, uterus removal, removal of stone from bladder etc. Since there is an assortment of illness, it is not possible to say which social class is more prone to this group of illness. Altogether 24 patients from 5 SES class in the urban area and 22 patients from 3 SES class in the slum suffered from other illness (i.e. diseases other than diseases due to infection and chronic illness) during the reference period of the study. Most of the patients in the slum are manual labourers working on daily wages and loss of working day would mean a loss of income for them. Similarly in the urban sample also the low class and very low class most of the workers are unskilled and are engaged in daily wages as manual labourers. So early and quick recovery from the illness is a must for them to bring bread for the family. Considering these factors, the lower class and very low class (SES_4 and SES_5) was in greater need of health services for the treatment of other illness.

Kind of Treatment : Utilization of particular medical system is influenced by different factors such as the nature of diseases, households or patients beliefs on particular medical system, the accessibility of the system available, the cost required for treatment and also the time taken for care etc. it can be seen that 95.8% of the urban, 95.4% of the slum patients of other illness used allopathic system of medicine. Only a few used (i.e. 4.2% in urban and 4.6% in slum) ayurvedic system for treatment of other illness. Since most of patients had either undergone surgeries or succumbed to injuries, all of them had gone for allopathic system, as other system is less useful and effective for such illness. People in the lower SES class preferred ayurvedic treatment for bone fractures, snakebite and insect bite, as it is less costly compared to allopathic.

Stay in Hospital : As most of the patients utilized the allopathic system, the type of health centre used by them for inpatient care is analysed. Table 6.18 provides the

Table 6.18: Type of Health Centre and Length of Stay of Other Illness Patients

Type of health centre	Urban				Slum			
	O.P.	I.P. short stay	I.P. long stay	Total	O.P.	I.P. short stay	I.P. long stay	Total
Public	4	4	1	9	6	9	-	15
	(50)	(30.7)	(33.3)	(37.5)	(46.1)	(100)		(68.2)
Private	4	9	2	15	7	-	-	7
	(50)	(69.3)	(66.7)	(62.5)	(53.9)			(31.8)
Total	8	13	3	24	13	9	-	22
	(100)	(100)	(100)	(100)	(100)	(100)		(100)

Source : Survey data. Figures in parentheses indicate percentage.

type of health centres utilized by other illness patients for inpatient care. From the table, it can be seen that most of the other illness patients in the slum preferred Govt. or public health centers. Whereas in the urban sample majority of them used private health centres. Those who used public health centres are the poor sections in the slum and urban areas because the inpatient care in the private hospital results in huge hospital bill. Though the facilities and treatment obtained from the public health centres were worse, these patients utilized the services of the same public health centres due to their poor economic status. In an informal talk with a respondent, who has admitted to hospital revealed the pathetic condition of treatment in the Govt. General hospital of the study area. He was admitted to the hospital for appendicitis operation and had undergone surgery. He was discharged from the hospital after 4 days and asked him to came back after two weeks. The most unfortunate thing is that, the 2nd day after discharging from the hospital, the stitched area of the stomach had broken and inner part of the stomach bulged outside. Immediately, again he was admitted to the hospital and a second surgery was done. The doctor who attended the surgery was not ready to explain his fault and informed him that these things may happen in certain cases. It can be seen that there exist several such cases of callousness on the part of doctors and medical personnel and sometimes this may lead to even death also. Such instances are more in Govt. hospitals at the same time they provide least significance for such cases.

The case of the respondent mentioned above give us the picture of the Govt. Hospital and the inhuman treatment offered by them. Even though this was the situation and environment of the Govt. hospitals, the poor and downtrodden section of the society (like SES_4 and SES_5 classes) had no other resort other than the Govt. hospitals. Actually they are approaching the Govt. hospital by expecting a hidden danger.

Kind of Health Centres

The tendency on the part of people to approach a particular health centre for treatment is also influenced by the economic status. Table 6.19 reveals the kind of health centres approached by patients in different SES classes for treatment of other illness. From the table it can be seen that as socio-economic status improves the proportion of patients using private health centres also rises and using Govt. health centres falls. In the urban sample 100% of patients in SES_1 and SES_2 depends on private health centres and totally avoid Govt. hospitals. In the slum households in different socio-economic classes are not revealing any specific trend, but 69% of the SES_5 and 75% of the SES_4 is utilizing Govt. health facilities.

Opinion About Health Services

A total of 24 patients in the urban and 22 patients in the slum used health services for other illness. Most of the patients who used Govt. health services were dissatisfied about the services rendered by them (i.e. 9 in case of urban and 15 in case of slum). Major complaints raised by them against Govt. hospitals include lack of

Table 6.19 : SES Class and Type of Health Centres Used for other Illness

Sex class	*Urban*			*Slum*		
	Type of health centre			*Type of health centre*		
	Private	*Govt.*	*Total*	*Private*	*Govt.*	*Total*
SES_1	2	-	2	-	-	-
	(100)		(100)			
SES_2	7	-	7	-	-	-
	(100)		(100)			
SES_3	4	2	6	1	-	1
	(66.7)	(33.3)	(100)	(100)		(100)
SES_4	1	4	5	2	6	8
	(20)	(80)	(100)	(25)	(75)	(100)
SES_5	1	3	4	4	9	13
	(25)	(75)	(100)	(30.7)	(69.3)	(100)
Total	15	9	24	7	15	22
	(62.5)	(37.5)	(100)	(31.8)	(68.2)	(100)

Source : Survey data. Figures in parentheses indicate percentage.

proper care, bribery, favouritism in allocating bed, irrational behaviour of nurses, lack of medicine etc. One respondent revealed to us from his experience at the Govt. hospital that, for conducting surgery in the Govt. hospital, the doctor concerned should be paid a good amount in advance. Then only he will be ready for surgery, otherwise the operation date will be postponed and the patient will be put in uncertainty. Bribery has become the hallmark of Govt. hospital, one that is meant for the vulnerable sections of the society.

Age of the Patients and the Agency of Treatment

The table 6.20 reveals the linkage between the age of the patients and type of agency utilized by them in the case of all the three type of illness. The data from table 6.20 reveals that in the case of diseases due to infections,

Table 6.20 : Age of the Infectious, Chronic and other Illness Patients and the Agency of Treatment sought

Age of patients	*Diseases due to infection*				*Chronic illness*				*Other illness*			
URBAN	*Private*	*Govt.*	*Voluntary*	*Total*	*Private*	*Govt.*	*Voluntary*	*Total*	*Private*	*Govt.*	*Voluntary*	*Total*
0-6	7	4	-	11	2	-	-	2	-	-	-	-
	(63.6)	(36.4)			(100)							
6-15	9	4	-	13	2	-	-	2	1	1		2
	(69.2)	(30.8)			(100)				(50)	(50)		
15-25	5	4	-	9	1	-	-	1	2	-	-	2
	(55.6)	(44.4)			(100)				(100)			
25-45	7	4	-	11	12	3	-	15	7	3	-	10
	(63.6)	(36.4)			(80)	(20)			(70)	(30)		
45-60	6	5	-	11	32	3	-	35	3	1	-	4
	(54.5)	(45.5)			(91.4)	(8.6)			(75)	(25)		
Above 60	1	1	-	2	24	6	3	33	2	4	-	6
	(50)	(50)			(72.8)	(18.2)			(33.3)	(66.4)		
Total	35	22	-	57	73	12	3	88	15	9	-	24
	(61.4)	(38.6)			(83)	(13.6)	(3.4)	(100)	(62.5)	(37.5)		

Contd....

Table 6.20 : (Contd....)

Age of patients	Diseases due to infection				Chronic illness				Other illness			
SLUM	*Private*	*Govt.*	*Voluntary*	*Total*	*Private*	*Govt.*	*Voluntary*	*Total*	*Private*	*Govt.*	*Voluntary*	*Total*
0-6	20 (46.5)	22 (51.2)	1	43	0	2 (100)	-	2 (100)	-	1 (100)	-	1
6-15	12 (63.2)	7 (36.8)	0	19	1 (100)	0	-	1 (100)	1 (50)	1 (50)	-	2
15-25	4 (22.2)	14 (77.8)	0	18	1 (33.3)	2 (66.7)	-	3	1 (33.3)	2 (66.7)	-	3
25-45	5 (33.3)	9 (60)	1 (6.7)	15	9 (52.9)	8 (47.1)	-	17	3 (37.5)	5 (62.5)	-	8
45-60	4 (26.7)	11 (73.3)	0	15	8 (40)	12 (60)	-	20	1 (16.7)	5 (83.3)	-	6
Above 60	0	8 (100)	0	8	8 (42.1)	11 (57.9)	-	19	1 (50)	1 (50)	-	2
Total	45 (38.1)	71 (60.2)	2 (1.7)	118	27 (43.5)	35 (56.5)	-	62	7 (31.8)	15 (68.2)	-	22

Source : Survey data. Figures in parentheses indicate percentage.

patients in the age group of 0-6 and 6-15 utilized more of private agency in the urban sample, whereas in slum all age group one way or other have interchangeably used both private and Govt. agency. Another fact, which is typical of the slum area, is that 100% of the patients in the age above 60 category utilized Govt. hospital. This may be due to lack of financial help from other members of the family to seek private medical aid. The family relationship in the slum is such that the youngsters usually neglect the aged people.

With regard to the use of private agency (both in the slum and urban sample) for the chronic illness, maximum thrust is given to the private agency for treatment. It is 83% for all age groups in the urban sample and 43.5% for the slum. In the case of slum, for chronic and other illness, the percentage that prefers voluntary hospital was totally absent, whereas the urbans totally avoided voluntary hospitals for diseases due to infection and other illness.

Age of the Patients and System of Treatment Utilised

Analysis of data related to age and system of medicine utilized revealed that at certain ages the patients utilized particular system of medicine. It is done in table 6.21. It can be seen that in urban sample around 86% of all the age groups and in slum around 89% use allopathy as the system of treatment for diseases due to infection. In slum nobody has utilized ayurveda for diseases due to infection and 11% used homoeopathy. The data about diseases due to infection shows that allopathy system dominates in almost all age groups both in the slum and urban sample under study. In the case of chronic illness, the first three age groups in urban and slum shows 100% preference for allopathy system. The 12.1% of the aged groups in urban (age above 60), 21% of the aged groups in slum utilized ayurvedic and homoeopathic system for chronic illness. In the case of other illness also allopathy is the leading system for all age groups both in the slum and urban areas. The age pattern and use of system of

Table 6.21: Age of the Patients (Infectious, Chronic and other Illness) and the System of Medicine utilised

Age of patients	*Diseases due to infection*				*Chronic illness*				*Other illness*			
URBAN	*Allo-pathic*	*Ayur-veda*	*Homoeo-pathic*	*Total*	*Allo-pathic*	*Ayur-veda*	*Homoeo-pathic*	*Total*	*Allo-pathic*	*Ayur-veda*	*Homoeo-pathic*	*Total*
0-6	11	-	-	11	2	-	-	2	-	-	-	-
	(100)				(100)							
6-15	11	-	2	13	2	-	-	2	2	-	-	2
	(84.6)		(15.4)		(100)				(100)			
15-25	6	-	3	9	1	-	-	1	2	-	-	2
	(66.7)		(33.3)		(100)				(100)			
25-45	9	2	-	11	13	2	-	15	9	1	-	10
	(81.8)	(18.2)			(86.7)	(13.3)			(90)	(10)		
45-60	11	-	-	11	30	4	1	35	4	-	-	4
	(100)				(85.7)	(11.4)	(2.9)		(100)			
Above 60	1	-	1	2	29	3	1	33	6	-	-	6
	(50)		(50)		(87.9)	(9.1)	(3)		(100)			
Total	49	2	6	57	77	9	2	88	23	1	-	24
	(56)	(3.5)	(10.5)		(87.5)	(10.2)	(2.3)		(95.8)	(4.2)		

Contd....

Table 6.21: (Contd....)

Age of patients	*Diseases due to infection*				*Chronic illness*				*Other illness*			
SLUM	*Allo-pathic*	*Ayur-veda*	*Homoeo-pathic*	*Total*	*Allo-pathic*	*Ayur-veda*	*Homoeo-pathic*	*Total*	*Allo-pathic*	*Ayur-veda*	*Homoeo-pathic*	*Total*
0-6	37 (86.05)	-	6 (13.95)	43	2 (100)	-	-	2	-	1 (100)	-	1
6-15	16 (84.21)	-	3 (15.79)	19	1 (100)	-	-	1	2 (100)	-	-	2
15-25	16 (88.89)	-	2 (11.11)	18	3 (100)	-	-	3	3 (100)	-	-	3
25-45	14 (93.33)	-	1 (6.67)	15	14 (82.35)	2 (11.76)	1 (5.88)	17	8 (100)	-	-	8
45-60	14 (93.33)	-	1 (6.67)	15	17 (85)	1 (5)	2 (10)	20	6 (100)	-	-	6
Above 60	8 (100)	-	-	8	15 (78.95)	2 (10.53)	2 (10.53)	19	2 (100)	-	-	2
Total	105 (88.98)	-	13 (11.02)	118	52 (83.87)	5 (8.06)	5 (8.06)	62	21 (95.45)	1 (4.55)	-	22

X^2 = 59.66375 df = 27 p = .00297 X^2 = 11.5498 df = 27 p = .995826 X^2 = 52.2423 df = 16 p = .00010

Source : Survey data. Figures in parentheses indicate percentage.

treatment reveals that the influence of western system of medicine is deeply rooted among the urban folks as the chances of quick relief is high in allopathic system of treatment. Statistical analysis revealed that the association between age group and use of allopathic system is highly significant in the case of diseases due to infection and other illness and not significant in the case of chronic illness.

Sex of the Patients and Type of Agency Utilized for Treatment

Some sort of association is noted between sex of the patients and the type of agency utilized for treatment of three types of diseases and the table 6.22 reveals this relationship.

The analysis of data related to agency revealed that in urban both male and female provided high priority for chronic illness. It is seen that 93.8% of the males and 76.8% of the females used private agency for treatment whereas in slum majority of the male and female uitlised Govt. hospitals. Another fact emerged from the study is that females utilized more of Govt. agency in the urban and male utilized more of Govt. agency in the slum for all the three type of illness. The reason behind this change is that in the urban all the males in one way or other are busy with their work or employment so they won't get enough time to wait in the Govt. hospitals. At the same time females are mostly unemployed in the urban setup so they utilized their time to seek the services of Govt. hospitals. In the slum the situation is different as mostly woman are in the working category. For immediate relief and to avoid the loss of one day's wage they prefer private clinic or hospitals, which function even in the evening or night. Moreover in the slum most of the illness-affected males are in the aged category, as they have no work and income they would like to utilize Govt. hospitals or health centres. As chronic diseases requires regular treatment and costly medicines most of the slum dwellers are

Table 6.22 : Sex of the Patients and the Type of the Agency Utilized for Treatment

Sex	*Diseases due to infection*				*Chronic illness*				*Other illness*			
URBAN	*Private*	*Govt.*	*Voluntary*	*Total*	*Private*	*Govt.*	*Voluntary*	*Total*	*Private*	*Govt.*	*Voluntary*	*Total*
Male	19	11	-	30	30	2	-	32	13	6	-	19
	(63.3)	(36.7)			(93.8)	(6.2)			(68.4)	(31.6)		
Female	16	11	-	27	43	10	3	56	2	3	-	5
	(59.3)	(40.7)			(76.8)	(17.9)	(5.3)		(40)	(60)		
Total	35	22	-	57	73	12	3	88	15	9	-	24
	(61.4)	(38.6)			(82.9)	(13.6)	(3.4)		(62.5)	(37.5)		
SLUM												
Male	27	42	-	69	10	15		25	5	12	-	17
	(39.1)	(60.9)			(40)	(60)			(29.4)	(70.6)		
Female	18	29	2	49	17	20		37	2	3	-	5
	(36.7)	(59.2)	(4.1)		(45.9)	(54.1)			(40)	(60)		
Total	45	71	2	118	27	35		62	7	15	-	22
	(38.1)	(60.2)	(1.7)		(43.5)	(56.5)			(31.8)	(68.2)		

Source : Survey data. Figures in parentheses indicate percentage.

Diseases due to infection	Chronic illness	Other illness
$X^2 = 13.5263$	$X^2 = 37.0169$	$X^2 = 5.81816$
df = 7	df = 7	df = 4
p = .060314	p = .000005	p = .213174

incapable of affording treatment from private sources. Statistical analysis revealed that the association between the sex and type of hospital utilized is highly significant in the case of chronic diseases. In the case of diseases due to infection and other illness in urban and slum both male and female have used Govt. and private hospitals for treatment and no serious sex difference is noted in this regard.

Sex and the System of Medicine Used

The analysis of data related to the utilization of health services with regard to the systems of medicine revealed certain interesting facts. The table 6.23 explains the relation between sex and the system of medicines utilized by the three categories of illness patients. From the table it can be seen that 90% males in urban and 93% males in slum utilized allopathy, whereas for the females it was 81.46% and 83.67% in urban and slum respectively. None of the males and females utilized ayurvedic system for diseases due to infection. In the case of chronic illness 84.38% urban males and 89.29% urban females used allopathic system and in slum this was 96% and 75.7% respectively for males and females.[2] The analysis of data from table 6.23 implies a higher male domination in the use of allopathy, as the males are the bread earners in most family, they want immediate relief, as such they prefer allopathic treatment which is supposed to provide quick relief. In the case of other illness homoeo treatment is totally absent as most of the illness in this category are of injuries, wounds and fractures, for all these they consider allopathy as the best method of treatment for quick relief.

Percapita Income and Type of Health Centre

Though the linkage of socio-economic status and type of health centre utilized were analysed, the influence of percapita income on the type of health centre was analysed separately to check the impact of income as a

Table 6.23 : Sex of the Patients and the System of Medicine Utilised

Sex	Diseases due to infection				Chronic illness				Other illness			
URBAN	Allo-pathic	Ayur-veda	Homoeo-pathic	Total	Allo-pathic	Ayur-veda	Homoeo-pathic	Total	Allo-pathic	Ayur-veda	Homoeo-pathic	Total
Male	27 (90)	2 (6.67)	1 (3.33)	30	27 (84.38)	4 (12.50)	1 (3.13)	32	19 (100)	-	-	19
Female	22 (81.48)	-	5 (18.52)	27	50 (89.29)	5 (8.93)	1 (1.79)	56	4 (80)	1 (20)	-	5
Total	49 (85.96)	2 (3.51)	6 (10.53)	57	77 (87.50)	9 (10.23)	2 (2.27)	88	23 (95.83)	1 (4.17)	-	24
SLUM												
Male	64 (92.75)	-	5 (7.25)	69	24 (96)	1 (4)	-	25	17 (100)	-	-	17
Female	41 (83.67)	-	8 (16.33)	49	28 (75.68)	4 (10.81)	5 (13.51)	37	4 (80)	1 (20)	-	5
Total	105 (88.98)	-	13 (11.02)	118	52 (83.87)	5 (8.06)	5 (8.06)	62	21 (95.45)	1 (4.55)	-	22

Source : Survey data. Figures in parentheses indicate percentage.

single factor influencing the decision of the choice of the type of hospital. This analysis is done in table 6.24. The table reveals that in general percapita income of the households increases, there is an aversion[3] to Govt. hospital in the urban setup. The trend of aversion to Govt. hospital is also visible in the urban slum, though the proportion of using private hospitals is not so high. Those households with percapita income below Rs.250 in slum, it can be seen that around 27% patients of the diseases due to infection and 30% chronic patients and 28.6% of the other illness patients utilized private hospitals. The reasons suggested by them is that, if they go to Govt. hospitals, their work will be affected due to the rush in Govt. hospitals and they have to purchase all medicines from outside. What they can save is only the doctors consultancy fees, for which they have to sacrifice one day's wage not only of the ill person but also of the accompanying person (if both of them were engaged in any type of work), whereas in the private hospital, they can visit either in the early morning or in the late evening without affecting their work. So many of them utilized private hospitals even if their income is low. If we consider all income categories together 61.4% utilized private hospitals and 38.6% Govt. hospitals for diseases due to infection in the urban areas whereas in slum it was 38.1% for private and 60.2% for Govt. hospitals. Again for chronic illness also the percentage of utilization of private agency in urban is (83%) almost double that of the slum utilized and this may be mainly due to the huge cost involved in the treatment of chronic illness from the private hospitals.

Education of the Head of the Households and Agency of Services Utilized

Table 6.25 revealed the educational status of the head, and the type of agency utilized for their morbidity problem of diseases due to infection, chronic illness and other illness. It shows that as educational status improves the tendency of using private health services increases with exception in certain cases. It can be seen that (table 6.25)

Table 6.24 : Percapita Income of Households and Type of Health Centre Utilised

Percapita Income (amount in rupees)	*Diseases due to infection*				*Chronic illness*				*Other illness*			
URBAN	*Private*	*Govt.*	*Voluntary*	*Total*	*Private*	*Govt.*	*Voluntary*	*Total*	*Private*	*Govt.*	*Voluntary*	*Total*
Below 250	2 (66.7)	1 (37.3)	-	3	4	-	1	5	7	-	-	7
250-500	10 (90.91)	1 (9.09)	-	11	24 (92.3)	1 (3.84)	1 (3.84)	26	3	-	-	3
501-1000	7 (63.6)	4 (36.4)	-	11	17 (80.9)	3 (14.3)	1 (4.8)	21	4	5		9
1001-1500	16 (61.5)	10 (38.5)	-	26	14 (77.8)	4 (22.2)	-	18	1	4		5
Above 1500		6	-	6	14 (77.8)	4 (22.2)	-	18				
Total	35 (61.4)	22 (38.6)		57	73 (82.9)	12 (13.6)	3 (3.4)	88	15 (62.5)	9 (37.5)		24

Contd....

Table 6.24 : (Contd....)

Percapita Income (amount in rupees)	*Diseases due to infection*				*Chronic illness*				*Other illness*			
SLUM	*Private*	*Govt.*	*Voluntary*	*Total*	*Private*	*Govt.*	*Voluntary*	*Total*	*Private*	*Govt.*	*Voluntary*	*Total*
Below 250	17	44	2	63	8	19	-	27	6	15	-	21
	(27)	(70)	(3)		(30)	(70)			(28.6)	(71.4)		
250-500	24	26	-	50	15	16	-	31	1	-	-	1
	(48)	(52)			(48.4)	(51.6)			(100)			
501-1000	4	1	-	5	4	-	-	4				
	(80)	(20)			(100)							
Total	45	71	2	118	27	35	-	62	7	5		22
	(38.1)	(60.2)	(1.7)		(43.5)	(56.5)			(47.8)	(52.8)		

Source : Survey data. Figures in parentheses indicate percentage.

Table 6.25 : Education of the Head of Households and Agency of Treatment

Education	*Diseases due to infection*				*Chronic illness*				*Other illness*			
URBAN	*Private*	*Govt.*	*Voluntary*	*Total*	*Private*	*Govt.*	*Voluntary*	*Total*	*Private*	*Govt.*	*Voluntary*	*Total*
Professional/	5	0	-	5	11	-	-	11	3	-	-	3
P.G	(100)				(100)				(100)			
Graduate	3	2	-	5	9	-	2	11	3	-	-	3
	(60)	(40)			(81.8)		(18.2)		(100)			
Intermediate	2	1	-	3	14	1	-	15	-	-	-	-
	(66.7)	(33.3)			(93.3)	(6.7)						
High School	13	5	-	18	27	4	1	32	6	2	-	8
	(72.2)	(27.8)			(84.4)	(12.5)	(3.1)		(75)	(25)		
Primary	5	10	-	15	12	5	-	17	3	7	-	10
	(33.3)	(66.7)			(70.6)	(29.4)			(30)	(70)		
Middle	6	2	-	8	-	1	-	1	-	-	-	-
	(75)	(25)										
Illiterate	1	2	-	3	-	1	-	1	-	-	-	-
	(33.3)	(66.7)										
Total	35	22	-	57	73	12	3	88	15	9	-	24
	(61.4)	(38.6)			(83)	(13.6)	(3.4)					

Contd....

Table 6.25 : (Contd....)

Education	*Diseases due to infection*				*Chronic illness*				*Other illness*			
SLUM	*Private*	*Govt.*	*Voluntary*	*Total*	*Private*	*Govt.*	*Voluntary*	*Total*	*Private*	*Govt.*	*Voluntary*	*Total*
Professional/P.G	-	-	-	-	-	-	-	-	-	-	-	-
Graduate	-	1 (100)	-	1	-	-	-	-	-	-	-	-
Intermediate	4 (57.1)	3 (42.9)	-	7	3 (60)	2 (40)	-	5	-	-	-	-
High School	8 (80)	2 (20)	-	10	5 (100)	-	-	5	1	-	-	1
Primary	16 (30.8)	35 (67.3)	1 (1.9)	52	12 (40)	18 (60)	-	30	4 (28.6)	14 (71.4)	-	18
Middle	11 (45.8)	12 (50)	1 (4.2)	24	5 (35.7)	9 (64.3)	-	14	1 (50)	1 (50)	-	2
Illiterate	6 (25)	18 (78)	-	24	2 (25)	6 (75)	-	8	1 (100)	-	-	1
Total	45 (38.14)	71 (60.17)	2 (1.69)	118	27 (43.5)	35 (56.5)	-	62	7 (31.8)	15 (68.2)	-	22

Source : Survey data. Figures in parentheses indicate percentage.

100% of the professionals and postgraduate's utilized private health services for diseases due to infection, chronic illness and other illness. Heads of households with graduate level of education also utilized Govt. health services. In the slum 60% of the chronic patients with intermediate level of education of the head and 100% of the chronic patients with high school level of education of the head utilized private agencies. In the urban sample 83% of all the chronic patients utilized private agencies, but this proportion was around 43.5% in the case of slum. In the slum none of the chronic and other illness patients had utilized voluntary hospital. Similarly in urban sample also, none of the infectious and other illness patients utilized voluntary hospital. The reason suggested by the respondents for their non-utilization is that the hospital cost is at par with that of the private hospitals, and there is no cost advantage, so they utilized the private hospitals, which are more accessible to them.

Untreated Cases of Chronic Illness

The chronic illness is such illness, which requires treatment for longer periods. Most of the patients in low class and very low class households find it difficult to continue treatment. As such data was collected to see the number of patients who stopped treatment and also the reason for discontinuing treatment. Table 6.26 provides the SES wise non-treatment of chronic illness.

From the table it can be seen that the problem of no treatment is very serious in the urban slum, as 6.5% of the chronic patients are not undergoing treatment, mainly due to financial constraints. From the table it is clear that the percentage of untreated illness comes down with an increase in the socio-economic status of households indicating that socio-economic status had an important role in the treatment pattern and the extent of utilization of health services. The reason for no treatment is so specific that 89% of such cases in slums and 75% in urban are due to financial constraints. Another reasons

Table 6.26 : SES Class with Number of Untreated Chronic Illness

Sex class	*Urban*			*Slum*		
	No. of patients with reasons for no treatment of chronic illness			*No. of patients with reasons for no treatment of chronic illness*		
	Financial	*Others*	*Total*	*Financial*	*Others*	*Total*
SES_1	-	-	-			
SES_2	-	-	-			
SES_3	-	1	1			
SES_4	-	-	1	1	1	2
SES_5	2	-	2		2-	2
Total	2 (66.7)	1 (33.3)	3 (100)	3 (75)	1 (25)	4 (100)

Source : Survey data. Figures in parentheses indicate percentage.

suggested are that there is no improvement even after long treatment. The most significant thing is that all these no treatment cases are clustered in the lower socio-economic classes and the better off sections seems to continue their treatment even if there is no improvement.

Utilization–A Comparison with National Data

The comparison of the field data of the present study with NCAER data (Sundar 1995) at the national level reveals that utilization of public hospitals for the non-hospitalised illness for urban was below the all India average and for slum it is above the national average. The all India average of utilization of public hospitals for non-hospitalised illness for urban India was 34%, private hospitals at 60% and charitable and medical shops at 6%. For urban Kerala it is 42.4% (43.5% for male and 41.4% for female) in public hospitals, 52.2% in private hospitals (51.8% males and 52.5% females) and the remaining 5.4% with (4.7% for male and 6.1% for female) medical shops or home remedy etc. In the present study only 16% had utilized private hospitals in the urban sample, whereas in the slum this proportion was 55% and 45% respectively for public and private hospitals. In the case of hospitalized treatment, NCAER data (Sundar 1995) for the country (Urban) as a whole for public hospitals was 60.1% and for private hospitals was at 39.1%. On urban Kerala it is 64.2% for public hospitals and 35.8% for private hospitals. The present study indicates that in the urban sample the public hospitals is used for hospitalized treatment only to the extent of 37.5% and 62.5% of them have utilized private hospitals, whereas in the slum 87.5% had utilized public hospitals and only 12.5% had utilized private hospitals.

Utilization data of inpatient and outpatient facilities in the public and private hospitals in the urban sample has some similarity with utilization studies conducted by Duggal and Amin (1989), Yesudian(1990), Visaria and Gumber (1994). According to them one third of inpatients and three quarters of outpatients utilize private health care facilities.

Regarding the utilization of different systems of medicines, the present study reveals that 88.2% of urban patients (as shown in table 6.27) utilized allopathic system and the remaining on homoeo (4.7%) and ayurveda system (7.1%). Another interesting thing is that, regarding the utilization of system of treatment, more or less the same urban trend is revealed by the slum households also.

Conclusion

The analysis of treatment process for curative care among different socio-economic classes revealed that the high classes have better perception about diseases and symptoms compared to lower socio-economic classes. Most of the high classes have utilized the curative care from private sources, whereas the low and very low social classes used Govt. health centres/hospitals. Govt. health centres are used more for inpatient care rather than outpatients, as inpatients care in private involves huge amount as hospital bill. The better classes like SES_1 and

Table 6.27 : Method of Treatment Followed by Patients of Different Illness

Type of illness	*Urban*				*Slum*			
	Allopathy	*Homoeo*	*Ayurveda*	*Total*	*Allopathy*	*Homoeo*	*Ayurveda*	*Total*
Diseases due to	49	6	2	57	105	13	0	118
infection	(86)	(10.5)	(3.5)	(100)	(89)	(11)		100)
Chronic illness	77	2	9	88	52	5	5	62
	(87.5)	(2.3)	(10.2)	(100)	(84)	(8)	(8)	(100)
Other illness	23	-	1	24	21	-	1	22
	(95.8)		(4.2)	(100)	(95.5)		(4.5)	
Total	149	8	12	169	178	18	6	202
	(88.2)	(4.7)	(7.1)	(100)	(88.1)	(8.9)	(3)	(100)

Source : Survey data. Figures in parentheses indicate percentage.

SES_2 in the urban area have utilized the voluntary health check-up scheme and most of them preferred one health centre for treatment specially a private hospital or private clinic which was quite alien for the low and very low class households. Similarly delayed treatment and no treatment is a phenomenon associated with households in the lower socio-economic status.

Though the slum folks are educationally backward, both the urban and slum shows the same trend regarding the utilization of system of medicine for curative care and maximum priority was given to allopathic system. The study proved that regarding the stage of treatment only 11.25% of the households prefer immediate treatment of illness, whereas this was 57.5% in the case of urban reflecting the impact of high percapita income. As income is increasing the stage of treatment of illness is becoming more and more immediate. The study of age and system of medicine utilized revealed that at the lower age (age upto 15) and at the age above 60 allopathy is utilized maximum both in the urban and slum for all the three type of illness. Similarly regarding the agency of treatment, for chronic illness all age groups in urban utilized maximum of private agency, whereas in slum they utilized maximum of Govt. service reflecting their financial status. Regarding the sex and system of medicines utilized a dominance of allopathic system among the male is noticed indicating the need for quick relief on their part. Similarly percapita income and type of medical agency utilized reveals that in most cases as income increases they prefer more of private agency and vice versa indicating the strong impact of economic status on the health services utilization. The overall analysis of treatment process of households in various socio-economic statuses revealed that, socio-economic status is in important determinant of health services utilization. At the same time demographic factors like age, sex, place of residence, nature of illness, etc. also influence in the degree of utilization of health services.

NOTES

1. Though Percapita income (PCI) of household is included in calculating the SES score of the households, a separate analysis of PCI and stage of seeking treatment is carried out here to see the influence of PCI alone on the stage of seeking treatment for illness.
2. Only in the case of chronic illness in urban a higher utilization of allopathic system by the females is noted. This may be due to the reasons that many of them are suffering from diabetes, blood pressure, asthma etc. and they consider allopathy only as the effective and no alternative at par to get quick relief.
3. There are certain exceptions to the aversion trend towards Govt. hospital. In the urban sample percapita income slab above Rs.1500, there are 6 cases of diseases due to infectious patients and they have utilized Govt. hospitals. This may be due to the fact that in the case of diseases like tuberculosis best treatment is offered in Govt. hospitals and for other illness also for claiming medical re-imbursement they utilized the services of Govt. hospitals.

REFERENCES

Duggal R. and Amin S., (1989), Cost of Healthcare : A Household Survey in an Indian District, F.R.C.H. Bombay.

Kannan K.P., Thankappan K.R., Kutty V.R., Aravindan K.P., (1991), Health and Development in Rural Kerala; A Study of Linkages Between Socio-economic Status and Health Status, Kerala Sastra Sahitya Parishad, Thiruvananthapuram.

Sunder Ramamani, (1995), Household Survey of Healthcare Utilization and Expenditure, NCAER, New Delhi, Working Paper No. 53.

Visaria P. and Gumber Anil, (1994), Utilization of and Expenditure on Health Care in India 1986-87, Gujarat Institute of Development Research, Goa.

Yesudian C.A.K., (1990), Utilization Pattern of Health Services and its Implication for Urban Health Policy. Take me Programme in International Health, Harvard School of Public Health.

7

Utilization of Government and Private Health Services

Barring a few Socialist countries like Cuba where the state is the sole provider of medical care, most of the developed and developing world largely has a mixed provisioning of services. The relative roles of public and private sectors in health care in developing countries have changed considerably over time. Although the state has played a central role in providing medical care in India, private interests were never curbed and as a result they have grown over the years. The focus of this chapter is to examine the utilization pattern of Govt. and private health care centres and the problems faced in general in the utilization of Govt. health care centres.

India does not have a well-developed private "health" sector. Despite the fact that the private sector is large and popular, its contribution to eradicating small pox, controlling malaria, bringing down the incidence of diarrhoeal deaths, and in general to lowering death rate and in increasing the life expectancy of the population of India is marginal. What exists is exclusively a 'private medical sector' isolated almost completely from efforts at providing health care to the people. The private medical sector in India is perhaps the largest in the world. Eighty percent of about 400000 registered allopathic and 85% of around 50,000 registered non-allopathic doctors' work in the private sector, of them over 85% was engaged in private medical practice (Uplekar and George 1994).

The private medical sector is vested with certain characteristics. The practitioners are like their counterparts in the public sector, trained in western type, hospital based urban oriented medical care system. Community health is perhaps the weakest and most neglected part of their curriculum. A licence to practice is issued to them soon after their training. Once they start practice, the phase of their education comes to an end and they are completely free to pursue their vocation. No monitoring, no organized arguments for continuing medical education, no regulation of fees they charge or the drugs they administer and prescribe and no system of renewal of the licence to practice (Uplekar and George 1994). But even then, regarding the provision of health care, most of the people in urban areas depends on private health care practitioners and private health care centres, because Govt. medical institution is fully vested with the bureaucratic dictation of medical professionals and the chance of getting best treatment to common people are very remote. Many of the doctors, nurses, and paramedical personnel working in the public health care system are not committed to their works, often greedy of making more and more money through private practice and other out of way methods. The health system has therefore to be de-mystified, de-professionalised, de-bureaucratised and de- commercialized to provide better services to the masses (Joseph et al 1983).

The private sector plays an important role in India's health care system. Through a wide network of health care facilities, this sector caters to the needs of both urban and rural population and has expanded widely to meet the increasing demands and challenges (Bhat 1999). Total health expenditure in India is estimated to be about 6% of G.D.P of which private health expenditure is 75% or

4.25% of G.D.P. About one third of this expenditure is on secondary and tertiary inpatient care, the rest meeting the curative needs at primary level (World Bank 1995). Private health care expenditure in India has grown at the rate of 12.5% per annum since 1960-61. For each 1% increase in percapita income, private health care expenditure has increased by 1.47% (Bhat 1996).

About 57% of hospitals and 32% of hospital beds are in the private sector. At present about 80% qualified allopathic doctors registered with medical councils in India are working in the private Sector (Jessani and Anantharam 1989, Bhat R. 1996). There are over 6,50,000 providers of other systems of medicine practicing in India (Govt. of India 1998) and most of them are in private practice. Utilization studies show that one third of the inpatients and three quarters of the outpatients utilize private health care facilities (Duggal and Amin 1989, Yesudian 1990, Visaria and Gumber 1994).

Government Health Services

Though Govt. health services are available freely to the poor, they are not fully used by them. Many factors are responsible for the under utilization of the Govt. hospital. Majority of the people used Govt. hospital for inpatient care as they can escape from the huge hospital bill levied by the private hospitals. The analysis of curative care in the earlier chapter revealed that, for outpatient care, only very few is using the Govt. hospitals, because they have to borrow entire medicines from private sources. This section deals with the utilization of Govt. hospital, causes for non-utilization of Govt. hospital and knowledge about various departments in the Govt. hospital and the opinion and complaints about Govt. hospital.

Table 7.1 provides the SES class with the number of households who Utilised Govt. hospitals/health centres, during the last 3 years prior to the survey. It shows that 43.3% households' in urban and 88.8% households' in

Table 7.1 : SES Class and Households Utilised Government Health Centres/Hospitals

Sex Class	*Urban*			*Slum*		
	No. of households Utilised by the Govt hospital/ health centres	*Not Utilised*	*Total*	*No. of households Utilised by the Govt hospital/ health centres*	*Not Utilised*	*Total*
SES_1	-	12 (100)	12	-	-	-
SES_2	7 (17.5)	33 (82.5)	40	-	-	-
SES_3	14 (41.2)	20 (58.8)	34	2 (22.2)	7 (77.8)	9
SES_4	17 (85)	3 (15)	20	30 (96.8)	1 (3.2)	31
SES_5	14 (100)	-	14	39 (97.5)	1 (2.5)	40
Total	52 (43.3)	68 (56.7)	120	71 (88.8)	9 (11.2)	80

Source : Survey data. Figures in parentheses indicate percen[illegible]e.

slum Utilised Government hospital during the last 3 years. From the table it can be seen that 100% of the very low class (SES_5) and 85% of the low class (SES_4) in urban areas used Govt. hospital in the last 3 years. For the urban slum this was 97.5% and 96.8% respectively for SES_5 and SES_4. Though the upper classes used Govt. hospital, it was very meagre and it is to be noted that nobody in the upper class (SES_1) used Govt. hospital during the last 3 years. In the slum as a whole 88.75% used Govt. hospital during the last 3 years, whereas this was only 43.3% in the urban sample. The analysis of data revealed that as socio-economic status improves, the percentage of household utilizing Govt. health services declines and vice-versa.

Percapita Income and Utilization of Government Hospital

Though the impact of SES on utilization of Govt. health services is analysed in table 7.1, the linkage of percapita income (though it is a constituent in measuring the SES of households) on the utilization of Govt. hospitals/ health centres is analyzed separately. Table 7.2 provides percapita income of households and the utilization of Government hospital/ health centres by the household members in the last 3 years prior to the survey. It reveals that as percapita income slab increases, the percentage of households who Utilised Govt. hospital services decreases and it is common for both urban and slum households. The decline in utilization of Govt. health services as percapita income increases is much deeper in the percapita income slab 501-750 in the case of slum compared to urban, where the decline is not so deeper. This indicates that even certain better income groups are utilizing Govt. hospital for getting either medical re-imbursement facility or for recording the treatment undergone under the Govt. doctors for availing medical leave. Thus percapita income and utilization of Govt. hospital is moving in the opposite direction.

Table 7.2 : Percapita Income of Households and Utilization of Govt. Hospital/Health Centres

Percapita Income (Amount in Rupees)	*Urban*			*Slum*		
	Utilised	*Not Utilised*	*Total*	*Utilised*	*Not Utilised*	*Total*
Upto 100	-	-	-	2 (100)	-	2
101 to 250	12 (92.3)	1 (7.7)	13	31 (96.9)	1 (3.1)	32
251 to 500	19 (86.4)	3 (13.6)	22	36 (94.7)	2 (5.3)	38
501 to 750	11 (47.8)	12 (52.2)	23	2 (25)	6 (75)	8
751 to 1000	4 (30.8)	9 (69.2)	13	-	-	-
1001 to 1500	6 (22.2)	21 (77.8)	27	-	-	-
Above 1500	-	22 (100)	22	-	-	-
Total	52 (43.3)	68 (56.7)	120 (100)	71 (88.8)	9 (11.2)	80 (100)

Source : Survey data. Figures in Parentheses indicate percentage.

Opinion about inpatient Services

Table 7.3 provides the opinion of respondents about test and treatment during the stay in Govt. hospital in the last 2 years. It can be seen that with regard to the inpatient services received from the Govt. hospital, 92% of the slum respondents and 78% of the urban respondents were totally dissatisfied indicating the poor and dismal performance of Govt. hospital. Most of the respondent in their informal talk with us disclosed that the test and treatment offered during their stay in hospital was very bad. As there is no other resort they stayed in the hospital for few days.

Table 7.3 : SES Class and Opinion about Inpatient Treatment in Government Hospitals

Sex Class	*Urban* Opinion about treatment				*Slum* Opinion about treatment			
	Good	Fair	Poor	Total	Good	Fair	Poor	Total
SES_1	-	-	-	-	-	-	-	-
SES_2	-	-	-	-	-	-	-	-
SES_3	-	-	3	3	-	-	1	1
SES_4	-	1	5	6	-	-	15	15
SES_5	1	2	6	9	2	1	19	22
Total	1 (5.5)	3 (16.7)	14 (77.8)	18	2 (5.3)	1 (2.6)	35 (92.1)	38

Source : Survey data. Figures in Parentheses indicate percentage.

Similarly the advice and information provided at the time of discharge is also significant as part of the follow up treatment. Most of the patients from the Govt. hospital would be discharged as early as possible to avoid the rush in the inpatient ward. But most of them are dissatisfied with the advice and information provided by the hospital authorities for follow up treatment. Table 7.4 gives opinion about the advice and information provided at the time of discharge from Govt. Hospital.

Table 7.4 : SES Class with Advice and Information Provided at the time of Discharge from Hospital

Sex Class	*Urban* Advice and information provided				*Slum* Advice and information provided			
	Good	Fair	Poor	Total	Good	Fair	Poor	Total
SES_1	-	-	-	-	-	-	-	-
SES_2	-	-	-	-	-	-	-	-
SES_3	1	2	-	3	-	1	-	1
SES_4	-	2	4	6	-	2	13	15
SES_5	-	3	6	9	3	3	16	22
Total	1 (5.6)	7 (38.8)	10 (55.6)	18 (100)	3 (7.9)	6 (15.8)	29 (76.3)	38 (100)

Source : Survey data. Figures in Parentheses indicate percentage.

Accessibility of a doctor is a must for the patient while staying in the hospital as inpatient. Table 7.5 gives the opinion about the accessibility of doctors in the Govt. hospital while as inpatient in the last 2 years prior to survey. The accessibility of the doctor is the vital factor, which prompt a patient to stay in the hospital. But according to many respondents who or their family members' Utilised Govt. hospital reveals that the accessibility is very poor. From the table 7.5 it is very clear that only very few (Just 5% both in the urban and slum) had fully satisfied about the accessibility of Government doctors while as inpatient in the hospital. The doctors try to finish the rounds in the wards as quickly as possible and sit in the outpatient wing for sometime and rush to residence before noon to attend the long queue of patients waiting there. In most cases the nurses on duty will cater the requirements of the patients and only on emergency cases the doctors will be conveyed or called for. The data related to inpatient services of Govt. hospitals reveals an inhuman picture of the Govt. doctors, whose education Govt. had incurred crores of rupees from the public exchequer. The most pitiable aspect of these deeds

Table 7.5 : SES class with Accessibility of Doctors While as Inpatient in Government Hospital

Sex Class	*Urban*				*Slum*			
	Opinion about accessibility of doctors				*Opinion about accessibility of doctors*			
	Good	*Fair*	*Poor*	*Total*	*Good*	*Fair*	*Poor*	*Total*
SES_1	-	-	-	-	-	-	-	-
SES_2	-	-	-	-	-	-	-	-
SES_3	-	2	1	3	-	1	-	1
SES_4	-	2	4	6	2	1	14	15
SES_5	1	2	6	9	2	3	17	22
Total	1 (5.6)	6 (33.3)	11 (61.1)	18 (100)	2 (5.3)	5 (13.1)	31 (81.6)	38 (100)

Source : Survey data. Figures in Parentheses indicate percentage

is that, it is the low class and very low class households' (SES_4 and SES_5) in the society who suffer a lot due to the sad state of affairs of Government hospitals. These sections find it difficult to approach private health care centres quite often, whereas the richer section always prefers private health centres alone.

Complaints and Allegations Against Govt. Hospitals

In order to get vivid picture about the service conditions of the Government hospitals, opinion about 7 items of services were asked to the respondents who Utilised Govt. hospital during the last 2 years.

From the Table 7.6 It can be seen that the major complaints raised by the respondents were against the check-up of doctors and poor medical equipment. As there is long queue in the outpatient department, the doctor in charge of the out patient counter may finish the check-up of each patient within seconds and give them prescriptions for one or two tablets and ask the next person to come. There is no proper diagnosis of the patient, as the doctor is busy to finish his work in the hospital and wanted to start private practice either from his residence or from the separate clinic setup for this. The lack of proper check-up of patients due to the callousness of the doctors is causing severe medical problems to the patients and in certain times even death. Lack of medical equipment is also causing severe problem for the patients. Though Government hospital is meant for the poor and vulnerable in the society, there are no medical equipment properly functioning in most of the hospitals. For X-ray, ECG etc. patients have to go outside. Even for blood test, sputum test, urine test etc. private sector is the only resort. Even if certain equipments were there, most of the time they will be in out of order or under damage and the authorities concerned would not take initiative to repair it due to pressure from outside private agencies, which render these services. Similarly the poor nursing care, favouritism, indifferent doctor's

Table 7.6 : SES Class and Complaints made Against Government Hospital

Complaints	*Urban*						*Slum*			
	SES Class						*SES Class*			
	SES_1	SES_2	SES_3	SES_4	SES_5	*Total*	SES_3	SES_4	SES_5	*Total*
Check-up	-	7 (100)	10 (71.4)	16 (94)	11 (78.5)	44 (84.6)	2 (100)	25 (83.3)	36 (92.3)	63 (88.7)
Doctor's behaviour	-	5 (71.4)	7 (50)	11 (64.7)	9 (64.2)	32 (61.5)	0	14 (46.6)	20 (51.2)	34 (47.8)
Nursing Care	-	5 (71.4)	9 (64)	14 (82.3)	9 (64.2)	37 (71.1)	2 (100)	23 (76.6)	29 (74.3)	54 (76)
Bribery	-	4 (57)	7 (50)	12 (70.5)	8 (57)	31 (59.6)	1 (50)	14 (46.6)	27 (69.2)	42 (59.1)
Favouritsm	-	4 (57)	4 (28.6)	13 (76.4)	9 (64.2)	30 (57.7)	1 (50)	19 (63.3)	25 (64)	45 (63.3)
Cleanliness	-	6 (85.7)	9 (64.3)	7 (41.1)	5 (35.7)	27 (51.9)	2 (100)	6 (20)	1 (2.5)	9 (12.6)
Medical equipment	-	7 (100)	12 (85.7)	17 (100)	12 (85.7)	48 (92.3)	2 (100)	30 (100)	37 (94.8)	69 (97.1)
No. of household Utilised Govt. hospitals	-	7	14	17	14	52	2	30	39	71
No. of complaints per household.	-	5.4	4.1	5.3	4.5	4.7	5	4.4	4.5	4.5

Source : Survey data. Figures in parentheses indicate percentage to total number of households' Utilised Government hospital.

behaviour etc. are also categorized as complaints against Govt. hospitals. Many respondents informed us that most of the nurses behave arrogantly and will not show any sympathy and if the patients raise any doubts about the medicine, they irritate on them. In the informal chat with the respondents and household members of the study area, we realised few more complaints against Govt. hospitals and doctors. Even if medicines were available in the Govt. hospital, the doctors in duty prescribe medicines to outside. Similarly for X-ray, ECG, Ultra Sound Scanning etc. they prescribe to outside private agencies and will not take interest to repair the existing equipment or install new one. As the doctors are receiving good amount as commission from these private agencies, they try their level best to continue the statusquo of Government hospitals for years. Those who raised complaints against the neatness in the General Hospital increased with the rise of socio-economic status. Since the houses of upper middle, upper class and lower middle class households were maintained clean and neat, the hospital environment looked unclean to them when compared to the cleanliness of their houses. On the other hand, the dwellings of the slum households and urban poor were not at all maintained properly and neatness was not a problem to them. In the slum, we often observed that on one side of the kitchen (most often only one room including kitchen) one child may be defecating, very close to it another child may be eating food. (This was observed during a rainy day). In the case of urban poor, their living situation is not as worse as that of slum dwellers, so some of them raised their voice against cleanliness. In General, for the poor, the hospitals were not unclean when compared to their own house.

On the whole 52 respondents in the urban areas made 249 complaints and 71 respondents in the slum areas made 316 complaints that Utilised Govt. hospitals (Table 7.6). The average number of complaints per household was 4.7 in urban and 4.5 in slum. In the urban sample the average number of complaints made by low class (SES_4) households was highest with 5.3 followed by upper middle class (SES_2) with 5.4 and minimum of 4.1 by lower middle class (SES_3). In the slum, it was the lower middle class (SES_3) whom raised maximum complaints with average rate of 5 followed by very low class (SES_5) with complaint rate of 4.5 and low class (SES_4) with complaint rate of 4.4.

Private Health Services

Private medical practice is the fundamental feature of urban health care system. The better off sections like SES_1, and SES_2 nurtures the private medical practice in urban areas. Due to the callousness and indifferent attitude of the Govt. doctors on the one side and sad state of affairs of the Govt. hospital on the other, even the poor sections are now utilizing the private health services. Private health centres in the study area is divided into three categories, namely private clinic, private hospital and voluntary hospital. Private hospital provide outpatient and inpatient services, and owned by either a single individual or a partnership. In private clinics the doctor either gives only prescriptions or medicines, from his own dispensary and voluntary hospitals in the study area are the Co-operative hospitals with outpatients and inpatient facility. It is managed by a board of directors as per the co-operative rules and regulations in practice. Table 7.7 explains the type of private health centres Utilised by the sample households. From the table it can be seen that 90.8% households in the urban, 66.3% households in slum Utilised private health services in the last two years. All the upper class (SES_1) and upper middle class (SES_2) households Utilised the private health services. Similarly most of the very low class (SES_5) low class (SES_4) and lower middle class (SES_3) households in both urban and slum had Utilised private health services. From the table it can be seen that the proportion of households utilizing private health services rises with rise of socio-economic status. Class wise analysis of urban

Table 7.7 : SES Class and Type of Private Health Centres Utilised

Sex Class	*Urban*				*Slum*			
	Private hospital/ Vol.	*Private clinic*	*Doctors residence*	*Total*	*Private hospital/ Vol.*	*Private clinic*	*Doctors residence*	*Total*
SES_1	4	3	5	12	-	-	-	-
	(33.3)	(25)	(41.7)					
SES_2	12	23	5	40	-	-	-	-
	(30)	(32.5)	(12.5)					
SES_3	7	25	1	33	3	5	1	9
	(21.2)	(75.8)	(3)		(33.3)	(55.6)	(11.1)	
SES_4	6	9	1	16	6	17	-	23
	(37.5)	(56.3)	(6.2)		(26)	(24)		
SES_5	2	6	0	8	7	14	-	21
	(25)	(75)			(33.3)	(66.7)		
Total	31	66	12	109	16	36	1-	53
	(28.4)	(60.5)	(11.1)	(100)	(30.2)	(67.9	(1.9)	(100)

Source : Survey data. Figures in Parentheses indicate percentage.

private health services utilization revealed that 60.5% of the private health service is met through private clinics, 28.4% through private hospitals and 11% through doctor's residence. It can be seen that slum households also exhibit somewhat similar trend. Doctors running private clinics near to the slum areas provide some concession to the poor people in the consultation fees charged by them which act as a blessing for the deprived groups in the slums and it augment the utilization of health services.

Reasons for Going to Private Health Centres

Though Government is incurring crores for running public health centres many poor people are compelled to go to private health centres for treatment. From the sample households in the urban area it can be seen that 109 households utilised private health services, whereas the Govt. health services was utilised only by 52 households. So the reason for the utilization of private health services were analysed and it is provided in table 7.8. From the table it is clear that most of the upper class (SES_1) and upper middle class (SES_2) used private health centres for good treatment and personal contact of the doctor. Major proportion of the low class (SES_4) and very low class (SES_5) households in urban and slum used private health centres mainly due to lack of medicines in Govt. hospitals. Many respondents expressed the view that what they can save after spending half day in front of the outpatient (O.P) counter of Govt. hospital is only the consultation fee of Rs.25/-, because they have to purchase the entire medicine from outside. In addition to this many households in the low class and very low class households prefer private clinic because it functions in night. So if the children or other members fall sick, the head of the household or other earning members in the family would have to take them to hospital or health centres. Since private clinic functions in night many prefers to take them to such clinic in the evening after earning their livelihood. So without causing any loss of income, they can consult doctors in the private clinic. Another reason suggested for the option of the private clinic or health centre is that, there is no need of long waiting as in the O.P. counter of Govt. hospitals. Due to the personal contact of the doctors, they can easily consult the doctor and long waiting can be avoided. The analysis of the reason for the choice of private health centre reveals

Table 7.8 : SES Class and Reasons for the Choice of Private Health Services

Reasons	*SES Class*					
	SES_1	SES_2	SES_3	SES_4	SES_5	*Total*
Good Treatment	9 (75)	28 (70)	14 (42.4)	-	-	51 (46.8)
No need of waiting	-	5 (12.5)	12 (36.4)	2 (12.5)	-	19 (17.4)
Doctor is known	3 (25)	4 (10)	4 (12.1)	-	-	11 (10.1)
Clinic functions in night	-	3 (7.5)	3 (9.1)	4 (25)	4 (50)	14 (12.8)
Lack of medicines in Govt. hospitals	-	-	-	10 (62.5)	4 (50)	14 (12.8)
Total	12 (100)	40 (100)	33 (100)	16 (100)	8 (100)	109 (100)
SLUM						
Good treatment	-	-	3 (33.3)	-	-	3 (5.7)
No need of waiting	-	-	6 (66.6)	4 (17.4)	-	10 (18.9)
Doctor is known	-	-	-	-	-	-
Clinic functions in night	-	-	-	13 (56.5)	14 (66.7)	27 (50.9)
Lack of medicines in Govt. hospitals	-	-	-	6 (26.1)	7 (33.3)	13 (24.5)
Total	-	-	9 (100)	23 (100)	21 (100)	53 (100)

Source : Survey data. Figures in Parentheses indicate percentage.

that both the urban and slum respondents differ widely in their attitude towards private health care. In the urban sample, around 58% prefer private health centres for good treatment and personal contact of the doctors, whereas in the slum this was only 5.7%. In the slum, the motivating force behind the utilization of private health service is accessibility of the doctors in the night and non-availability of medicines from Govt. hospitals, which accounts for 76% of the reasons pointed out by them.

Complaints Against Private Hospital

The complaints raised against private hospital/ health services were few. As they are charging good amount for the services rendered, it is upto the mark in every sense. But the major complaint on the part of private health service users was that the rate charged by them was abnormal and treatment is expensive. But this complaint had little relevance, as the study made by Aravindan (2001) revealed that the cost of an illness episode as outpatient is somewhat same in private and Govt. hospitals in Kerala. Out of 109 respondents in urban sample who used private health services, 10.1 % of them complaint that it is costly and in slum 22.6% of 53 respondents also complaint about high cost of private health care service. Many upper class and upper middle class respondents informed us that doctors practicing in big hospitals are unnecessarily advising for undergoing MRI Scanning, ECG, and X-ray etc. for raising hospital resources. Such charges are even too heavy for the lower middle class (SES_3) and upper middle class households (SES_2).

Utilization of Private and Government Health Services

As the health care system is covered by both public and private agencies, there exist many households', which utilize both public and private health services. In order to get a clear picture of the utilization pattern of Govt. and private health services, only a combined data can provide these results. Table 7.9 provides the utilization pattern of Government and private health services together. From the table 7.9 it is clear that there is a marked difference in the utilization pattern of Government and private health services.

Table 7.9 : SES Class and Utilization of Private and Government Medical Services

Sex Class	Urban: Type of health services utilised				Slum: Type of health services utilised			
	Govt. alone	Private alone	Both	Total	Govt. alone	Private alone	Both	Total
SES_1	0	12	0	12	-	-	-	-
SES_2	0	33	7	40	-	-	-	-
SES_3	1	20	13	34	0	7	2	9
SES_4	4	3	13	20	8	1	22	31
SES_5	6	0	8	14	19	1	20	40
Total	11 (9.2)	68 (56.7)	41 (34.2)	120 (100)	27 (33.8)	9 (11.3)	44 (55)	80 (100)

Source : Survey data. Figures in Parentheses indicate percentage.

The very low class and low class households with their meagre income may be compelled to go to private health centres for their health needs. They normally go to private health centres when the government health services fails to meet their health needs. Certain upper middle class (SES_2) and certain lower middle class (SES_3) households utilize Government health services for getting medical benefits. It is noticed that those who did not go to Govt. hospital for treatment of fever would like to go for treatment of some serious ailments in Govt. hospital for getting medical benefit, since the treatment cost is high. The analysis also reveals that only 9% of the urban sample depends on Govt. health services alone for all health needs and in slum it is 34%. Similarly another 34.2% in urban and 55% in slum depends on both private and Govt. health centres for the medical assistance.

Annual Medical Expenditure

The utilization of health services and the medical expenditure are highly correlated. The intensity of utilization depends on the capacity of the medical aid seeker to pay for it. But by the linking of medical aid with the expenditure capacity, it could not be possible to judge utilization of health services by the low class and very low class sections, because these two classes mainly use freely available public health services.

Medical expenditure items of the community differ widely from one SES class to another. The expenditure data of the present study reveals that the upper class (SES_1) and upper middle class (SES_2) spend good amount for medical care. Their expenditure items include special food, transportation, tests, medicines, consultant fees etc. Whereas most of the low class and very low class (SES_4 and SES_5) restricted their expenditure in one or two items like either medicines or medicines and transportation. Table 7.10 analyses the medical expenditure of different SES classes during the last one year prior to survey. From the table it can be seen that in the urban sample 50% of the upper class (SES_1) and 27.5% of upper middle class (SES_2) had expenditure above Rs.3500. Similarly 50% of the very low class (SES_5) and 40% of the low class (SES_4) had annual medical expenditure of less than Rs.1000 per month. Another thing to be noted here is that 5.8% of the urban sample had no health expenditure at all for the last one year and in high classes we assumes that the no expenditure may be due to their good luck in escaping from diseases due to infection and in the case of lower sections this may be due to their lacunae to go for treatment. In the urban sample out of 15 households, which had health expenditure of above Rs.5000, 80% belongs to upper class (SES_1) and upper middle class (SES_2). In the slum only very few (i.e 10%) had expenditure beyond Rs.2500. On the whole it is revealed that as socio-economic status rises, the amount incurred for medical expenditure also increases. In the slum also 6.3% had

Table 7.10 : SES Class and Annual Medical Expenditure

Medical Expenditure (Amount in Rupees)	*Urban*						*Slum*			
	Socio-economic class						*Socio-economic class*			
	SES_1	SES_2	SES_3	SES_4	SES_5	*Total*	SES_3	SES_4	SES_5	*Total*
No Expenditure	0	1	1	2	3	7 (5.8)	0	2	3	5 (6.3)
Upto Rs.1000	2	5	8	6	4	25 (20.8)	1	4	4	9 (11.2)
1001 to 1500	1	9	8	2	5	25 (20.8)	0	8	12	20 (25)
1501 to 2500	1	7	4	2	1	15 (12.5)	6	14	18	38 (47.5)
2501 to 3500	2	7	7	5	1	22 (18.3)	2	3	3	8 (10)
3501 to 5000	1	4	4	2	-	11 (9.2)	-	-	-	-
Above 5000	5	7	2	1	-	15 (12.5)	-	-	-	-
Total	12	40	34	20	14	120	9	31	40	80

Source : Survey data. Figures in Parentheses indicate percentage.

no health expenditure and this may be due to avoiding treatment for illness by practicing home remedy.

Average Expenditure on Health

In order to see the differences among SES class in the amount of expenditure incurred for health services utilization, the annual average percapita expenditure on health and annual average percapita income was analysed. Table 7.11 explains the annual average percapita income and annual average percapita expenditure on health. From the table it can be seen that in the case of urban sample as socio- economic status falls proportion of income spend on health rises. It is 2.4% only in the case of upper class, but reached to the maximum of around 5 times (i.e 10.44%) in the case of very low class. Similarly the annual average percapita expenditure on health incurred by households falls as socio- economic status falls. It is 695.87 in the case of upper class (SES_1) but only 360.49 in the case of very low class. The same trend is visible in the slum sample also though the differences between the lower middle class (SES_3) and very low class are not wide.

Priority of Medical Expenditure

In order to examine the significance of medical expenditure in the household expenditure, respondents were asked about the priority of different expenditure item in their household budget. The major items of expenditure asked include 1) Food, 2) Dress items, 3) Water current and telephone, 4) Medical, 5) Recreation, 6) Education, 7) Rent and 8) Maintenance of house roof. The table 7.12 shows the priority of expenditure items of households. The data analysis reveals that nobody neither in urban nor in slum had provided first priority to health expenditure. Around 9% in urban and 11% in slum had given second priority to medical aid in the expenditure. There are certain households with members ailing from chronic illness, like asthma, diabetes, pain in joint, epilepsy, cancer etc. for such illness continuous treatment

Table 7.11: SES Class with Annual Average Percapita Expenditure on Health and Annual Average Percapita Income

Reasons	*Urban*			*Slum*		
	Annual Average percapita expenditure on health in Rs.	*Annual Average percapita income in Rs.*	*Percentage on health*	*Annual Average percapita expenditure on health in Rs.*	*Annual Average percapita income in Rs.*	*Percentage on health*
SES_1	695.87	28956	2.4	-	-	-
SES_2	654.14	20696.10	3.16	-	-	-
SES_3	475.40	8847	5.37	313.58	7640	4.1
SES_4	420.76	5499.60	7.65	262.29	4031.61	6.5
SES_5	360.49	3451.70	10.44	273.33	2860.80	9.6
All groups	546.72	14491.61	3.77	272.33	3868.60	7.03

Source : Survey data.

Table 7.12 : SES Class with Priority of Medical Expenditure

Priority order	*1*	*2*	*3*	*4*	*5*	*6*	*7*	*8*	*Total*
Urban									
SES Class									
SES_1	-	-	3	3	6	-	-	-	12
SES_2	-	1	2	14	14	9	-	-	40
SES_3	-	3	2	14	11	4	-	-	34
SES_4	-	5	3	5	7	-	-	-	20
SES_5	-	2	3	5	4	-	-	-	14
Total	-	11	13	41	42	13	-	-	120
		(9.2)	(10.8)	(34.2)	(35)	(10.8)			(100)
Slum									
SES_3	-	-	1	3	5	-	-	-	9
SES_4	-	3	8	15	5	-	-	-	31
SES_5	-	6	15	16	3	-	-	-	40
Total	-	9	24	34	13	-	-	-	80
		(11.3)	(30)	(42.5)	(16.2)				(100)

Source : Survey data. Figures in Parentheses indicate percentage.

is a must. These households have to keep separately a good amount for the purchase of medicines and conducting of medical tests, such households' medicine is most urgent after food. Most of the households in upper class (SES_1) and upper middle class (SES_2) did not provide any high priority for medical expenditure and provide 4th, 5th, or 6th priority only. The number of households given last priority increased with rise of socio- economic status.

The high class spent good amount as health expenditure (table 7.12) but their priority to medical expenditure was very low. Though the absolute amount spent on health services was high, but this amount formed only a small percentage of their total income as they earns huge amount as monthly income and they spend bigger amount on other household expenditure. In our informal talk with the respondents certain respondents in the upper class households revealed that, current, water, and telephone charge occupy the first priority in their expenditure items. At the same time smaller amount incurred for the health expenditure by the low class and very low class households, formed a bigger percentage of their total income as they earn only a minimum income, that too was not fixed in character.

REFERENCES

Aravindhan, K.P., (2001), Kerala Aroghya Mathruka, Puthiya Noottandilekku, Kerala Sastra Sahithya Parishad, Kochi.

Bhat Ramesh, (1996), Regulation of Private Health Sector in India. International Journal of Health Planning and Management, Vol.11, pp. 253-274.

Bhat Ramesh, (1999), Characteristics of Private Medical Practice in India, a Provider Perspective, Health Policy and Planning Vol.14 No.1, pp. 26-37.

Duggal R. and Amin S., (1989), Cost of Health Care, A Household Survey in an Indian District, FRCH, Bombay.

Government of India (1998), Approach Paper to Ninth Five Year Plan 1997-98 Planning Commission, New Delhi, p. 87.

Jessani A. and Anatharam S., (1989), Private Sector and Privatization in the Health Care Services, F.R.C.H., Bombay.

Joseph George, Desrochers John Kalathil Mariamma, (1983) Heath Care in India, Centre for Social Action, Banglore.

Uplekar Mukund and George Alex, (1994), Access to Health care in India, Present Situation and Innovative Approaches, R.C.H. Bombay, p.10.

Visaria P. and Gumber Anil, (1994), Utilization of and Expenditure on Health care in India 1986-87, Gujarat Institute of Development Research, Goa.

World Bank (1995), India Policies and Finance Strategies for Strengthening Primary Health care Services, Report No. 13042 Population and Human Resources Division, Washington D.C.

Yesudian C.A.K., (1990), Utilization Pattern of Health Services and its Implications for Urban Health Policy, Take me Programme in International Health, Harvard School of Public Health.

8

Utilization of Maternal and Child Health Services

Introduction

Utilization of health services is a complex behavioural phenomenon affected by multitude of factors including availability, distance, cost and quality of care as well as personal attitudes and socio- economic characteristics. In an attempt to understand the factors that determine women's utilization of health services, Chatterjee (1990) posited the role of need, permission, ability and availability. He argued that when permission and ability interact with need, a demand for health services is generated. Actual utilization of health services occurs when this generated demand overlaps with availability. In the Indian context the situation is further complicated by women's perception of illness, which are affected by their cultural conditioning to tolerate suffering. Because of this tolerance of suffering, the perceived need for health services can be small, even when the actual need is great.

Another factor affecting women's health seeking behaviour is that, traditionally women in India considered pregnancy as a natural state rather than a condition requiring medical attention and care. Such perception and beliefs constitute the 'lay health culture' that is an intervening factor between the presence of a condition and its corresponding treatment. Post natal care, infant and child health care are similarly affected by this culture with the result that women often do not avail themselves of preventive and curative medical services, intended to safeguard their own and their children's health and well being. The lay health culture presumably has substantial effects on the utilization of maternal and child health services in regions of the country, where poverty and illiteracy are widespread. The role of this culture is difficult to measure directly, but it is possible to control for a number of socio- economic factors that affects its importance. Many studies conducted in the utilization at the national level revealed that (RCH Project 1998, NFHS* 1992-1993, NFHS 1998-1999), the role of health culture is least in Kerala compared to other Indian states and it is mainly due to improved women literacy which is estimated as 87.8% (Govt. of India 2001) for woman aged 6 years and above, whereas all India average was only 51.4% (NFHS-2, 1998-99) which is the highest in India.

Mothers and children are considered the most vulnerable groups in the community, as they are susceptible to certain health problems to which other sections of the community are not exposed. It is estimated that, there occurred 10 lakhs annual deaths related to pregnancy and childbirth in India and it accounts for 20% of the global maternal mortality (Aravindan 2001). The maternal mortality rate in India was estimated at 570 per one lakh (UNDP 1999) live birth, whereas it was 7 in Sweden, 12 in USA and 10 in Ireland. The average maternal mortality rate is 26 for countries having high human development index. In Srilanka it is 140, Cuba 95, China 95, Vietnam 160, Pakistan 340 and South Africa 230 per one lakh live birth. The most pitiable thing is that maternal mortality rate in India is higher than the average for the developing countries as a whole of 491

---

* National Family Health Survey.

and the world average of 437. When maternal mortality for India as a whole was 555 in 1982-86, the average for U.P, Bihar, Madhya Pradesh and Rajasthan it was 823, at the same time it was 234 for Kerala and 319 for Tamil Nadu indicating high regional difference. The maternal mortality rate now in Kerala is estimated at 87 (Aravindan 2001).

An important proximate determinant of maternal mortality is access to and use of quality health services (Mc Carthy and Maine 1992). Access to quality reproductive health services is also crucial for improved child survival and increased contraceptive use and consequent fertility decline in the developing countries (Ramachandran 1989).

In this section the current levels of knowledge about the maternal and child health care and utilization of maternal and child health services are assessed. For analysing the utilization of maternal and child health services, data was collected from among those woman (from the 120 households already selected as sample for the urban and 80 households for the slum) who had a live birth within the last three years prior to the survey and had a child in the age group of 12 to 36 months. If there were more than one such woman in the households only one was taken into account and the last woman was taken as the respondent and data was collected from her. As such a total of 35 women respondent was obtained from the urban sample and 49 women respondent from the slum. The important maternal and child care facts related to utilization was collected from them which include utilization of antenatal care (ANC) with coverage and source of ANC (Ante Natal Care), type of ANC, pregnancy complications and treatment, natal care with place of delivery and assistance during delivery, post natal care with post delivery complications etc. In addition, the immunization status of children and childcare practices were also assessed. (If the woman respondents had more than one child in the age group of 12 to 36 months at the time of survey only the last child was recorded). This chapter is divided into two parts, maternal health care and childcare practices.

Maternal Health Services

As mentioned earlier, maternal health services is a package of health care measures adopted during pregnancy, childbirth and after childbirth. Studies conducted in this regard reveals that educated women take more advantage of maternal health services utilization than uneducated women and the degree of utilization will be maximum among the educated than the illiterate (Cald well et al 1983, Mosley and Chen 1984, Cleland J and Vani Ginnekan J 1988). The NFHS-1 for the year 1992-93 indicates a very high degree of maternal health care services utilization in rural Kerala (Das etal 2001) with 98% antenatal check up 91% consumed IFA tablets, 90% had taken tetanus injection and 86% had institutional delivery. All these figures are the highest in India and without analyzing much it can be proved that women education is the main factor responsible for this high degree of utilization of maternal and child health services. Education is not a magic pill, but it can boost a young woman's confidence and teach her life skills equipping her to make her own judgments. Female education along with employment and income are decisive for the improvement in the quality of family life and a steady reduction in fertility (Mirasiva 1997). In the present study among the urban sample a high degree of maternal health services utilization was recorded. Table 8.1 provides education status of women respondent from whom maternal and child health services utilization data were collected and it forms the sample size for the study of utilization of maternal and child health services. As revealed by table 8.1, 16.4% of the slum woman who utilized maternal and child health services are illiterate, whereas in the urban area no illiterate women respondent was obtained and 83% of them are with above 10 years of education. Table 8.1 also reveals that as social and economic status rises the proportion of women respondent with 10 years and above education increases and this reflects in better maternal health services utilization.

Table 8.1: SES Class and Education Status of Women Respondent

Sex Class	*Urban*				*Slum*			
	Level of education				*Level of education*			
	Illiterate	*1 to 9 years*	*10 years & above*	*Total*	*Illiterate*	*1 to 9 years*	*10 years & above*	*Total*
SES_1	-	-	4	4	-	-	-	-
SES_2	-	2	11	13	-	-	-	-
SES_3	-	1	9	10	-	1	3	4
SES_4	-	-	5	5	-	14	7	21
SES_5	-	3	-	3	8	8	8	24
Total	-	6 (17.1)	29 (82.9)	35 (100)	8 (16.4)	23 (46.9)	18 (36.8)	49 (100)

Source : Survey data. Figures in Parentheses indicate percentage.

Utilization of Ante Natal Care (ANC)

Antenatal care comprises of a variety of preventive measures during pregnancy including regular check ups, tetanus toxoid injections, iron and folic acid tablets and educating woman about nutrition, delivery care, and postpartum care. Antenatal care may enable women to have safe delivery even in cases of high-risk pregnancies. Table 8.2 explains the proportion of households who utilized antenatal care.

In the urban sample ANC coverage was 100% and in slum it was 95.9%. The NFHS survey 1992-93 reveals that the ANC Coverage for India as a whole is only 62.3% and for Kerala it is 97.3%. The NFHS survey 1998-99 reveals that the ANC Coverage has increased to 65.4% for India and 98.8% for Kerala. The present study also indicates results in this direction that only 4.1% of the

Table 8.2 : SES with Utilization of Ante Natal Care

SES Class	*Urban*			*Slum*		
	ANC used	*Not used*	*Total*	*ANC used*	*Not used*	*Total*
SES_1	4	-	4	-	-	-
SES_2	13	-	13	-	-	-
SES_3	10	-	10	4	-	4
SES_4	5	-	5	21	-	21
SES_5	3	-	3	22	2	24
Total	35 (100)	-	35	47 (95.9)	2 (4.1)	49

Source : Survey data Figures in Parentheses indicate percentage.

slum households avoided ANC, whereas 100% of the urban mothers utilized the ANC. The poor perception of the slum mothers mainly due to their illiteracy was responsible for this reduction of antenatal care.

Type of Health Centre Utilized for ANC

The utilization of type of health centre is an important aspect to be considered regarding the extent of utilization. As private agency charge for every antenatal visit, lower income household prefer public agencies. Table 8.3 provides the type of agency used for antenatal care. The Govt. agency utilized by the people of the study area is the General hospital Thalassery with a bed capacity of 541 situated in the heart of the city and another dispensary close to the slum area. The private agencies utilized by the respondents include private hospitals, voluntary hospitals private clinics etc. The table 8.3 shows that as SES scale raises the proportion of household choosing private health centres for ANC increases. In the urban sample 100% of the SES_2 utilized private health services, and in the SES_5 100% utilized Govt. centres for antenatal care. As a whole for the urban sample 74.3% utilized private and 25.7% used public health centres. The RCH project 1998 (Govt. of India 1999) Indicates that

ANC utilized by the urban woman in Kerala through the public agency was at 38.1% and private agency at 61.6%. In the slum sample as a whole 89.4% utilized public health centres and remaining 10.6% used private centres. The utilization data of ANC reveals that as SES scale rises they prefer private agencies and if it falls they prefer public agencies.

Table 8.3 : SES Class and Type of Agency Used for Antenatal care

SES Class	*Urban*			*Slum*		
	Govt.	*Private*	*Total*	*Govt.*	*Private*	*Total*
SES_1	-	4 (100)	4 (100)	-	-	-
SES_2	2 (15.4)	11 (84.6)	13 (100)	-	-	-
SES_3	1 (10)	9 (90)	10 (100)	1 (25)	3 (75)	4 (100)
SES_4	3 (60)	2 (40)	5 (100)	20 (95.2)	1 (4.8)	21 (100)
SES_5	3 (100)	-	3 (100)	21 (95.5)	1 (4.5)	22 (100)
Total	9 (25.7)	26 (74.3)	35 (100)	42 (89.4)	5 (10.6)	47 (100)

Source : Survey data. Figures in Parentheses indicate percentage.

Number of Times Gone for Antenatal Care

The number of ANC visit indicates the intensity of utilization of maternal health care services by the pregnant woman. The table 8.4 shows the SES class and number of antenatal care attended by the pregnant woman. From the table it can be seen that the urban mothers utilized the maximum antenatal care services. The RCH survey for urban Kerala reveals that 99.4% of them attended more than 3 ANC services. The NFHS 1998-99 revealed that 98.3% had more than 3 ANC visit in Kerala. In the present study, in the urban area the utilization of ANC was 100%, whereas in the slum it was only 95.9%. Most interesting is that 97% had visited more than 6 times for ANC in the urban areas and in slum this was only 69.4%. This indicates that even poor people are alert in the utilization of maternal health care services in Kerala.

Table 8.4 : SES with No. of Antenatal Care Visit

Sex Class	*Urban*			*Slum*			
	No. of ANC visit			*No. of ANC visit*			
	3 to 5	*6 and above*	*Total*	*No. visit*	*3 to 5*	*6 and above*	*Total*
SES_1	-	4	4	-	-	-	-
SES_2	-	13	13	-	-	-	-
SES_3	-	10	10	-	-	4	4
SES_4	-	5	5	-	7	14	21
SES_5	1	2	3	2	6	16	24
Total	1 (2.9)	34 (97.1)	35 (100)	2 (4.1)	13 (26.5)	34 (69.4)	49 (100)

Source : Survey data. Figures in Parentheses indicate percentage.

Month of Pregnancy Gone for Antenatal Care

The month of pregnancy in which antenatal care is attended is divided into three trimesters. Those who attended ANC in the first three months of pregnancy is catalogued as under 1st trimester, and those who attended ANC in four to six months of pregnancy is included under the 2nd trimester and those attended after six months is included under the third trimester. The month of pregnancy in which antenatal care sought indicates the expectant mothers consciousness of the need for such care as well as the quantum of services consumed. Those who go early for antenatal care tend to have larger period of antenatal care and the chance of any complications during delivery can be detected earlier. Table 8.5 explains the month of pregnancy in which ANC is sought. From the table it can be seen that 94.3% pregnant women started ANC in the first trimester itself, whereas in the slum this was only 68% and the remaining started ANC in the second trimester. When we asked about the reason for the delay in starting of ANC, many respondents reacted that, if they started ANC at an early period and decided to go every month, the doctor will prescribe lot of medicines and tonics. As they could not purchase such tonics and medicines, they decided to start ANC only in the later period of pregnancy. Thus, their poor perception and financial hazards are responsible for the lower health services utilization by them. In the urban sample only one respondent in the SES_5 started ANC in the second trimester, all other have gone for ANC in the first trimester itself indicating seriousness of maternal care on the part of urban mothers. The RCH project 1998 (Govt. of India 1999) reveals that 85.2% of the urban women in Kerala started ANC in the first trimester and the present study shows that in the urban sample it is 94.3%. The NFHS data for 1998-99 shows that those started ANC in the first trimester for Kerala as a whole is 81.1% and for India as a whole it is only 33%. Compared to NFHS and RCH survey hike in the utilization of antenatal care in the first

Table 8.5 : SES Class and Month of Pregnancy Gone for Antenatal Care

Sex Class	*Urban*				*Slum*			
	First trime-ster	*Second trime-ster*	*Third trime-ster*	*Total*	*First trime-ster*	*Second trime-ster*	*Third trime-ster*	*Total*
SES_1	4	-	-	4	-	-	-	-
SES_2	13	-	-	13	-	-	-	-
SES_3	10	-	-	10	4	-	-	4
SES_4	5	-	-	5	14	7	-	21
SES_5	1 (33.3)	2 (66.7)	-	3	14	18	-	22
Total	33 (94.3)	2 (5.7)	-	35 (100)	32 (68.1)	15 (31.9)	-	47 (100)

Source : Survey data. Figures in Parentheses indicate percentage.

trimester is high in the present study. This may be mainly due to the bifurcation of urban and slum samples separately and also due to the small size of the sample. In the slum, it can be seen that as SES status rises, the proportion of women who attended ANC also rises and vice versa.

Mother's Education and Period of Antenatal Care Started

The influence of mother's education in the starting of ANC was also tested in the study. Table 8.6 reveals the education of mothers and period of ANC started. From the table it can be seen that in the urban sample there is no illiterate mothers. Out of mothers with 1 to 9 years of education, only 66.6% started ANC in the first trimester itself, whereas in the case of mothers with 10years and above education 100% of them started ANC in the first trimester itself, indicating that education is significant determinant in the extent of utilization ANC. In the case of slum 66.7% of the illiterate mothers (32% of the slum mothers as a whole) started ANC only in the 2nd trimester indicating the significance of maternal education in the better utilization of maternal health care services.

Table 8.6 : Education of Mothers and Period of Antenatal care started

Mothers education	*Urban*			*Slum*		
	First trimester	*Second trimester*	*Total*	*First trimester*	*Second trimester*	*Total*
Illiterate	-	-	-	3 (33.3)	6 (66.7)	9
1 to 9 years	4 (66.6)	2 (33.4)	6	16 (76.2)	5 (23.8)	21
10 years and above	29 (100)	-	29	13 (76.5)	4 (23.5)	17
Total	33 (94.3)	2 (5.7)	35	32 (68)	15 (32)	47

Source : Survey data. Figures in Parentheses indicate percentage.

Utilization of Antenatal Care

To know the full extent of utilization of ANC, in addition to the number of visits, one must know the type of ANC received during the pregnancy period. The table 8.7 explains the type of ANC received by woman of different SES classes. Important item of ANC services used were measurement of weight and blood pressure, consumption of iron and folic acid tablets (IFA) tetanus toxoid injections (TTI) and abdominal check-up. From the table (8.7) it can be seen that though there exist 49 women in the slum, 2 did not utilized any of the antenatal care services.

In the urban and slum sample 100% of the woman who utilized ANC, irrespective of the SES class utilized the measurement of weight and blood pressure. 85.7% in urban and 85.1% in slum utilized IFA tablets. But the consumption of 100 and above IFA tablets during pregnancy period is very few among the upper and upper middle classes and only 25% of the urban upper class (SES_1) consumed more than 100 IFA tablets, 38.5% by the upper middle class and other classes consumed more than 50%. It can be seen that between the slum and urban woman, the consumption of 100 and above tablets increases as SES classes falls indicating the high deficiency of iron and other vitamin contents among the woman in the lower socio-economic status. Another antenatal item, which is most vital, is the tetanus injections. It can be seen that women belongs to lower socio-economic status (2 in urban and 5 in the slum) neglected one dose of T.T. injections indicating high alertness even among the poor sections for maternal health care. Similar is the case of abdominal check up as 94.3% of the urban and 97% of the slum had also utilized this service. The analysis of the availing of ANC services like 2 TT injection, plus IFA tablets plus at least 3 ANC visit among the urban and slum women reveals that as SES status falls, the proportion of women utilizing these antenatal package measures also falls (with the exception of SES_3, in slum, may be due to the short size of the

Table 8.7 : SES Class and Type of Antenatal Care Received

Type of ANC received	Urban						Slum			
	Socio-economic class						Socio-economic class			
	SES_1	SES_2	SES_3	SES_4	SES_5	Total	SES_3	SES_4	SES_5	Total
1. Weight taken	4 (100)	13 (100)	10 (100)	5 (100)	3 (100)	35	4 (100)	21 (100)	22 (100)	47
2. Blood Pressure Measured	4 (100)	13 (100)	10 (100)	5 (100)	3 (100)	35	4 (100)	21 (100)	22 (100)	47
3. IFA tablets consumed	4 (100)	12 (92.3)	8 (80)	4 (80)	2 (66.6)	30 (85.7)	3 (75)	18 (85.7)	19 (86.4)	40 (85)
Below 100	3 (75)	7 (53.8)	3 (30)	1 (20)	-	14 (40)	-	1 (4.1)	1 (4.5)	2 (4.3)
Above 100	1 (25)	5 (38.5)	5 (50)	3 (60)	2 (66.6)	16 (45.7)	3 (75)	17 (80.9)	18 (81.8)	38 (80.9)
No IFA tablets	-	1 (7.7)	2 (20)	1 (20)	1 (33.3)	5 (14.2)	1 (25)	3 (14.3)	3 (13.6)	7 (14.9)
4. T.T. Injection taken	4 (100)	13 (100)	10 (100)	5 (100)	3 (100)	35 (100)	4 (100)	21 (100)	22 (100)	47 (100)
One T.T	-	-	-	1 (20)	1 (33.3)	2 (5.7)	-	1 (4.8)	4 (18.2)	5 (10.6)
Two T.T	4 (100)	13 (100)	10 (100)	4 (80)	2 (66.6)	33 (94.3)	4 (100)	20 (95.2)	18 (81.8)	42 (89.4)

Contd....

Table 8.7 : (Contd....)

Type of ANC received	*Urban*						*Slum*			
	Socio-economic class						*Socio-economic class*			
	SES_1	SES_2	SES_3	SES_4	SES_5	*Total*	SES_3	SES_4	SES_5	*Total*
5. Abdominal check up	4 (100)	13 (100)	10 (100)	5 (100)	3 (100)	35 (100)	4 (100)	21 (100)	22 (100)	47 (100)
Less than three	-	-	-	-	2 (66.6)	2 (5.7)	-	1 (4.8)	-	1 (2.1)
Three or more	4 (100)	13 (100)	10 (100)	5 (100)	1 (33.3)	33 (94.3)	4 (100)	20 (95.2)	22 (100)	46 (97.9)
6. Women with 2 TT + IFA + At least 3 ANC visit.	4 (100)	12 (92.3)	8 (80)	4 (80)	2 (66.7)	30 (85.7)	3 (75)	18 (85.7)	19 (79.2)	40 (81.6)
Total Woman	4	13	10	5	3	35	4	21	24*	49

Source : Survey data. Figures in Parentheses indicate percentage.

* Total woman in the slum is 49, but two woman did not utilized (SES_5) any antenatal care services. For calculating serial No.6 of Table 8.7 under slum total is taken as 49 with SES_5 as 24 (i.e including 2 women who avoided antenatal care).

sample in the group) indicating that the extent of utilization of ANC services is influenced greatly by the socio-economic status of the household. The RCH project 1999 reveals that 99.4% of the urban woman in Kerala had undergone more than 3 ANC visits, 85.3% had taken two tetanus injections, 89% had taken IFA tablets. The RCH project also reveals the data related to ANC package as a whole, that is those who had 2TT + IFA + at least 3 ANC in urban Kerala account for 74.6%. The NFHS data for 1998-99 reveals that in Kerala 86.4% had taken two T.T. injections, 95.2% had taken IFA tablets. The present study reveals utilization proportion higher than RCH data related to utilization of ANC services that is 85.7% for the urban and 81.6% for the slum. This may again be due to the small size of the sample and also due to lack of wide coverage in selecting the sample compared to RCH project.

Pregnancy Complications

Complications during pregnancy can adversely affect woman's health or the outcome of pregnancy. World wide about 500,000 women die every year from pregnancy and childbirth related causes and most of these deaths occur in developing countries (WHO 1999). Early identification of pregnancy complications and its timely treatment are the important components of safe motherhood programme. Women's were asked about the pregnancy complications and health problems they experienced during pregnancy and the type of treatment they sought. Incidence of pregnancy complications was assessed by the reported systems associated with the complications Viz Anemia, eclampsia, ante-partum bleeding etc. In the urban sample 77.14% (i.e 27 women) and in slum 87.8% (43 women) women had pregnancy complications. Table 8.8 shows SES with the pregnancy complications.

From the table (8.8) it can be seen that the problem of pregnancy complications is associated more with urban slum compared to urban sample. This is mainly due to lack of proper maternal care during pregnancy by the slum

Table 8.8: SES with Pregnancy Complications

SES Class	Urban			Slum		
	Pregnancy Complications			Pregnancy Complications		
	Yes	No	Total	Yes	No	Total
SES_1	3	1	4	-	-	-
SES_2	8	5	13	-	-	-
SES_3	9	1	10	4	-	4
SES_4	5	-	5	17	4	21
SES_5	2	1	3	22	2	24
Total	27 (77.14)	8 (22.6)	35 (100)	43 (87.43)	6 (12.57)	49 (100)

Source : Survey Data. Figures in Parentheses indicate percentage.

women. The table 8.9 explains the incidence of pregnancy complications with SES character of women households. The table reveals the variety of pregnancy health problems faced by women in different SES categories. The common problems reported were weakness by 60% of the urban and 73.5% of the slum, paleness by 54.3% of the urban, 53.1% of the slum, dizziness felt by 51.4% of the urban and 55.1% of the slum.

The health problems like the swelling on hands and feet as reported by 45.7% of urban women and 42.8% of the slum, bleeding felt by 8.5% for urban and 14.3% for slum. Another thing which can be realized from the data on pregnancy complications is that, prevalence of most of the complications are more among the low class and very low class (SES_4 and SES_5) households in urban and slum indicating their weak financial position and low socio-economic status as paleness and weakness or tiredness etc. are generally associated with the lack of nutrient food on the part of pregnant women.

Type of Health Centre Used for Pregnancy complications

The entire women who had felt pregnancy complications had not undergone for treatment. Twenty

Table 8.9 : SES Class with type of Pregnancy Complications

Type of pregnancy complications	Urban						Slum			
	Socio-economic class						Socio-economic class			
	SES_1	SES_2	SES_3	SES_4	SES_5	Total	SES_3	SES_4	SES_5	Total
1. Swelling	2	6	5	2	1	16	1	10	10	21
	(50)	(46.2)	(50)	(40)	(33.1)	(45.7)	(25)	(47.6)	(41.7)	(42.8)
2. Paleness	2	7	5	3	2	19	3	11	12	26
	(50)	(53.8)	(50)	(60)	(66.6)	(54.3)	(75)	(52.4)	(50)	(53.1)
3. Weakness	-	9	6	4	2	21	2	15	19	36
		(69.2)	(60)	(80)	(66.6)	(60)	(50)	(71.4)	(79.1)	(73.5)
4. Dizziness	1	6	6	3	1	17	1	12	14	27
	(25)	(46.2)	(80)	(60)	(33.3)	(48.6)	(25)	(57.1)	(58.3)	(55.1)
5. Bleeding	-	-	1	1	1	3	-	2	3	5
			(10)	(20)	(33.3)	(8.5)		(9.5)	(12.5)	(10.2)
6. Others	-	-	-	2	1	3	1	2	4	7
				(40)	(33.3)	(8.5)	(25)	(9.5)	(16.6)	(14.3)
Total woman.	4	13	10	5	3	35	4	21	24	49

Source : Survcy Data. Figures in Parentheses indicate percentage of total women in each SES class.

two per cent of the urban and 34.9% of the slum women did not go for treatment, considering that these are not serious ailments and some women in the very low class (SES_5) felt financial hurdles in going to the hospital for treatment. The table 8.10 presents the type of health centre and number of women gone for treatment of pregnancy complications. It shows 18.5% of those sought treatment for pregnancy complications in urban sample consulted Govt. doctors and 59.3% to private doctors. In the slum 53.5% sought the services of Government doctors and 10.6% from the private doctors.

Table 8.10 : SES Class with type of Health Centre Utilized for Pregnancy Complications

Sex Class	*Urban*				*Slum*			
	Type of Health Centre				*Type of Health Centre*			
	Govt.	*Private*	*No treat-ment*	*Total*	*Govt.*	*Private*	*No treat-ment*	*Total*
SES_1	-	3	-	3	-	-	-	-
SES_2	-	6	2	8	-	-	-	-
SES_3	1	6	2	9	1	1	2	4
SES_4	3	1	1	5	8	3	5	17
SES_5	1	-	1	2	14	1	7	22
Total	5 (18.5)	16 (59.3)	6 (22.2)	27	23 (53.5)	5 (10.6)	15 (34.9)	43

Source : Survey data. Figures in Parentheses indicate percentage.

Opinion on Antenatal care

Of the 35 women in the urban sample only 9 had sought the ANC from Government doctors and 26 sought ANC from private doctors. Similarly in the slum out of 49 only 47 sought ANC and only 5 women approached private doctors. In the urban sample only 4 persons were dissatisfied about the ANC. They were 2 from upper middle class (SES_2) 1 from lower middle class (SES_3) one from low class (SES_4). The interesting thing is that all the four dissatisfied were consulted with Government doctors and nobody is dissatisfied with private doctors, even though they think that cost of private treatment is higher. Similarly in the urban slum, out of 47 who used ANC, 16 (38.1% of those utilized Govt. doctors service) of them dissatisfied, unfortunately all those dissatisfied belong to those utilized Govt. hospitals. These group complaint that the check-up of Govt. hospital doctors is very poor and often they did not provide any medicines. As there is no alternative, which they can afford, they are compelled to go to Govt. hospitals. To know the reasons for the dissatisfaction on the part of women respondents, the researcher consulted the Govt. doctors and also discussed with those who are in charge of maternal and child health care. They opines that the overcrowded condition of the out patient counter of the Govt. hospitals [Where most of the low class (SES_4) and very low class (SES_5) approached] compelled the doctors to cut short the consulting time allotted to each patient, as such a thorough examination of the pregnant women is quite impossible within that limited time. This might have caused some dissatisfaction on the part of pregnant women.

Natal Care

The place of delivery and assistance during delivery is highly significant as far as the health of the mother and child is concerned. The selection of the delivery place is mostly determined by one's socio-economic status. The NFHS-1 for 1992-93 reveals that community access variables like distance to the health centre, family welfare or health worker visit, access to mass media etc. had an important influence on the utilization of antenatal, natal, post natal care. The section deals with the utilization of natal care by mothers in the study sample.

Place of Childbirth

Place of delivery is divided into three categories including Govt. hospital, private hospital and home. The place of delivery would indicate the type of health services used and the extent of its utilization by mothers. The place of delivery is an important determinant for reducing the risk of infant and maternal death. The table 8.11 presents the choice of delivery place by mothers. The problems of home delivery is absent among the urban mothers, whereas this system still exist among the few slum dwellers. The table reveals that 14.3% of the deliveries in the slum are occurred in home, assisted by Nurse/ANM (Auxiliary Nurse Midwife) and relatives. It also reveals that SES scale has a vital role in the selection of delivery place as 100% of the upper class (SES_1), upper middle class (SES_2), lower middle class (SES_3), in the urban sample utilized private hospitals for delivery. As SES scale of household rises, the proportion of women who utilized private hospital for delivery rises and utilization of Govt. hospital falls. This trend is quite common in both urban and slum. Since people of low class and very low classes occupy the slum area, 75.5% of them have utilized Govt. hospital for delivery. The RCH (Reproductive child Health) project 1998 for Kerala reveals

Table 8.11: SES Class and Choice of Delivery Place

SES Class	*Urban*			*Slum*			
	Govt.	*Private*	*Total*	*Govt.*	*Private*	*Home*	*Total*
SES_1		4 (100)	4	-	-	-	-
SES_2		13 (100)	13	-	-	-	-
SES_3		10 (100)	10	1 (25)	2 (5.0)	1 (25)	4
SES_4	3 (60)	2 (40)	5	16 (16.2)	2 (9.5)	3 (14.3)	21
SES_5	3 (60)	-	3	20 (83.3)	1 (4.2)	3 (12.5)	24
Total	6 (17.1)	29 (82.9)	35 (100)	37 (75.5)	5 (10.2)	7 (14.3)	49 (100)

Source : Survey data. Figures in Parentheses indicate percentage.

that in urban Kerala 39% of the deliveries are occurred in Govt. hospital and 61% in private institutions. The RCH project 1998 also reveals that 99% urban had institutional deliveries, but in this micro study 100% of the urban had institutional deliveries, whereas in the slum, institutional delivery is only 85.7% and 14.3% is reported as home delivery.

Percapita Income and Choice of Delivery Place

The choice of delivery place is significant in assessing the delivery and post delivery complications of a woman. Recently there is an increasing trend of institutional delivery, which culminated in reducing delivery and post delivery complications on the part of mother and child. But the choice of delivery place is determined by some socio- economic variables. The family per capita income is treated as one such vital variable and it is analysed in Table 8.12.

It is very clear from the table that percapita income of the family is also the most vital determinant in choice of delivery place. Household with lower percapita income preferred the Govt. hospital and home delivery whereas high percapita income groups preferred private hospital. It can be seen that 100% of the Below Rs.100 percapita income households in the slum, 100% of the households in the per capita income slab of Rs.100-250 in urban opted Govt. hospital as the choice of their delivery place. Similarly 77.8% of woman in the PCI slab of Rs.100 to 250 in slum opted Govt. hospital for delivery and the remaining 22% home deliveries. Similarly all those with per capita income more than Rs.500 utilised private hospital for delivery indicating that income is an important determinant in the choice of delivery place and associated health services utilization. As income increases their preference of opting private hospital for delivery and related health services utilization increases and vice versa. The low-income groups avoid private hospital due to its high cost at the same time the better off section is not

Table 8.12 : Percapita Income of the Family and Choice of Delivery Place

Urban				
Percapita Income Slab (Amount in Rupees)	*Choice of delivery place*			
	Govt.	*Private*	*Home*	*Total*
Below 100	-	-	-	-
100-250	2	-	-	2
	(100)			
251-500	4	3	-	7
	(57.1)	(42.9)		
501-750	-	2	-	2
		(100)		
751-1000	-	7	-	7
		(100)		
1001-1500	-	14	-	14
		(100)		
Above 1500	-	3	-	3
		(100)		
Total	6	29	-	35
	(17.1)	(82.9)		
Slum				
Below 100	1	-	-	1
	(100)			
100- 250	14	-	4	18
	(77.8)		(22.2)	
251-500	21	(11.1)	(11.1)	
	(77.8)	3	3	27
501-750	1	2	-	3
	(33.3)	(66.7)		
751-1000	-	-	-	-
1001-1500	-	-	-	-
Above 1500	-	-	-	-
Total	37	5	7	49
	(75.5)	(10.3)	(14.2)	

Source : Survey data. Figures in Parentheses indicate percentage.

ready to share their privacy by opting Govt. hospital though the cost is less.

Reasons for the Choice of Delivery Place

The reason for the choice of delivery place may vary from individual to individuals, may be personal or economic or quality of health services. Table 8.13 presents the reasons for the choice of delivery place based on the socio-economic status of households.

Table 8.13 : SES Class and Reasons for the Choice of Delivery place

URBAN						
Reasons	SES_1	SES_2	SES_3	SES_4	SES_5	Total
Free or less expenditure	-	-	-	3 (60)	3 (100)	6 (17.2)
Good medical care	3 (75)	9 (69.2)	7 (70)	1 (20)	-	20 (57.1)
Doctor is known	1 (25)	4 (30.8)	3 (30)	1 (20)	-	9 (25.7)
Others	-	-	-	-	-	-
Total	4	13	10	5	3	35
SLUM						
Free or less expensive	-	-	1 (25)	16 (76.2)	20 (83.3)	37 (75.5)
Good medical care	-	-	2 (50)	1 (4.8)	1 (4.2)	4 (8.2)
Doctor is known	-	-	-	1 (4.7)	-	1 (2.0)
Others	-	-	1 (25)	3 (14.3)	3 (12.5)	7 (14.3)
Total	-	-	4	21	24	49

Source : Survey data. Figures in Parentheses indicate percentage.

There was wide difference in the criteria selected for the choice of health centres by mothers for delivery place.

The table 8.13 reveals that as socio economic status rises the proportion preferring good medical care as the reason for the choice of delivery place, rises both in urban and slum. Financial constraints compel the low class (SES_4) and very low class (SES_5) women to go to Govt. hospitals for delivery, as it is less costly compared to private hospitals. The 100% of the very low class (SES_5) and 60% of the low class in urban and 83.3% of the very low class and 76.2% of the low class in slum reported that free treatment prompted them to prefer Govt. hospital for delivery. Other reasons pointed out by slum households include lack of bystanders in hospital, and financial hurdles, which compels them to opt for home deliveries. As most of the slum women are manual workers or rag pickers, once a woman is admitted to the hospital for delivery, somebody must stay with the patient as bystander. Lack of such persons compelled them to opt for home delivery, which is supplemented by financial hurdles because, even in Govt. hospital for delivery some amount of expenditure is inevitable.

Percapita Income and Choice of Delivery Place

Table 8.14 reveals percapita income and reason for the choice of delivery place. In the urban sample 100% of the women with percapita income in the range 100-250 opines that free or less expensive motivated them to opt Govt. Hospital. In the urban 17.1% of women and in slum 75.5% expressed that free or less expensive prompted them to choose Govt. hospital. In slum as most of them are economically deprived groups only 8.2% have thought in terms of good care, whereas in urban areas 57.1% have expressed this as the reason for the choice of delivery place. The table reveals that as income status raises all of them chase behind good medical care or decides to consult a doctor who is very close to them. Thus the analysis reveals that percapita income is an important determinant in deciding the type of health services utilized by the household members.

Table 8.14 : Percapita Income Slab and Reasons for the Choice of Delivery Place

Percapita Income Slab (Amount in Rupees)	Urban					Slum				
	Reasons for the choice of delivery place					Reasons for the choice of delivery place				
	Free or less expensive	Good medical care	Doctor is known	Others	Total	Free or less expensive	Good medical care	Doctor is known	Others	Total
Below 100	-	-	-	-	-	1 (100)	-	-	-	1
100-250	2 (100)	-	-	-	2	14 (77.7)	-	-	4 (22.3)	18
251-500	4 (57.1)	2 (28.5)	1 (14.2)	-	7	21 (77.8)	2 (7.4)	1 (3.7)	3 (11.1)	27
501-750	-	1 (50)	1 (50)	-	2	1 (33.3)	2 (66.7)	-	-	3
751-1000	-	5 (71.4)	2 (28.6)	-	7	-	-	-	-	-
1001-1500	-	10 (71.4)	4 (28.6)	-	14	-	-	-	-	-
Above 1500	-	2 (66.7)	1 (33.3)	-	3	-	-	-	-	-
Total	6 (17.1)	20 (57.1)	9 (25.7)	-	35 (100)	37 (75.5)	4 (8.2)	1 (2.1)	7 (14.3)	49 (100)

Source : Survey data. Figures in Parentheses indicate percentage.

Delivery Complications

Delivery complications are also significant in the maternal health as serious complications may lead to the death of the mother or newborn. The common delivery health problems reported from the field are pre-mature labour, obstructed labour and prolonged labour. Table 8.15 presents common delivery complications felt by the mothers. The most common delivery problem observed was obstructed and pre- mature labour. It is to be noted that such health problem persist more with the lower class (SES_4) and very low class in both urban and slum.

Postnatal Care

Postnatal care covers health check-up of the mother and child and treatment of all post delivery complications. The utilization of postnatal care varies according to the socio-economic status of the woman households. We from our field experience realized that most of the very low class women (SES_5) utilized postnatal care only if they happened any post delivery complications. At the same time most of the upper class and upper middle class (SES_1 and SES_2) women had gone for health check-up even if the delivery is normal. It was observed that utilization of maternal health services is high among the upper class sections of the community. One thing which we realised from our field experience is that, though there is no dearth of health care facilities in terms of hospital beds, equipments, sophisticated treatment methods and highly specialized health man power, still the health status of large section of mothers and children in urban areas remain very poor. The data related to post delivery complication indicates thoughts in this regard. Table 8.16 gives the number of women who had post delivery complications. From the table it can be seen that 25.7% women in urban and 40.8% women in slum had post delivery complications. The table 8.16 reveals the type of post delivery complications on the part of women. It shows the morbidity problems arising out of delivery during the

Table 8.15 : SES Class and Type of Delivery Complications

SES Class	Urban				Slum			
	Type of Delivery Complications				*Type of Delivery Complications*			
	Pre-mature labour	*Obstructed labour*	*Pro-longed labour*	*Total*	*Pre-mature labour*	*Obstructed labour*	*Pro-longed labour*	*Total*
SES_1	1	1	-	2	-	-	-	-
SES_2	-	2	-	2	-	-	-	-
SES_3	1	2	-	3	-	-	-	-
SES_4	1	-	1	2	1	3	2	6
SES_5	1	1	-	2	5	3	3	11
Total	4	6	1	11	6	6	5	17
	(36.4)	(54.5)	(9.1)	(100)	(35.3)	(35.3)	(29.4)	(100)

Source : Survey data. Figures in Parentheses indicate percentage.

first week after delivery. The post delivery complications are high among lower SES classes both in the slum and urban. It reveals that as SES status falls the incidence of post delivery complications rises.

Table 8.16 : SES Class and No. of Women who had Post Delivery Complications

SES Class	Post delivery Complications	No complications	Total
Urban			
SES_1	1	3	4
SES_2	1	12	13
SES_3	2	8	10
SES_4	2	3	5
SES_5	3	-	3
Total	9 (25.7)	26 (74.4)	35 (100)
SLUM			
SES_3	1	3	4
SES_4	7	14	21
SES_5	12	12	24
Total	20 (40.8)	29 (59.2)	49 (100)

Source : Survey data. Figures in Parentheses indicate percentage.

Another fact, which is emerging from the data presented in table 8.17 which can be related with this issue, is that more of the post delivery complications are associated with those who opt Govt. hospital for delivery. As better classes preferred private hospitals, most of the low class and very low class only utilized Govt. hospitals for delivery and post delivery complications. It is clustered more among the very low class both in the slum and urban. It is expected that this might be due to lack of proper check-up done by Govt. doctors who on their part is suffering from heavy load of patients as inpatient and outpatient in Govt. hospitals.

Table 8.17 : SES Class and Type of Post Delivery Complications

Type of post delivery complication	Urban						Slum			
	Socio-economic class						Socio-economic class			
	SES_1	SES_2	SES_3	SES_4	SES_5	Total	SES_3	SES_4	SES_5	Total
High fever	1 (25)	1 (7.6)	-	1 (20)	3 (100)	6 (17.1)	-	3 (14.2)	5 (20.8)	8 (16.3)
Lower Abdominal pain	-	-	2 (20)	1 (20)	3 (100)	6 (17.1)	-	3 (14.2)	4 (16.7)	7 (14.3)
Excess bleeding	-	-	-	-	-	-	-	-	1 (4.2)	1 (2)
Dizziness, severe headache	-	1 (7.6)	2 (20)	1 (20)	-	4 (11.4)	1 (25)	3 (14.2)	7 (29.2)	11 (22)
Total	1	2	4	3	6	16	1	9	17	27
Total Women in the sample	4	13	10	5	3	35	4	21	24	49

Source : Survey data. Figures in Parentheses indicate percentage of total women in each class.

Note : Percentage may exceed 100 due to reporting of more than one post delivery complications by same women.

Utilization of Health Centres for Post Delivery Complications

Of the 9 post delivery complications cases in urban, all the 9 persons had gone for treatment. Whereas in the slum, of the 20 post delivery complications cases only 17 had gone for treatment. Table 8.18 shows the type of health centres and doctors utilized for post delivery complications.

Table 8.18 : SES Class and the Type of Health Centres Utilized for Post Delivery Complications

SES Class	*Urban*			*Slum*		
	Govt.	*Private*	*Total*	*Govt.*	*Private*	*Total*
SES_1		1	1	-	-	-
SES_2		1	1	-	-	-
SES_3		2	2	-	1	1
SES_4	1	1	2	5	1	6
SES_5	2	1	3	8	2	10
Total	3 (33.3)	6 (66.7)	9 (100)	13 (76.4)	4 (23.6)	17 (100)

Source : Survey data. Figures in Parentheses indicate percentage.

For the post delivery complications also most of the low class and very low class women used Govt. hospital. Of the total who sought post delivery complications in slum 76.4% sought treatment from Govt. sources and 23.6% from private. For the urban 33.3% of those sought treatment approached Govt. hospital, all of them belonged to low class and very low classes and remaining 66.7% sought treatment from private hospitals. The RCH study for Kerala reveals that 37.9% of the post delivery complicated cases were treated from Govt. hospital and the remaining by the private doctor. Most important findings emerged from the study is that selection of a particular institution for the utilization of antenatal, natal and post natal care is determined primarily by their socio-economic status.

Child Health Services

The primary object of family welfare programme is the promotion of health of mothers and children. Good health of children engenders a sense of security in the minds of parents, that the children born will survive and live a healthy life, which in turn, contributes greatly to the acceptance of small family norm. Hence under basic maternal and child health services, the mothers should be provided with much needed care during antenatal, natal and post natal periods. Infants and pre-school children are to be monitored for their growth and development, adequate protections with immunization and early detection and treatment of diarrhoea and other childhood diseases is to be provided.

Childhood is an important stage where the child is prone to certain illness for which others are not exposed. The child faces a group of communicable diseases like polio, diphtheria, whooping cough, etc. and also many deficiency diseases. Only through proper immunization all these can be prevented among children.

Infant mortality is the most frequently used index for the assessment of health status of population. A declining infant mortality rate (IMR) usually is considered to reflect an improvement in the health of the population. However the empirical evidence indicates that IMR has been declining in almost every country in recent years, irrespective of the economic cycles affecting these nations. Even during periods of economic recession, infant mortality is seen to have declined. For instance, in the state of Sau Paulo, Brazil that suffered serious necessary impact, IMR registered a significant and consistent decline during 1979-82 (Macedo Robert 1984). The experience of Chile another Latin American country, which experienced a more protracted recession, also conforms to the pattern. (Alenjandro Foxley, and Daymar Raizyasky 1984). This apparent Paradox is not difficult to resolve. For one thing IMR (Infant Mortality Rate) does not necessarily reflect the overall health situation of children in a community. In other words IMR can continue to decline even when there is no perceptible improvement in the morbidity condition and nutritional status of the child population. Nearly 60% of all deaths of infant occur in the neo-natal period (in the first four weeks) and the major causes underlying neo-natal deaths are infectious and congenital malformation and pre-maturity. In the post neo- natal period an important additional factor is enteric infection. An improvement in birth weight of babies is normally associated with a decline in infant mortality (Panicker and Soman 1985). The IMR represents only the survival prospects of a child in the first year of life. But a reduction in the risk of death in infancy does not necessarily imply an improvement in the health of the children who survive.

Though Kerala a small state in India is noted for its low level of infant mortality rate of 13 per 1000 for both rural and urban (Registrar General 1998), the morbidity problems among the children in Kerala is maximum compared to other Indian states. In 1999 alone the (Govt. of Kerala 1999) important communicable diseases reported from Government hospitals in Kerala amounts to 5,88,116 acute diarrhoeal diseases, 53,60,644 acute respiratory infections, 293 whooping cough 24,996 pneumonia, 35,937 pulmonary tuberculosis 15,162 enteric fever, 9585 chicken pox, 6693 measles etc. The above data reveals that mere reduction of infant mortality is not an index for better health status of the child population, they should be free from all types of illness (Communicable and others) in the childhood so as to be healthy in the future.

In this section the important immunization coverage of children is studied along with the type of immunization covered, the health centre utilized for coverage, if not immunized the reasons for non-immunization etc. The problem of underweight among the newborn is also examined since underweight is causing many morbidity problems among children.

For analysing the child health care and immunization coverage of children, data was collected from 35 mothers in the urban and 49 mothers in the slum (only one from each household, if there is more than one, only the last one was taken into account, as the women respondent) who had children in the age group of 1 to 3 years. If there were more than one child in this age group for the woman respondents only the case of last child was taken into account.

Utilization of Immunization Methods

Regarding the immunization coverage of children below 3 years, the respondents were asked about the vaccinations and inoculations given to the last child before attaining one year of age. The table 8.19 reveals the coverage of all vaccinations to be given to a child before attaining one year of age including BCG (Bacillus Calmatte Guerin) + Oral polio, DPT (Diptheria, Pertusis, Tetanus)

Table 8.19 : SES Class and Vaccination Given to Children

SES Class	*Urban*			*Slum*			
	Vaccination given	*Not given*	*Total*	*Vaccination given*	*Not given*	*Not remember*	*Total*
SES_1	4 (100)	-	4	-	-	-	-
SES_2	13 (100)	-	13	-	-	-	-
SES_3	8 (80)	2 (20)	10	3 (75)	1	-	4
SES_4	1 (20)	4 (80)	5	16 (76.2)	4	1	21
SES_5	2 (66.7)	1 (33.3)	3	19 (79.2)	4	1	24
Total	28 (80)	7 (20)	35 (100)	38 (77.6)	9 (18.4)	2 (4)	49 (100)

Source : Survey data. Figures in Parentheses indicate percentage.

polio three doses, and measles. The available data shows that only 80% of the urban and 77.6% of the slum respondent had given all the vaccinations to the children. The problem of not giving vaccination is high among low and very low economic classes both in the urban and slum. As many of the woman respondents in slum are illiterate, they are not familiar with the names of immunization vaccine. We had asked them about the immunization card and verified whether all doses of immunization is given or not. The field data shows that all most all children in the upper class (SES_1) and upper middle class (SES_2) had taken all immunization vaccine, but many children in the low class and very low class (SES_4 and SES_5) had missed/ avoided certain doses of immunization vaccine.

Table 8.20 presents item wise coverage of immunization vaccine so as to find out which vaccine was neglected and which one was taken and also to examine the percentage of children who has got the full doses of immunization. The table 8.20 shows the immunization coverage to children in the study area was very high. In the urban sample major vaccinations like BCG, DPT measles polio etc had better utilized by all five SES classes and in better classes like SES_1 and SES_2, the utilization was 100%. In the urban sample 100% of the children below one year had taken BCG and DPT vaccination and a small reduction occurred in the case cf polio (85.7) and measles (94.3%). If we consider the full dose of immunization (i.e BCG + DPT + 3 polio + measles) the urban coverage was 85.7% indicating a better utilization coverage and got full protection against 6 vaccine preventable diseases. The RCH Project of 1998 (Govt of India 1999) estimated that the urban coverage of full dose of immunization was 80.8% and it is also same for the Kerala as a whole. The NFHS survey 1998-99 reveals that for Kerala as a whole 96.2% had taken BCG and 84.6% had taken measles, but the full dose was taken only by 79.7% of the children. In the slum under study the utilization of immunization coverage is comparatively weak as the full dose of immunization coverage is only 79.6%, though certain vaccination like BCG (98%) DPT (93.9%) Polio (81.6%) and measles (85.7%) had taken better coverage. Though there exist differences in the proportion of utilization of immunization

Table 8.20 : SES Class and Type of Vaccinations Given

SES Class	BCG +Oral polio	DPT	Polio 3 doses	Measles	Full dose (BCG+3DPT +3Polio +Measles)	Total
Urban						
SES_1	4 (100)	4 (100)	4 (100)	4 (100)	4 (100)	4
SES_2	13 (100)	13 (100)	12 (92.3)	13 (100)	12 (92)	13
SES_3	10 (100)	10 (100)	8 (80)	10 (100)	8 (80)	10
SES_4	5 (100)	5 (100)	4 (80)	4 (80)	4 (80)	9
SES_5	3 (100)	3 (100)	2 (66.7)	2 (66.7)	2 (66.7)	3
Total	35 (100)	35 (100)	30 (85.7)	33 (94.3)	30 (85.7)	35
Slum						
SES_3	4 (100)	4 (100)	4 (100)	4 (100)	4 (100)	4
SES_4	21 (100)	20 (95.3)	17 (80.9)	20 (95.3)	17 (80.9)	21
SES_5	23 (95.8)	22 (91.7)	19 (79.2)	18 (75)	18 (75)	24
Total	48 (98)	46 (93.9)	40 (81.6)	42 (85.7)	39 (79.6)	49

Type of vaccination given spans columns BCG through Full dose.

Source : Survey data. Figures in Parentheses indicate percentage to total women.

vaccination by the SES classes, it is not significant. The reason is that almost all these immunization is provided free of cost from the Govt. health centres, and if the mothers are alert then the chance of missing any dose of immunization is very rare.

Reasons for not Giving Vaccination

From the table 8.20 it is clear that 14.3% children in urban and 20.4% children in slum had not taken the full dose of immunization. When the respondents were asked about the reason for non-vaccination of their children, respondents in the lower socio-economic classes revealed that they were ignorant and not aware of all doses. In certain cases mothers informed that the child was ill during the due date/period of vaccination and in certain cases they deliberately avoided the vaccination. Certain upper class mothers avoided polio vaccination by fearing its side effects. The problem of ignorance, lack of awareness about all doses, avoidance of vaccination due to sickness etc. was reported more from the slum areas, as there exist illiterate mothers. The slum folks are not exposed to mass media like television, and news papers as such the significance of immunization and inoculation is quite alien to them.

Sources of Immunization

Irrespective of the socio-economic status most of the children were immunized from Government health centres. Table 8.21 presents data on sources of immunization by SES characteristics. It shows the universalization of Government hospitals for the immunization of children. About 77% of the immunization of children in urban is carried out from Govt. institutions. The RCH project 1998 for Kerala reveals that 67.8% of the immunization in urban Kerala is covered by Government hospitals or institutions and 32.2% by private institutions and hospitals. In the slum sample 100% of the immunization is taken from Govt. hospitals. The important factor, which prompted people to go to

Govt. hospitals/ Institutions for immunization is the credibility of the people in the immunization scheme developed and implemented by the Government as part of eradication of 6 major vaccine preventable diseases.

Table 8.21: SES with Sources of Immunization

SES Class	*Urban*			*Slum*		
	Govt.	*Private*	*Total*	*Govt.*	*Private*	*Total*
SES_1	2	2	4	-	-	-
	(50)	(50)	(100)			
SES_2	7	6	13	-	-	-
	(53.8)	(46.2)	(100)			
SES_3	10	-	10	4	-	4
			(100)			(100)
SES_4	5	-	5	21	-	21
			(100)			(100)
SES_5	3	-	3	23	-	23
			(100)			(100)
Total	27	8	35	48	-	48*
	(77.1)	(22.9)	(100)	(100)		(100)

Source : Survey data. Figures in Parentheses indicate percentage.

* One child in the slum did not take any immunization at all.

Birth Weight of Babies

A major outcome of inadequate maternal nutrition is low birth weight babies, infant weight below a viable 2.5 kilograms. The incidence of this problem continues to be extremely high in India. While an average estimate for the country as a whole is 'over one third'. A major study reported the low birth weight incidence ranging from 25.9% to 40.8% in rural communities (ICMR 1985).

Birth weight trends serve as important indicators of health status of a community. Birth weight is one of the aspects suggested by WHO as an index to monitor progress towards health for all (WHO 1981). In developing countries proportion of low birth weight babies (those whose birth weight is less than 2500 gms) usually exceed 10 percent. (Vijayakumar and etal. 1990) The risk of mortality in the first year of life especially in the neo-natal period increases dramatically with the lowering of birth weight (Ghosh Shanti 1976).

The table 8.22 presents the problem of underweight among the children in the study sample.

Table 8.22 : SES Class and the Problem of Underweight Among Children

SES Class	*Urban* Weight of the children			*Slum* Weight of the children			
	Below 2.5kg	*Above 2.5kg*	*Total*	*Below 2.5kg*	*Above 2.5kg*	*Not weighed due to home delivery*	*Total*
SES_1	-	4	4	-	-	-	-
SES_2	-	13	13	-	-	-	-
SES_3	1 (11.1)	9	10	0	3	1	4
SES_4	1 (20)	4	5	4	14	3	21
SES_5	1 (33.3)	2	3	10	11	3	24
Total	3 (8.6)	32 (91.4)	35 (100)	14 (33.3)	28 (66.7)	7	49 (100)

Source : Survey data. Figures in Parentheses indicate percentage

The table 8.22 shows the problem of underweight among the children in the study sample. The children with less than 2.5kgms were usually treated as underweight children. (R.C.H. Survey 1999) From the table it can be seen that the problem of underweight is much more grave in the slum compared to urban areas. Of the total 49 children in the sample under slum 7 had been not weighed immediately after delivery (being home delivery). Out of 42 children weighed 33.3% had been below the minimum weight of 2.5kgm at the time of birth indicating that such children are susceptible to frequent illness and the problem is grave in slum. In the urban sample the proportion of under weight children is very meager with only 8.6% of the total children weighed after delivery (All the children in the sample were weighed immediately after delivery).

Percapita income of Household and Underweight Problem of Children

The table 8.23 shows the per capita income of the household and the problem of the underweight of the newborns. It clearly reveals that percapita income of household is an important determinant in influencing the problem of underweight. The birth weight below 2.5kgm is treated as underweight children. From the table it can be seen that the problem of underweight children is specially felt in the low P.C.I households and it steadily disappears as income slab increases. The problem is so serious in slum, where of the 42 child's birth weight collected, 33.3% of them is underweight, another 14.3% of the total child's did not undergone weight testing since it being home delivery. As it is clear the problem of underweight is due to low calorie intake of the mother during pregnancy period and low intake of food due to poverty resulting from low percapita income of the family. The problem of malnutrition and poverty resulting from low per capita income is responsible for the underweight children in the urban and slum areas of the country. Such children require high level of health services in the childhood to survive and to protect from different illness due to ill health and low immunization power. Thus per capita income is an important determinant of health services utilization on the part of children and other members of the family.

The R.C.H project 1998 for Kerala reveals that the proportion of underweight children in urban Kerala is

Table 8.23 : Per Capita Income of Household and Underweight Problem of Children

Per capita Income (Amount in Rupees)	Urban: Weight of the children: Less than 2.5kgm	Urban: More than 2.5kgm	Urban: Total	Slum: Weight of the children: Less than 2.5kgm	Slum: More than 2.5kgm	Slum: Don't know	Slum: Total
Below 100	-	-	-	-	1 (50)	1	2
100-250	2 (100)	-	2	8 (36.4)	8 (36.4)	6 (50)	22
251-500	1 (20)	4 (80)	5	6 (27.3)	16 (72.7)	-	22
501-750	-	5 (100)	5	-	3 (100)	-	3
751-1000	-	6 (85.8)	6	-		-	-
1001-1500	-	14 (100)	14	-		-	-
Above 1500	-	3 (100)	3	-		-	-
Total	3 (8.6)	32 (91.4)	35	14 (33.3)	28 (66.7)	7	49

Source : Survey data. Figures in Parentheses indicate percentage.

14.1%. The sample data provides that the underweight problem of the children in the study area is below the RCH average, indicating that the problem is not serious in urban at the same time it is acute in the slum. The underweight problem is an important indicator to be taken into account for improving the health status of the children. This phenomenon is mainly due to lack of proper nutrient food on the part of mothers during pregnancy, adolescent pregnancies (common in slums) and lack of full-fledged antenatal care services.

REFERENCES

Aravindan, K.P., (2001), Kerala Aroghya Mathruka, Puthiya Noottandilekku, Kerala Sastra Sahithya Parishad, Kochi.

Caldwell J.C., Reddy P.H. and Caldwell P., (1983), The Social Component of Mortality Decline : An Investigation in South India–employing Alternative Methodologies, Population Studies Vol. 37 (2), pp. 185-205.

Chatterjee, M., (1990), Indian Women, their Health and Economic Productivity, World Bank Discussion Paper No. 109 Washington D.C.

Cleland J. and Van Ginneken J., (1988), Maternal Education and Child Survival in Developing Countries. The Search for Pathways of Influence, Social Science and Medicine Vol. 27, (12) pp. 1357-1368.

Das N.P., Misra K. Vinod and Saha P.K., (2001), Does Community Access Affect the use of Health and Family Welfare Services in Rural India? NFHS Subject Reports. No.18 International Institute of Population Sciences, Mumbai.

Foxley Alenjandro and Raizyasky Daymar, (1984), Vulnerable Groups in Recessionary Situation The use of Children and Young in Chile, The Impact of World Recession on Children, UNICEF, New York, p. 58.

Ghosh Shante, (1976), The Feeding and Care of Infants and Young Children, UNICEF, New Delhi, p. 70.

Govt. of India, (1999), Rapid Household Survey, RCH Project 1998, Ministry of Health & Family Welfare Population, Research Centre, Institute for Social & Economic Change, Banglore.

Govt. of India, (2001), Provisional Population Totals, Census of India 2001. Series–33 (Kerala) Paper 2 of 2001, Director of Census Operations, Thiruvananthapuram.

Govt. of Kerala (1999), Statement Showing Institutional Cases of Diseases and Deaths due to Communicable Diseases in 1999, Directorate of Health Services, Thiruvananthapuram.

Indian Council of Medical Research, (1985) Birth Weight, A Major Determinant of Child Survival, Future Perspectives on Children 17, ICMR, New Delhi.

International Institute of Population Science (1995), National Family Health Survey 1992-93, I.I.P.S Mumbai.

International Institute of Population Science (2000) National Family Health Survey 1998-99 (NFHS-2) I.I.P.S, Mumbai.

Mcarthy and Maine D., (1992), A Frame Work for Analyzing the Determinants of Maternal Mortality Studies in Family Planning Vol 23 (1).

Mira Siva, (1997), Freedom from Illness, Health Status of Woman, Social Welfare Vol. 44, No. 6, pp. 28-32.

Mosley W.H. and Chen L.C., (1984), An Analytical Frame Work for the Study of Child Survival in Developing Countries in W.H. Mosely and L.C Chen (eds) Child Survival Strategies for Research, Population and Development Review 10 (Supplement).

Panicker P.G.K and Soman C.R., (1985), Recent Trends in the Health Status of Urban Children, A Reappraisal, Working Paper No. 209, Centre for Development Studies, Thiruvananthapuram.

Ramachandran A., (1989), The Effect of Antenatal and Natal Services on Pregnancy Outcome and Health of the Mother and Child, Journal of Family Welfare Vol. 35, (5) pp. 34-36.

Registrar General of India (1998), Sample Registration Bulletin Vol. 32, No.1, New Delhi.

Robert Macedo, (1984), Brazilian Children and Economic Crisis, Evidence from the State of Sauopaulo, The Impact of World Recession on Children, UNICEF, New York, p.43.

U.N.D.P., (1999), Human Development Report 1999, Oxford University Press, New Delhi.

Vijayakumar K. Ramankutty V. and Soman C.R., (1990), Trends in Birthweight in Kerala, A Hospital Based Study, Health Population Perspectives and Issues. Vol. 13, No.1 and 2 p.52.

W.H.O., (1981), Development Indicators for Monitoring Progress Towards Health for all by the year 2000, Health for all Series No. 4, WHO Geneva.

W.H.O., (1999), World Health Report 1999, Making a Difference, WHO Geneva.

9

Summary and Conclusions

Result of urbanization and shortage of resources in many cities in both developing and developed countries are increasingly unable to provide the infrastructure and services required to meet the needs of their population. In low income and slum areas, in particular the effects of environmental degradation and lack of housing, drinking water and sanitation coupled with inaccessible or poor quality and inefficient health services are precipitating an urban health crisis.

The utilization of health care services depends on the availability of quality of health care services at a reasonable and on the ability of people to utilize the health services effectively. The provision of appropriate health infrastructure is a necessary but not a sufficient condition for health care utilization. A number of factors such as economic status, caste, occupation, education and gender have great influence on the perceived need for medical care and affect the access to health care facilities. In this chapter an attempt is made to summarize the data analyzed so far to bring out the differential utilization pattern of health services of five important socio-economic classes identified and also the major problems in the field of urban health system.

Summary of Findings

The socio-economic context of medical care utilization in a developing society like India becomes the focal point of investigation for understanding the nature and extent of the efficacy of health services utilization system. There are also some factors responsible for not utilizing existing medical facilities by the urban masses and the mounting problems of urban health.

Problems of Urban Health

The findings of the present study proved that rapid urbanization is the root cause of all urban health problems. The world urbanization trend is rising fastly and India too had experienced rapid urbanization in the last 3 decades. Among the states Mizoram records the highest degree of urbanization followed by Goa, Tamil Nadu and Maharashtra. Kerala too is in the forefront of urbanization with 25.97%, which is very close to the national average of 27.8% in the 2001 census. Among the districts, Kannur district record the highest degree of urbanization where the present study was focused.

The problem of accessibility of public medical facilities is an important problem in the urban health environment of Kerala. The bed population ratio (availability of Govt. hospital beds) also varies from district to district and the position of Kannur district is less than the state average of 3.1 beds per 1000 population. The inter district disparity in the availability of Govt. doctors to the urban community compared to their rural counterparts is another finding of the study. Two districts, (Thirssur and Kannur) face the problem of lower doctor population ratio. In the study district (Kannur) 50.46% of the urban population is served by only 47.5% of the doctors available in the district and in the case of Thrissur 28.1% of the urban population of the district gets services from only 21.2% of the doctors working in the district. The lower doctor-population ratio is an important finding of the study, which has an important bearing on the utilization of health services in urban areas. Accessibility of public and private health services varies from country to country and from region to region. In Cali (Columbia) the private sector caters only 15% of the medical care, whereas in Bombay the proportion is almost 50% and 75% of the urban poor in Bombay use private sector for minor ailments. This is mainly due to the inability of the public health centres to cater the needs of the people who approached such centres. The data related to health expenditure of Govt. of Kerala revealed that major chunk of the Govt. health budget is devoted to paying salary and allowances (i.e. 67.69%) and other expenditure associated with day-to-day administration and only a very meagre amount was incurred (17.83%) for the purchase of medicines. As such they could not meet the requirements of the people and compelled even the poor ones to switch over to private institutions for medical care.

The poverty related health hazards is increasing in the urban set up. These include infectious and gastro-intestinal diseases, often called 'diseases of poverty' chronic de-generative diseases associated with poor living and working conditions and pathogenic conditions associated with stress resulting from social isolation and insecurity. The findings of the study (analysis of secondary data about the problem) indicates that the health problem is severe among the urban poor mainly due to overcrowding, lack of sanitation, lack of proper drainage, lack of pure drinking water and lack of good housing. This support the hypothesis formulated for the study that living environment is the important determinant of health status.

Severe threat to maternal health due to unnecessary medical intervention is another finding of the study. Hike in caesarean rates causes a lot of morbidity problems among the mothers and the newborns. Doctors in the private medical institutions are encouraging caesarean for getting maximum fees and also to augment the hospital income. The conditions of Govt. maternity hospitals are such that once they enter the hospital for delivery they cannot return in normal health. As such in certain circumstances even poor people become victims of caesarean sections of private hospitals. An examination of the performance of each state on the different safe motherhood indicators reveals that the performance is below the national average in most of the states including Bihar Madhya Pradesh, Rajasthan, Nagaland, Uttar Pradesh, Madhya Pradesh, Sikkim, Assam and Arunachal Pradesh. The performance of Kerala is better when compared to all the other states.

Urban morbidity is rising steadily in all the urban centres and it is mainly due to bad living environment. Regarding the type of morbidity, both communicable and chronic diseases are on the rise and communicable diseases affect the poor living in the slum area more. The infant death statistics of Kerala in 1995 reveals that the problem of infant death is high in urban Kerala where out of the 5664 total infant deaths, 71.5% was reported from the urban centres. This hike in infant deaths is mainly due to concentration of maternity hospitals and delivery clinics in urban areas on the one hand and presence of larger proportion of urban poor and slum population on the other. Morbidity of the aged is another serious concern in the urban areas and they are subject to more of chronic diseases. Another important finding of the study is that, urban Kerala records the highest number of chronically ill elderly in India. In Kerala it is the females, who dominate over the males in the category of the chronically ill aged persons. It is also found that housing conditions, food consumption pattern, educational status of households, living environment, drinking water, and sanitary facilities and above all their economic soundness are the important determinants of health.

Morbidity and Socio-economic Status

Morbidity and its linkage with various socio-economic variables analysed reveals the impact of socio-economic status on the morbidity pattern. The morbidity commonly faced by the urbans was divided into three categories, namely diseases due to infection, chronic diseases, and other diseases. The major diseases due to infection identified among the population are Typhoid, Jaundice, chicken pox, malaria, Tuberculosis, filariasis, leprosy, dysentery, fever, diarrhoea etc. Morbidity of chronic infectious disease like filariasis and tuberculosis is very high in the slum dwellings. Morbidity rate of filariasis is 7.44 and tuberculosis is 11.9 for every 1000 population in the slum and it is only 3.9 in the case of tuberculosis and filariasis in the urban area. The major chronic diseases found in the study sample are diabetes, heart disease, cancer, mental illness, asthma, epilepsy, kidney diseases, blood pressure, arthritis, ulcer etc. Among chronic illnesses diabetes accounts for 22.73% in urban areas followed by asthma, blood pressure, and heart disease. In the slum the major chronic illness found are asthma (65%) followed by blood pressure, diabetes, and heart disease. The major other illnesses found in the study area are surgeries undergone for cataract, appendicitis, insect bite, accidental injuries, eye diseases etc.

Morbidity analysis with socio-economic status shows that as socio-economic status decreases from upper class to very low class (SES_1 to SES_5) both in the case of slum and urban, the morbidity prevalence of infectious illness increases. The morbidity trend of chronic illness shows that as socio-economic status decreases, the morbidity prevalence of chronic illness also decreases, indicating that chronic illness dominates among the affluent and better off sections. The trend of chronic illness in the slum reveals that, though its magnitude is less in the SES_3 and SES_4 (lower middle class and low class), it is slightly higher in the lowest socio-economic status group (SES_5) indicating that there are certain chronic illness which are diseases of poverty like asthma, and diseases of affluence like hyper tension. The SES_5 (very low class) is more affected by asthma and its morbidity rate is 40 per 1000 population, whereas in the urban sample its morbidity rate is 13.38 per 1000 population. Another trend that is found in the study is that morbidity prevalence of chronic illness, including heart disease, blood pressure, and diabetes together accounts 61 per 1000 persons in the urban areas, whereas this was only 34.2 in the urban slum, which supports the idea that chronic diseases are the diseases of affluence. This is in conformity with the hypothesis formulated for the study, as SES status comes down morbidity of communicable (infectious) illness increases, whereas chronic illness decreases. In the case of other illness also it is observed that as socio-economic status decreases, the morbidity prevalence rate increases. The findings of the study about overall morbidity picture reveal that as socio-economic status falls from SES_1 to SES_5 (upper class to very low class) the overall morbidity prevalence rate also increases both in the urban and slum areas. These findings support the hypothesis formulated that as SES status comes down overall morbidity prevalence rate increases steadily. The morbidity and its linkage with educational status reveal that, morbidity prevalence of infectious illness is high among illiterate and those with primary and below primary level of education. Similarly for chronic illness also its magnitude is high among the illiterates both in the urban and slum indicating that education is a vital determinant of health status. The prevalence of morbidity on the basis of occupation shows that its intensity is high among the unskilled, semi-skilled and unemployed categories both in the urban and slum, which indicates that occupation also acts as an important determinant in the health status of the urban dwellers. In other words morbidity prevalence is high among blue collars (unskilled and skilled) and less among white collars (clerical, semi-professional etc). The analysis of morbidity prevalence and type of housing reveals that morbidity cases are reported more from Kachcha and semi-pucca type of houses. In the case of urban the prevalence rate of illness is high among children in the age group of 4-15, those in the age group of 36 to 55 and those exceed 55, whereas the slum morbidity is high in all the age group except in the category of 16 to 35. These findings indicate the need for targeted health intervention in certain specific age groups to reduce morbidity prevalence. The study also reveals that infectious illness is also high among those household who have no proper sanitation, safe drinking water and good drainage system. The analysis of the primary data of the study approves the hypothesis formulated that the living environment is the important determinant of health status.

Treatment Process and Curative Care

The data related to seeking of treatment for different illness reveals that as socio-economic status declines the percentage of households seeking treatment for all illness declines. It is found that people in the lower SES class go for treatment only in the case of illness of serious nature and in such cases too they wait and see the severity of illness. The study also found that as socio-economic status improves the perception or awareness of households about different diseases increases and the tendency of opting immediate treatment for illness also increases. This behaviour pattern of households support the hypothesis formulated for the study, which is that, the better the social and economic position, the better would be the perception of people about different diseases and higher would be the utilization of health services. The health check-up, which is another indicator for health services utilization reveals that the practice of health check-up is restricted among the better socio-economic class in the urban areas and none in the slums have gone for health check-up. This also indicates that volume of health services utilization is high among the better socio-economic class.

Type of Health Centre Utilized : The type of health centre used by different socio-economic classes for different illness reveals that the utilization pattern differs widely across the socio-economic class. In the urban sample 75% of them preferred private clinic and private hospitals, whereas in slum this proportion was very meagre about 12.5%. .

Choice of Health Centre : Analysis of data regarding the reasons for the choice of particular health centre shows that, the better SES class prefer one particular hospital or health centre either for obtaining highly specialized treatment or for good treatment, whereas the lower SES class opt for a particular health centre for obtaining free or concession treatment. It is found that 100% of the SES_5 in the urban and 89% of the SES_5 in the slum preferred one health centre for obtaining only free or concession treatment. This reveals the significance of socio-economic status in the utilization of health services. The study found that regarding the stage of treatment only 11.25% of the households prefer immediate treatment of illness, whereas this was 57.5% in the case of urban reflecting the impact of high percapita income. As income increases the stage of treatment of illness becomes more and more immediate. The relation between age and system of medicine utilized reveals that at the lower age (age upto 15) and at the age 60 above allopathy is utilized maximum both in the urban and slum for all the three type of illness. The age of the infectious patients and the type of medical agency utilized reveals that in the urban set up lower age group (age upto 15) utilized more of private agencies, whereas in the slum all age group upto to 60 have inter-changeably used both private and Government agency. It is found that 100% of the slum patients in the age of 60 plus utilized Govt. hospital alone. This is mainly due to financial stringency; the family set up in the slum is such that youngsters usually neglect the aged people. In the case of chronic illness 83% of the urban in all age group preferred private agencies, whereas in slum this was only 43.5%.

The education of the head of the household and the type of medical agency utilized reveals that as educational status improves, there is a tendency for opting more of private medical services which is quite common both in the urban and slum, and is also common in the case of all the three type of illness. They consider allopathy as the only source. Similarly among those who used Govt. allopathic centres for treatment of infectious illness, all of them were dissatisfied about the services rendered and the major complaints raised include lack of medicine, careless treatment, rough behaviour of the doctors and early discharge from the hospital.

Treatment related to chronic illness reveals that 83% of the urban and 43.5% of the slum utilized private hospital. As these diseases require intensive treatment and medicines, Govt. health centres and hospitals could not provide this. The SES wise analysis reveals that patients in the low class (SES_4) and very low class (SES_5) in the slum and very low class (SES_5) in the urban, where 50% and above utilized Govt. hospital for chronic illness. It is their poor economic status, which compelled them to opt for Government hospitals even if they are rendering services, which give rise to a lot of complaints. Due to the callousness of the Govt. doctors and lack of medicine in Govt. hospitals, people who are leading a hand to mouth existence are compelled go to private hospitals for treatment. Regarding the method of treatment for chronic illness 87.5% of the urbans and 83.8% of the slum patients utilized allopathic system. The better off sections in the urban in the SES_1 and SES_2 category has shown much interest for ayurvedic and homoeopathic systems with the expectation that the system is free from all side effects. The study found that, the utilization of Govt. hospital is high in the case of inpatient care. For undergoing treatment, as inpatient in the private hospitals requires huge amount, so many low class and very low class socio-economic status patients in the slum utilized Govt. hospitals for inpatient care to escape from the huge hospital bills. With respect to the inpatient care the study reveals that 85.7% of short stay and 80% of long stay of chronic patients in the slum area is in the public health centres. Among the urban dwellers this was 20% and 40% respectively indicating the better financial status of urban dwellers. This reveals the impact of socio-economic status in the selection and utilization of health services. Regarding the sex and system of medicines utilized, the allopathic system is more popular among the males, which they consider as the means of quick relief and early recovery. Similarly percapita income and type of medical agency utilized reveals that in most cases as the income increases, they prefer more of private agencies indicating the impact of economic status on the health services utilization. In the case of other illness, which include surgeries undergone and injuries occurred, major chunk of the urban and slum patients utilized allopathic system. Patients who belong to lower SES class prefers ayurvedic treatment for bone fractures, snakebite and insect bite, as it is less costly compared to allopathic system. Similar to that of chronic and infectious illness patients, most of the other illness patients who utilized Govt. hospital services were also dissatisfied. Major complaints raised against Govt. health centres or hospitals are lack of proper care, bribery, favouritism, irrational behaviour of nurses, lack of medicine etc. The relation between percapita income and type of medical agency utilized for curative care by the ill persons reveals that in most cases as income increases they prefer more of private agency indicating the impact of economic soundness on the utilization of private health services. In the urban sample, it is found that in most cases as income increases they steadily switch over to private health services with rare exceptions. In the slum also, increase in percapita income inspired them to go for private medical services. According to them, if they go to Govt. hospital, their work will be affected due to the rush in Govt. hospitals and they have to purchase all the medicines from outside. What they can save is only doctor's fees, for the same they have to sacrifice their day's wage not only of the ill person but also of the accompanying person. The timings of the private hospital is such that, they can go in the morning or in the evening without any loss of earning. In certain cases the poor financial status of the household resulted in non- treatment of chronic illness and thereby non-utilization of health services. The data analysis shows that as socio-economic status comes down the percentage of untreated illness cases increase, which shows that financial status has an important role in the treatment pattern and extent of utilization of health services. The reason for no- treatment is so specific that in most of the cases both in the slum and urban, it is mainly due to financial constraints. Regarding the system of medicine utilized, the study found that allopathic system is most popular both in the urban and slum households and only a smaller percentage resort to homoeopathic and ayurvedic system. The overall analysis of treatment process of households in various socio-economic status reveals that socio-economic status is an important determinant of health services utilization. At the same time demographic factors like age, sex, place of residence, nature of illness etc. also exert an influence in the degree of utilization of health services.

Utilization of Government and Private Hospitals

Analysis of data related to percapita income and utilization of Govt. hospital for the last 3 years by the household reveals that as income increases, the percentage of households who utilized Govt. hospital services diminished steadily (with the exception of one income slab in the urban) and it is quite common for the urban and slum households.

Opinion About Inpatient Services and Accessibility of Doctors : The study found that 92% of the slum respondents and 78% of the urban respondents were totally dissatisfied about the inpatient services rendered by the Govt. hospitals. They consider the service as poor and dismal even in the case of accessibility of doctors in the inpatient ward. The major complaints raised against

Government hospitals were poor check-up, bad behaviour of doctors, bribery, favoritism, lack of cleanliness, medical equipment, medicines and doctors were more money minded.

Private Health Services : The data related to the utilization of private health services found that 90.8% households in the urban and 66.3% households in the slum utilized private health services in the last two years. The analysis shows that the proportion of households who utilize private health services increases with rise of socio-economic status. The major reason suggested by the households for the choice of private health services are good treatment, doctor is known, no need of waiting for long time, clinic functions in night and lack of medicine in Govt. hospitals. The only complaint against private hospital services is about its cost.

The analysis of data related to utilization of private and Govt. health services for the last 2 years reveals that only 9% of the urban samples utilized Govt. health services alone for all health needs, and in slum this proportion is 34%. Similarly another 34.2% in urban and 55% in slum utilized both private and Govt. health centres.

Medical Expenditure : The amount of medical expenditure incurred is considered as an important indicator of health services utilization. It is found that as socio-economic status increases, the amount incurred for medical expenditure also increases. In order to see the differences between SES classes in the amount of expenditure incurred for health services utilization, the annual average per capita expenditure on health and annual average per capita income was analysed. It reveals that in the case of urban sample, as socio-economic status falls, proportion of income spends on health rises. It is 2.4% only in the case of upper class but reached to the maximum of around 5 times (i.e. 10.44%) in the case of lower class. Similarly the annual average percapita expenditure on health incurred by household fall as socio-economic status falls. It is 695.87 in the case of upper class (SES_1) but only Rs.360.49 in the case of very low class (SES_5). The same trend is visible in the slum sample also, though the differences between the lower middle class (SES_3) and very low class (SES_5) is not wide.

Utilization of Maternal Health Services

The utilization of maternal health services which is another indicator of health services utilization reveals wide differences between urban and slum dwellers. In the case of utilization of antenatal care services by pregnant women, it can be seen that, 100% of the urban dwellers utilized it, whereas this was only 96% in the case of slum. In the selection of agency for the utilization of antenatal care, 75% of the urban mothers utilized private agencies, whereas this was only 10.6% in the case of slum. It is found that in the urban as socio-economic status rises the mothers are utilizing more and more of private agencies for their antenatal care services and it is common for both urban and slum. It is found that 100% of the SES_1 or upper class in urban utilized private agencies for antenatal care, whereas 100% of the SES_5 or very low class utilized Govt. health centers, indicating that the SES status is an important indicator of the selection of agency for the utilization of ante-natal care services. The upper class (SES_1) and upper middle class (SES_2) mothers started antenatal care earlier than the low class (SES_4) and very low class (SES_5). Similarly the number of times the antenatal care sought was also increased with rise of socio-economic status. Majority of the upper class and upper middle class (SES_1 and SES_2) mothers in the urban received full dose of antenatal care services (check-up, tests, IFA tablets, T.T. injection and advice) whereas this proportion was comparatively less in the case of low class (SES_4) and very low class (SES_5) mothers in urban and slums and as a whole urban mothers are better placed in the utilization of antenatal care services compared to slums. This pattern of antenatal care services utilization supported the hypothesis formulated for the study.

Regarding the selection of place of delivery, SES class differed widely and the reason suggested by them is such that free or less expensiveness prompted the mothers of low SES classes to opt for Govt. health centres, whereas the need for good medical care and rapport with the doctors prompted the better SES class to opt for private health services. It is found that as socio-economic status increases, the proportion preferring good medical care as the reason for the choice of delivery place increases both in urban and slum. Another finding of the study is that, the problem of under weight children is more associated with lower SES class group both in the urban and slum and the poverty and malnutrition are responsible for the creation of such children. Another finding of the study related to immunization is that, as far as the full dose of immunization is concerned (i.e. BCG + 3DPT + 3 Polio + Measles) the urban coverage is 85.7% and got full protection against 6 vaccine preventable diseases, whereas this proportion was only 79.6% in the case of slums. This also supports the hypothesis formulated in the beginning that urban mothers utilized the M.C.H (Maternal and child health) services at a higher rate than the slum mothers.

The finding of the study clearly reveals that the low class and very low class (SES_4 and SES_5) both in the slum and urban areas did not consume health services to the fullest extent they required. Apart from their incapacity to consume private health services, they also fail to utilize the freely available public health services. So any health services package which aims to augment the volume of health services utilization by the whole community should take steps to eradicate the agonies of these urban poor.

Suggestions and Recommendations

Health and nutritional programme for the urban poor should be designed and implemented according to their needs and environmental content. Special programmes through a comprehensive package of shelter, health care and economic support programmes are urgently required for this group. For improving the accessibility and utilization of health services by the urban poor and slum dwellers, it would be better if the authority can provide mobile health care vans in their dwelling place during night and in the evening. Specific health risks such as traffic accidents, suicidal attempts, food poisoning and tuberculosis are health problems that are more frequent in urban and urban slum than in rural communities and require varied type of services. Facilities should be created in urban dispensaries to treat the accident victims so that un- necessary delay and heavy rush in the General hospitals and District head quarter hospitals can be avoided and many accident victims can be saved from death. Significant steps must be taken to make health care affordable and accessible. In the health care budget of the Government more allocation of funds should be earmarked for medicines and supplies, so that the vulnerable and urban poor utilizing Govt. hospitals and dispensaries will be benefited a lot. Similar to the rural health infrastructure set up through the primary health centres, an urban health infrastructure should be created by setting up new-dispensaries or health centres and strengthening the existing dispensaries in the urban areas. In other words establishment of a regional health care delivery system suited for the urban areas is most inevitable to mitigate the problems of urban health. For this survey of the existing resources and facilities in the urban set up is to be measured along with the actual needs. Similarly earmarking of institutions is to be started or upgraded, estimate personnel needed, available and also their potential. Moreover specific standards should be fixed for organization and maintenance of equipments and also for services to be provided. Above all proper examining machinery for supervision, monitoring and evaluation should be created to ensure quality of services rendered.

The basic infrastructure facilities like good drinking water, sanitation facilities and drainage facilities etc should be provided in the residential areas of urban poors and some income generating activities should also be undertaken for alleviating their poverty.

For the improvement of the slums the following policy implications are suggested.

For the overall development of the human resources more thrust should be given to the children of slum areas. Health, education, sports and recreational facilities should be provided to them within the slums at reasonable distance. In all the existing slums the basic amenities for human needs should be provided as under the scheme of Environmental Improvement of Urban Slums (EIUS). Some income generating activities should be undertaken by the Government in these areas for the betterment of slum dwellers. Activities, which help in the social and cultural assimilation of slum dwellers in the city life, should be taken up. Non-governmental agencies can be used for devising ways of narrowing the gap between city culture and slum culture. For improving the housing facilities of the slum dwellers, a housing scheme with Governmental subsidy should be devised to rehabilitate the slum dwellers. Most of the slums identified and selected for the study are low lying areas and are inundated during rainy seasons. Measures should be taken to raise their levels in order to avoid problems of flooding and sledging in such slums.

The unhygienic living conditions and unhealthy working conditions of the low class and very low classes expose them to a variety of communicable diseases, occupational diseases, injuries and physical disabilities. Whereas the upper classes and upper middle classes are mostly free from these health problems due to their better living and working conditions. But their eating habit and stressful occupational environment create ample chances of chronic diseases. To get rid of this urban health problems fast food habit should be avoided and balanced diet high in fibre and low in calorie to be consumed. People should be encouraged to follow a habit of moderate exercise in order to have a positive and cheerful attitude. For reducing the morbidity problems of the aged population, old age homes providing gainful activities and entertainment to the aged should be created in the urban centres. The health services scheme proposed above will reduce the gap that exists between urban and slum dwellers in the utilization of health services and also make the health services scheme affordable and accessible to the entire urban community.

Bibliography

BOOKS

Ali S. Manazir, (1993), Status of Morbidity and Mortality of New Borns Delivered to Urban Mothers, in Umashankar P.K.and Misra K. Girish, (eds), Urban Health System, Reliance Publishing House, New Delhi.

Anderson W. Odin, (1963), The Utilization of Health Services in Howard Freeman and other (eds) Handbook of Medical Sociology, Prentice Hall Inc, New Jersy, p. 363.

Andrew Mason, (1996), Population Housing and the Economy in Denni's A. Albery (ed), The Impact of Population Growth in Developing Countries, Springer, Berlin.

Antia W.H., (1999), The Social Path to Kerala's Health, in Rethinking Development, Kerala's Development experience ed. by Ommen M.A., Concept Publishing Company, New Delhi.

Aravindan K.P., (2001), Kerala Aroghya Mathruka, Puthiya Noottandilekku, Kerala Sastra Sahithya Parishad, Kochi.

Banerjee, (1996), Political Economy of Public Health in India, in Das Gupta Monica, Krishnan T.N, and Chen Lincoln. C. eds. Health Poverty and Development in India, Oxford University Press, Delhi.

Berg Robert, (1973), Health Status Indexes, Hospital Research and Education Trust, Chicago.

Bhatnagar S., (1985), Magnitude of Morbidity and Mortality Among Children Below 5 years of Age in Urban Slums of Delhi, National Institute of Health and Family Welfare, Delhi.

Blexter M., (1976), Social Class and Health in Equalities in Co-carter and John Peel (eds), Equalities and in-equalities in Health, Academic Pres, London, pp.11-124.

Cemper G.E., (1984), Determinants of Health levels in Developing

Countries, Research Studies Press Ltd., England.

Dandekar Kumudini, (1996), The Elderly in India, Sage Publications, New Delhi.

Dean T. Jameson et. al. (eds), (1993), Disease Control Parasites in Developing Countries, Oxford University Press, pp. 100-101.

Donaldson R.J., (1976), Urban and Suburban Differentials in Co Carter and John Peel (eds), Equalities and in Equalities in Health, Academic Press, London, pp. 127-140.

Dreze, Jean and Sen Amartya, (2002), India Development and Participation, Oxford University Press, New Delhi.

Elo Irma T., (1987), Utilization of Maternal Health Services in Peru, the Role of Women's Education, Populations Centre, University of Pennsylvania, Philadelphia.

Gupta J.P., (1993), Referral Services in Urban Health Care Delivery System in Umashanker P.K. and Missra K. Girish (eds), Urban Health System, Reliance publishing house, New Delhi. p.152.

Gupta M.C. and Mahajan B.K., (1995), A Text Book of Preventive and Social Medicine, Japee Brothers, Medical Publishers, New Delhi, p. 35.

Hazari Kamal, (1993), Contraceptive Acceptance and Immunization Status in Urban Slums in Umashankar P.K. and Misra Girish (eds), Urban Health System, Reliance Publishing House, New Delhi.

Heller Celia S., (1969), Structural Social in Equality and Social Stratification, Macmillan Company, New York.

Jah S.S., (1986), Structure of Urban Poverty the Case of Urban Slums, Popular Prakashan, Bombay.

Joseph George, Desrochers John Kalathil Mariamma, (1983), Heath Care in India, Centre for Social Action, Banglore.

Kannan K.P. Thankappan K.R. Kutty V.R., Aravindan K.P., (1991), Health and Development in Rural Kerala, A Study of the Linkage between Socio-economic Status and Health Status, Kerala Sastra Sahitya Parishad, Thiruvananthapuram.

Khandekar, Mandakini, (1974), Utilization of Social and Welfare Services in Greater Bombay, Tata Institute of Social Services, Bombay, pp. 65-70.

Kirit S. Parikh, (1999), India Development Report 1999-2000, Indira Gandhi Development Research Institute, Oxford University Press, New Delhi, p. 51.

Kumar M. and Kumar R., (1987), Environmental Impact of Slums on Health in R. Kumar (ed), Environmental Pollution and Health Hazards in India, Ashish Publishing House, New Delhi, p. 58.

Kundu Amitab, (1994), Cited in Patterns Causes and Consequences of Urbanization by D. Retnaraj in Kerala's Economic Development Issues and Problems ed. B.A. Prakash, Sage publications, New Delhi, 1999.

Kunhikannan T.P., Aravindan K.P., (2000), Changes is Health Status of Kerala 1987-1997, Kerala Shastra Sahitya Parishad, Thiruvananthapuram.

Leela Gulathi and Rajan Irudaya, (1989), Ageing of Population in Kerala, Centre for Development Studies, Thiruvananthapuram.

Mahajan B.K. and Gupta M., (1995), Text Book of Preventive and Social Medicine, Japee Brothers Medical Publishers, New Delhi.

Malati Damodaran, Soman C.R., Paniker P.G.K., (1994), A Study of Infant Feeding and Child Rearing Practices in Thiruvanahtapuram City and Rural Areas, Centre for Development Studies, Thiruvananthapuram.

Mathur Indu and Sharma Sanjay, (1995), Health Hazards, Gender and Society, Rawat Publications, New Delhi.

Mukherjee, R.K., (1971), Six Villages of Bengal, Popular Prakashan, Bombay.

Murray C.J.L. and Lopez A.D., (1996), (eds), The Global Burden of Disease, M.A. Harvard University Press, Cambridge.

Nayar K.R., (1999), Housing and Health Another Kerala Conandrum in Rethinking and Development, Oommen M.A (ed), Vol. 2, Concept Publishing Company, Delhi.

Odin W. Anderson, (1963), The Utilization of Health Services in Howard Freeman and others (eds), Hand Book of Medical Sociology, New Jersey, Prentice Hall Inc., p. 363.

Panicker, P.G.K., (1985), Health care System in Kerala and its Impact on Infant Mortality in S. Halstead et. al., (eds), Good Health at Low Cost, Rock Feller Foundation, New Delhi.

Panicker, P.G.K., (1999), Health Transition in Kerala, Kerala Research Programme on Local Development, C.D.S Thiruvananthapuram, p.11.

Panicker P.G.K. and Soman C.R., (1994), Health Status of Kerala, The Paradox of Economic Backwardness and Health Development, Centre for Development Studies, Thiruvananthapuram.

Panikar P.G.K. and Soman C.R., (1981), Health Status of Kerala Paradox of Economic Backwardness and Health Development, Centre for Development Studies, Thiruvananthapuram, pp. 72-77.

Peach G.C.K., (1970), Urbanization in India in Beckinsale and Houston J.M. (eds), Urbanisation and its Problem, Blackwell, Basil, p. 297.

Pickering et. al., (1989), Cited in Health and Nutrition of the Urban Poor, the Case of Calcutta Slums in Dasgupta Monica, Chine Lincoln, Krishnan T.N. (eds), Health Poverty and Development in India, Oxford University Press, Delhi, p.190.

Raja Bala, (1986), Trends of Urbanization in India, Rawat Publications, Jaipur.

Rama V. Baru, (1999) The Structure and Utilization of Health Services, An inter-state Analysis in Mohan Rao (ed), Disinvesting in Health, Sage Publications, New Delhi, pp. 127-140.

Ramachandra Sastry K., (2000), Promoting Responsible Sexual Behaviour Among Youths in Banglore in Sunil Misra (ed), Voluntary Action in Health and Population, Sage Publications, New Delhi, pp.156-166.

Rodhe J.E., (1983), Why the other Half Dies, The Science and Politics of Child Mortality in the Third World, Assignment Children pp. 61-62.

Sachar R.K. and Gill P.V.S., (1993), Development and Urbanization. Its Implication for Childhood Mal Nutrition in Umashankar P.K. and Misra K. Girish, (eds), Urban Health System, Reliance Publishing House, New Delhi, p. 24.

Sen N.K., (1987), Commodities and Capabilities, Oxford University Press, Bombay.

Sharma Omprakash, (2000), Rural Health and Medical Care in India, Manak Publications, New Delhi.

Shreekant V. Khandewala, (1996), Health Administration and the Weaker Sections in an Indian Metropolis, Devika Publications.

Sjobery O.G., (1973), The Origin and Evolution of Cities in Davis K., (ed), Cities their Origin, Growth and Human Impact, L.H Freeman and Co. Sanfransisco p. 20.

Smith K.R., (1987), Bio–fuels Air Pollution and Health, Plennum Press, New York.

Soman C.R., (2000), Mode of Living and Diseases in Janakeeya Arogyam, A Group of Writers, Kerala Sastra Sahitya Prishad, Thiruvananthapuram, pp. 75-92.

Stanley H. King (1962), Perception of Illness and Medical Practice, Russel, Sage Foundation, New York.

Sundar Ramamani, (2000), The Fertility Reduction Project in a low Income re-settlement Colony in Sunil Misra (ed) Voluntary Action in Health and Population, Sage Publications, New Delhi, pp. 178-188.

Sureender K., (2000), Health and Family Welfare Through Community Participation. Dharavi Slum Bombay in Sunil Misra (ed) Voluntary Action in Health and Population, Sage Publications, New Delhi, pp. 167–177.

Umashankar P.K. and Misra Girish (eds), (1993) Urban Health System, Reliance Publishing House, New Delhi.

Underwood C.F. and Margett S., (1987), Cited in Adair L.S. Vanderslice and Zohoori urban- rural Differences in Growth and Diarrhoeal Morbidity of Filipino Infants, Urban Ecology and Health in Third World (ed), by Schell C.M. Smith M.T. and Bilsborough, Cambridge University Press, Cambridge.

Yesudian C.A.K., (1990), Utilization Pattern of Health Services and its Implications for Urban Health Policy. Take me Programme in International Health, Harvard School of Public Health.

JOURNALS

Anderson R. and Adey L.A., (1978), Access to Medical Care in the U.S. Realised and Potential, Medical Care Vol. 16, pp. 533-46.

Anderson R. Newman J.F., (1973), Societal and Individual Determinants of Health Care Utilization in the U.S. Milbank Memorial Fund Q. 8, pp. 32-142.

Antonovsky, Aaron, (1967), Social Class, Life Expectancy and Overall Mortality, Milbank Memorial Fund, Quarterly, Vol. 45, pp. 31-73.

Azurin J.C. and Alvero M., (1974), Field Evaluation of Environmental Sanitation, Measures Against Cholera, Bulletin of World Health Organisation Vol. 51, No.1, p.21.

Banerjee D., (1973), Health Behaviour of Rural Population, Impact of Rural Health Services, Economic and Political Weekly Vol 18.

Basta, (1976), Nutrition and Health in Low Income Urban Areas of Third World, Ecology of Food and Nutrition, pp.113-124.

Belcher D.W. et. al., (1976), Cited in Sodani P.R. and Gupta S.D Health Care Expenditure, Results from a Study in Tribal areas of Rajasthan, Margin, Vol.31, No.1, 1998, p.70.

Benyoussef A. Wessen A.R., (1974), Utilization of Health Services in Developing Countries, Tunisia, Social Science and Medicine, Vol. 8, pp. 287-304.

Bhat Ramesh, (1996), Regulation of Private Health Sector in India. International Journal of Health Planning and Management, Vol.11, pp. 253-274.

Bhat Ramesh, (1999), Characteristics of Private Medical Practice in India, a Provider Perspective, Health Policy and Planning Vol.14, No.1, pp. 26-37.

Bhatnagar, et. al., (1988a), Utilization of Health Care Facilities in an Urban Slums of Delhi. Health Population Perspective and Issues, Vol. 11, No. 4, pp. 162-170.

Bhatnagar S. Dosajh V. and Kapoor S.D., (1988), Maternal and Child Health Status and Patterns of Health Care in Urban Slums of Delhi. Health Population Perspectives and Issues, Vol II, No.3.

Brink L.S.G. and Nader P.R., (1981), Pattern of Primary Care Utilization in a Tri-ethnic Urban Population of School Children, Medical Care, Vol.19, pp. 591-599.

Caldwell J.C. Reddy P.H. and Caldwell P., (1983), The Social Component of Mortality Decline, An Investigation in South India–employing Alternative Methodologies. Population Studies Vol. 37, (2) pp. 185-205.

Chojhacka H. and O. Adeybola, (1984), The Determinants of Infant and Child Morbidity and Mortality in Lagus, Nigeria, Social Science and Medicine, 19 (8) pp. 799-810.

Cleland J. and Van Ginneken J., (1988), Maternal Education and Child Survival in Developing Countries, The Search for Path ways of Influence, Social Science and Medicine Vol. 27 (12), pp.1357-1368.

Daksh Pandit, et. al., (1996), Evaluation of MCH Services Provided by an Urban Health Centre, Health and Population Perspectives and Issues, Vol. 19, No.1, pp. 41-49.

Davids Salvekar, (1975), Economic Class Differentials, Access to Care, Comparison Among Health Care System, International Journal of Health Statistics Vol. 15, No. 3, pp. 373-396.

Delizan et. al., (1999), Cited in Unwanted Medical Intervention, Caesarean Sections as a Case Study, Madhukar Pai, Economic and Political Weekly, Vol.XXXV, No.31, 2000 July 29 -August 4.

Dhanalakshmi N. Moorthy M.S.K., (1973), Socio-economic and Demographic Factors Influencing Child Morbidity, Indian Journal of Social Work, Vol. LIV, No.3, pp. 429-436.

Duraiswamy, P., (1998), Morbidity in Tamil Nadu, levels Differentials and Determinants, Economic and Political Weekly XXXIII No.17.

Ebraham G.T., (1984), Primary care and the Urban Poor, Journal of Tropical Paediatrics No.1.

Engelman Robert, (1997), Why Population Matters, Population Action International, Washington DC.

Fein Stein Jonathan S., (1993), The Relationship Between Socio-economic Status and Health, A Review of Literature, Milbank Memorial Fund, Quarterly, Vol. 71, pp. 279-322.

Fergussan D.M., Dineoad M.E., Horwood C.J. and Shannoi F.T., (1984), The Utilization of Pre-school Health and Education Sources, Social Science and Medicine, Vol.19, No.11, pp. 1173-1180.

Garg B.S. and Singh J.V., (1985), Belief About Causation of Diseases and Preference of Utilization of Health Agencies by Elderly Persons in Urban Community, Health and Population Perspectives and Issues, Vol.8, No.1.

Gerald Rosenthal, (1965), Factors Affecting the Utilization of Short Term General Hospital, American Journal of Public Health and Nations Health, Vol. 55, p. 1739.

Gesler W.M. and Meade M.S., (1988), Locational and Population Factors in Health Care Seeking behaviour in Savannah, Georgian Health Services Research, Vol. 23, pp.443-462.

Gopalan C., (1985), The Mother and Child in India, Economic and Political Weekly Vol. 20, No.4, p.162.

Guendelman Sylvia and Sebwalbe Joan, (1986), Medical Care Utilization by Hispanics Children, Medical Care, Vol. 24, No. 10, pp. 925-940.

Gumber Anil and Berman Peter, (1997), Measurement and Pattern of Morbidity and the Utilization of Health Services: Some Emerging Issues from Recent Health Interview Surveys in India, Journal of Health and Population in Developing Countries, Vol.1, (1) Fall pp.16-43.

Hamza A., (1989), An Appraisal of Environmental Degradation in Bogota, Columbia, Urbanization and Environment. Vol. 1, No.1, pp.16- 21.

Haynes R., (1991), In-equalities in Health and Health Service use, Evidence from the General Household Survey, Social Science and Medicine Vol. 33, pp. 361-368.

Irudaya Rajan S. and Navaneetham K., (1994), Maternal and Child Immunisation on Infant Survival in Kerala, India, Janasamkhya, Vol. 12, No. 1 and 2.

Jatindar Bajaj, (1999), Knowledge and Utilization of Maternal and Child Health Services in Delhi Slums, The Journal of Family Welfare. Vol. 45, No.1.

Jeffrey Robin, (1987), Govt. and Culture, How Woman made Kerala Literate, Pacific Affairs, Vol. 6, No. 3.

Jerry A. Solon, (1966), Pattern of Medical care Variation Among a Hospital Outpatients, American Journal of Public Health and Nations Health, Vol. 56, p. 883.

Johansson S.R., (1991) The Health Transition, the Cultural Inflation of Morbidity During the Decline of Mortality, Health Transition Review Vol.1, No.1, pp. 39-68.

Jyothi Prakash and Vijayalakshmi, (2000), Bio-fuels Pollution and Health Linkages, A Survey of Rural Tamil Nadu, Economic and Political Weekly, Vol. 35, No. 47, pp. 4125-4137.

Kapilalakshmi M.C., (2000), Review of the Present Health Status of India. Emerging Health Problems and their Solutions.

Health Population Perspectives and Issues, Vol. 23, No.1, pp. 1-10.

Kaplan and Taylor C., (1985) Bio-social Factors in the Epidemiology of Childhood Asthma in British National Sample, Journal of Epidemiology and Community Health, Vol. 39, pp. 152-156.

Kutty V.R. Thankappan K.R., Kannan K.Pand Aravindan K.P. (!993), How Socio-economic Status Affects Birth and Death Rates in Rural Kerala, India, Results of a Health Study, Indian Journal of Health Services, Vol.23, No.2.

Kutty V.R., Balachandran K.G. Jayasree A.K. and Jessy Thomas (1993a), Prevalance of Coronary Heart Disease in Rural Population of Thiruvananthapuram District, Kerala, India, International Journal of Cardiology, Vol. 39, pp. 59-70.

Mackenbach, Johan P. and Anton E. Kust, (1997), Measuring the Magnitude of Socio-economic in-equalities in Health, An Overview of Available Measures Illustrated with 2 Examples from Europe, Social Science and Medicine, Vol. 44, No.6, pp. 757-771.

Madhava Menon, (2000), The Health Status of Kerala, Health for Millions Vol. 26, No.2.

Mahadevia Darshini, (2000), Health for all in Gujarath, Is it Achievable, Economic and Political Weekly, Vol. XXXV No. 35 and 36, p. 3204.

Mcarthy and Maine D., (1992), A Frame Work for Analyzing the Determinants of Maternal Mortality Studies, Family Planning Vol. 23 (1).

Mira Siva, (1997), Freedom from Illness, Health Status of Woman, Social Welfare, Vol. 44, No. 6, pp. 28-32.

Mosely W.H. and Chen C.C., (1987), An Analytical Frameworks for the Study of Child Survival in Developing Countries, Population and Development Review, Supplement to Vol. 10, No.4, pp. 25-45.

Mosley W.H. and Chen L.C., (1984), An Analytical Frame Work for the Study of Child Survival in Developing Countries in W.H. Mosely and L.C., Chen (eds) Child Survival Strategies for Research. Population and Development Review 10 (Supplement).

Mukherjee J. and Samaddar J.C., (1995) How Safe is Caesarean Section, Journal of Obstetrics and Gynaecology, Vol. 21, No.1, pp.17-21.

Mutatkar R.K., (1995), Public Health Problems of Urbanization, Social Science and Medicine, Vol. 4, No.7.

Nangia Praveen, Kamla Gupta and Tiwari N.C., (1996), Emergence of Slums : A Case Study of Thane Urban Agglomeration, Indian Journal of Social Work, Vol. 57, No.4.

Nayar K.R., (1997), Housing Amenities and Health Improvement, Some Findings, Economic and Political Weekly Vol. XXXII, No. 2.

Pai Madhukar, (2000), Unwanted Medical Intervention: Caesarean Section as a Case Study, Economic and Political Weekly Vol. XXXV, No. 31, pp. 2755-2761.

Panicker P.G.K., (1979), Resources Not the Constraint on Health Improvement, A case Study of Kerala, Economic and Political Weekly, No.14, No.44.

Pawar R.G., (1983), Utilization of Preventive Services, A Study of Vaccine Acceptors, Indian Journal of Preventive and Social Medicine, Vol. 14, No.1 and 2.

Pawl W. Newacbeck and Halfon, (1986), The Association between Mothers and Children, The use of Physician's Service, Medical Care, Vol. 24, No.11, pp. 30-38.

Purohit Brijesh C. and Siddique Tasleem, (1994), Utilization of Health Services in India, Economic and Political Weekly, Vol. 29, No. 17.

Rajan Irudaya and Mohana Chandran P., (1999), Estimating Infant Mortality in Kerala, Economic and Political Weekly, Vol. 34, No. 20.

Rajan Irudaya and Navaneetham, (1994), Maternal and Child Health Immunization on Infant Survival in Kerala, Janasamkhya Vol. 12, No.1 and 2.

Rajna and et.al., (1998), Impact of Maternal and Child Health Services on Child Mortality in Uttar Pradesh, Asia Pacific Population Journal, Vol.13, No. 2, pp. 27-36.

Ramachandran A., (1989), The Effect of Antenatal and Natal Services on Pregnancy Outcome and Health of the Mother and Child, Journal of Family Welfare Vol. 35, (5) pp. 34-36.

Ramankutty V., (1989), Rational Medialcare in Kerala : Price and Non-price Mechanisms, Economic and Political Weekly Sept. 2-9, pp. 1991-1992.

Ramankutty V. Thankappan K.R. Kannan K.P. and Aravindan K.P. (1993) How Socio-economic Status Affects Birth and

Death Rates in Rural Kerala, India : Results of a Health Study, International Journal of Health Services Vol. 23, No.2.

Ratna Raj, (2001), Kerala Maintains Better Urban Health, Yojana Vol. 45, pp. 46-47.

Ray C.N., Rout P.R., (2000), Environmental Risk, Assessment of Municipal Corporation of Gujarath, Nagarlok Vol. XXXII, No. 2, pp. 11-30.

Rodney M. Coe and Albert M. Wessen, (1965), Social Psychological Factors Influencing the use of Community Health Resources, American's Journal of Public Health and Nations Health, Vol. 55.

Rosen, (1993), Cited in K.R. Nayar's Housing Amenities and Health Environment, Some Findings, Economic and Political Weekly, Vol. XXXII, No. 2, pp. 1275-1279.

Rupert Samuel G.E, Gupta J.P. and Wadha V.S., (1992), Satisfaction and Utilization of Primary Health Services Facilities in Karnataka, Population Perspectives and Issues, Vol.15, No. 3 and 4, pp. 140-152.

Shanon G.W., Sinner J.C. Buschar R.C., (1973), Time and Distance, The Journey for Medical Care, International Journal of Health Studies, Vol. 3, No. 2, pp. 237-244.

Shariff Abusaleh, Gumber Anil, Duggal Ravi and Alam Moneer, (1999), Health Care Financing and Insurance Perspectives for the Ninth Plan-1997-2002, Margin Vol. 31, No. 2, p. 40.

Shelah S. Bloom, David Wypij and Monica Das Gupta, (2001), Dimensions of Woman Autonomy and the Influence on Maternal Health Care Utilization in a North Indian City, Demography, Vol. 38, No.1, pp. 67-76.

Sivarajan, (1987), Factors Influencing Differential Utilization of Government Hospitals Across two Contrasting Regions, Hospital Administration, Vol. XXIV, No.13 and 4.

Smith G.D. Bartley M. and Blane D., (1990), The Black Report on Socio-economic in Equalities, in Health 10 years on, British Medical Journal No. 371.

Sodani P.R. and Gupta S.D., (1988), Health care Expenditure, Results from a Study in Tribal areas of Rajasthan, Margin Vol. 13, No.1, pp. 66-76.

Soman C.R., Malati Damodharan, Rajasree S., Kutty V.R. and Vijaya Kumar K., (1990), High Morbidity and low Mortality,

The Experience of Urban Pre-school Children in Kerala, Journal of Tropical Paediatrics Vol. 37, pp.17-41.

Sreenivasa Reddy, (1998), Health Care Services for Maternal and Child Health through Primary Health Centre, An Innovative Approach. Health and Population Perspectives and Issues, Vol. 21, No.1, pp. 45-51.

Sundar Ramamani, (1992), Household Survey of Medical Care, Margin, Vol. 24, No.2, pp.169-175.

Tangerose Suezanne et. al., (1984), Differences in Use of Health Services by Children According to Race, Medical Care, Vol. 22, No. 9, pp. 848-853.

Tessler R. and Mechanil P., (1978), Factors Affecting Children's use of Physician Services in a pre-paid Group Practice, Medical Care, Vol. 16, p. 933.

Thankappan, (1999), Caesarean Section Deliveries on the Rise in Kerala, National Medical Journal of India, Vol. 12, No.6, p. 297.

Victoria C.G., Smith P.G. Vanghan J.P., (1988) Water Supply Sanitation and Housing in Relation to the Risk of Infant Mortality from Diarrhoea, International Journal of Epidemiology Vol. 17, pp. 651-654.

Vijayakumar K. Ramankutty V. and Soman C.R., (1990), Trends in Birthweight in Kerala, A Hospital based Study, Health Population Perspectives and Issues, Vol.13, No.1 and 2 p. 52.

Vijayanthimala, (2000) Women and Health, The Role of Internal Environment, Environment and People Vol. 7, No. 6, p. 30.

Wan T.T.H. and Soifer S.J., (1974), Determinants of Physician Utilization, A Casual Analysis, Journal of Health and Social Behaviour Vol. 15, pp.100 –108.

Yesudian, (1981), Differential Utilization of Health Services in a Metropolitan City, Indian Journal of Social Work. Vol. 12, No.4.

Yesudian C.A., (1984), Primary Health Care in Urban Areas, Problems and Issues, Indian Journal of Social Work, Vol. XLV.

REPORTS

Agarval A., (1982), The State of India's Environment, A Citizens Report, Centre for Science and Environment, New Delhi.

Benchmark Survey, (1993) Report on UBSP, Benchmark Survey of Thalassery Municipality, 1993, Loyola College of Social Science, Thiurvananthapuram.

Chatterjee M., (1990) Indian Woman, their Health and Economic Productivity, World Bank Discussion Paper No.109, Washington D.C.

Das N.P., Misra K. Vinod and Saha P.K., (2001), Does Community Access Affect the Use of Health and Family Welfare Services in Rural India? NFHS Subject Reports, No.18, International Institute of Population Sciences, Mumbai.

Duggal R. and Amin S., (1989), Cost of Health Care, A Household Survey in an Indian District, FRCH, Bombay.

Espagnet Ross, (1984) A Primary Health Care in Urban Areas Reaching the Urban Poor in Developing Countries, A State of the Art Report, Unpublished UNICEF/WHO Document, SHS 84.4 Cited in WHO's Urbanization and its Implication for Child Health, Geneva, 1988.

Foxley Alenjandro and Raizyasky Daymar, (1984), Vulnerable Groups in Recessionary Situation, The Use of Children and Young in Chile, The Impact of World Recession on Children, UNICEF, New York, p. 58.

Ghosh Shante, (1976), The Feeding and Care of Infants and Young Children, UNICEF, New Delhi, p.70.

Government of India (1998), Approach Paper to Ninth Five Year Plan 1997-98, Planning Commission, New Delhi, p.87.

Govt of India (1991), Census of India 1991, Office of the Census Commissioner, Series-12, Ministry of Home Affairs, New Delhi.

Govt. of India (1985), National Health Policy, Loksabha Secretariat, New Delhi.

Govt. of India (1991), Census of India, Population of Kerala Series 12 paper 2, Director of Census Operations, Thiruvananthapuram.

Govt. of India (1997), Compendium of Environmental Statistics 1997, Central Statistical Organization, Dept of Statistics, Ministry of Planning and Programme Implementation, New Delhi.

Govt. of India (1998), Indian Population : Some Salient Facts and Figures, Central Statistical Organization, Ministry of Planning and Programme implementation, New Delhi.

Govt. of India (1999), Rapid Household Survey, RCH Project 1998 Ministry of Health and Family Welfare, Population Research Centre, Institute for Social and Economic Change, Banglore.

Govt. of India (2001), Census of India, Population of Kerala, Series 33 paper 2 of 2001, Provisional Population Totals, Director of Census Operations, Thiruvananthapuram.

Govt. of Kerala (1995), Malaria Persistence in the District, Records in the District Medical Office, Kannur.

Govt. of Kerala (1996), Survey of Private Medical Institutions in Kerala, Dept. of Economics and Statistics, Thiruvananthapuram.

Govt. of Kerala (1997), Urban Slums in Kerala 1995-1996, Town Planning Department, Thiruvananthapuram.

Govt. of Kerala (1998), List of Allopathic Medical Institutions in Kerala, Directorate of Health Services, Thiruvananthapuram.

Govt. of Kerala (1998), Report of the Steering Committee on Health Water Supply, Sanitation and Nutrition, Ninth Five Year Plan, 1997-2002, State Planning Board p. 63.

Govt. of Kerala (1999), Statement Showing Institutional Cases of Diseases and Deaths Due to Communicable Diseases in 1999. Directorate of Health Services, Thiruvananthapuram.

Govt. of Kerala (2001), Urban Family Survey, Household level Data Prepared by the Municipal Corporation, Thalassery as Part of Urban Family Survey in Kerala.

Indian Council of Medical Research (1985), Birth Weight : A Major Determinant of Child Survival, Future Perspectives on Children 17, ICMR, New Delhi.

International Institute of Population Science, (1995), National Family Health Survey–1992-93 International Institute of Population Science, Mumbai.

International Institute of Population Science (2000), National Family Health Survey–1998-99 International Institute of Population Science, Mumbai.

ISEC, (1999), Rapid Household Survey Phase I, Reproductive Child Health Project, Population Research Centre, Banglore.

Jessani A. and Anatharam S., (1989), Private Sector and Privatization in the Health Care Services, F.R.C.H., Bombay.

Kutty V.R. and Thankappan K.R., (1994), Morbidity Profile in Kerala with Respect to Age, Education, Gender and Income, International Congress on Kerala Studies, Abstracts, AKG Centre for Research Studies, Thiruvananthapuram 27-29 August.

Misra H.N., (1987), Popular Settlements in the City of Allahabad (India) and the Health Problems of their Inhabitants: Findings from Three Case Studies, International Institute of Development Research, Allahabad.

Mukhopadhyay, (1997), Report of the Independent Commission on Health in India, Voluntary Health Association of India, New Delhi, p. 87.

Paul P. Appaswamy, (1993), Health and Environment, the Interaction in Urban Areas, 23rd Inter Disciplinary Research Methodology Workshop on Health and Human Resources Development, Madras Institute of Development Studies, Madras.

Rao P.S., (1981), Study on Socio-economical and Demographic Correlation of Medical Care Utilization and Health Behaviour, Research Report, Indian Council of Social Science Research, New Delhi.

Registrar General (1996), Population Projection for India and States 1996-2016, Census of India 1991, New Delhi, Table 2.

Registrar General (1998), Sample Registration Bulletin Vol. 32, No.1, New Delhi.

Robert Macedo, (1984), Brazilian Children and Economic Crisis: Evidence from the State of Sauopaulo, The Impact of World Recession on Children, UNICEF, New York, p. 43.

Rossi Espagnet A., (1984), Primary Health Care in Urban Areas: Reaching the Urban Poor in Developing Countries, A State of the Art Report by UNICEF and WHO, Geneva.

Shariff, Abusaleh (1999), India, Human Development Report, Oxford University Press, New Delhi.

Shenoy K.T., (1997), Determinants of Health Care Service Utilization in Kerala, Clinical and Epidemiological, Project of the United Nation Development Programme.

U.N.D.P., (1999) Human Development Report 1999, Oxford University Press, New Delhi.

U.N.D.P., (1999), Human Development Report 1999, Oxford University Press, New Delhi.

Uplekar Mukund and George Alex, (1994), Access to Health care in India, present situation and innovative approaches, R.C.H. Bombay, p.10.

Visaria P. and Gumber Anil, (1994), Utilization and Expenditure on Health Care in India 1986-87, Gujarat Institute of Development Research, Goa.

WHO, (1981), Development Indicators for Monitoring Progress Towards Health for All by the year 2000, Health for all Series No. 4, WHO Geneva.

WHO, (1999), World Health Report 1999, Making a Difference, WHO Geneva.

WHO, (1988), Urbanization and Implication for Child Health, Potential for Action, Geneva.

WHO, (1988), Managing System for Better Health Facilitator Guide, WHO, Geneva.

WHO, (1991) Indoor air Pollution from Bio-mass Fuel, Geneva.

WHO, (1992) The Role of Health Centres in the Development of Urban Health Systems : Report of the WHO Study Group on Primary Health Care in Urban Areas, Geneva.

WHO, (1993), The Urban Health Crisis, Strategies for Health for all in the Face of Rapid Urbanization, Report of the Technical Discussions at 44th World Health Assembly, World Health Organization, Geneva.

World Bank, (1993), World Development Report 1993, Washington.

World Bank, (1995), India Policies and Finance Strategies for Strengthening Primary Healthcare Services, Report No. 13042 Population and Human Resources Division, Washington D.C.

World Bank, (1998), World Resources 1998-99 Oxford University Press, New York.

World Bank, (1999), World Development Report, Oxford University Press, p. 41.

World Bank, (2000), The World Development Report 1999-2000, Oxford University Press, Page to 19.

World Bank, (2001a), India's Future Health Systems : Issues and Options, Draft Report, World Bank, New Delhi.

World Bank, (2001b), World Development Indicators 2001, Table 27, World Bank, Washington DC.

OTHERS

Charles C.C., (1997), Health Status and Health Care System Among Fisher Folk : A Micro level Analysis, Unpublished M.Phil Thesis Submitted to Jawarhalal Nehru University, Centre for Development Studies, Thiruvananthapuram.

Deolalikar, Anil and Vashishtha, Prem, (1996), The Health and Medical Sector in India : Potential Reforms and Problems, IRIS Working Paper 9 Center for Institutional Reform and the Informal Sector, University of Mary Land.

Duraiswamy P., (2000), 'Health Status and Health care in Rural India' Mimeo, Department of Econometrics, University of Madras, Chennai.

Govt. of Kerala, (1999), Malaria Persistence in Kerala, Records with the Directorate of Health Services, Thiruvananthapuram.

Kabir M. and Krishnan T.N., (1991), Social Intermediation and Health Transition : Lessons from Kerala, Paper Prepared for a Seminar on Human Development in India Jointly Sponsored by the NCAER and Harvard University Centre for Population and Development Studies, Held in New Delhi, January 2-4.

Kumar B.G. and Vidyanathan, (1988), Morbidity in India some Problems of Measurement : Interpretation and Analysis, Paper Presented at the Sixth Annual Conference of Indian Society of Medical Statistics, Hyderabad Oct. 27-29.

Kutty, V.R. and Thankappan K.R., (1994), Morbidity Profile in Kerala with Respect to Age, Education, Gender and Income, International Congress on Kerala Studies, Abstracts AKG Centre for Research Studies, Thiruvanthapuram 27-29 August, p. 9.

Malayala Manorama, (2000), July 26, Kottayam.

Murugan G., (1994) Investment in Rural Water Supply and its Impact on Water Borne Diseases of Kerala, International Congress on Kerala Studies, A.K.G. Centre for Research Studies Vol. 5, Thiruvananthapuram.

National Council of Applied Economic Research (NCAER) (2000), Who Benefits from Public Health Spending in India, Mimeo, NCAER, New Delhi.

Nayar M.D., (2000), Needed Multi pronged Strategy, The Hindu, 25th April.

Panda, Pradeep Kumar, (1997), The Effects of Safe Drinking Water and Sanitation on Diarroheal Diseases Among Children in Rural Orissa, Working Paper No. 278, C.D.S. Thiruvananthapuram, p.14.

Panicker, P.G.K. and Soman C.R., (1985), Recent Trends in the Health Status of Urban Children : A Reappraisal, Working Paper No. 209, Centre for Development Studies Thiruvananthapuram.

Panikar, P.G.K. (1999), Health Transition in Kerala, C.D.S. Working Paper No.10, Thiruvananthapuram, p. 31.

Pio, A.,(1984), The Magnitude of the Problem of Acute Respiratory Infection in Children, Proceedings of an International Workshop, University of Adelaide, Sydney, p.376.

Schultz, T.P., (1980), Assessing the Causes and Consequences of the Incidence of Disease and Death : Interpretation of Relations Among Health, Household Economies and the Health Environment, WHO Mimeo.

Shariff Abusaleh, (1995), Health Transition in India : Differentials and Determinants of Morbidity in India by Disaggregated Analysis Working Paper No. 57, NCAER, New Delhi.

Soman C.R., (1993), Health and Fertility Transition : Lessons from Kerala, K.S. Sajeevani Lecture, Madras, April.

Sundar Ramamani, (1995), Household Survey of Healthcare Utilization and Expenditure, the Working Paper No.53, NCAER, New Delhi.

Surekha G., (1999), Health Care Utilization : Differential by Socio Economic Groups and by Sex, Unpublished M. Phil, Thesis, Centre for Development Studies Thiruvananthapuram.

The Hindu, (2001) 1st May.

Vaidyanathan, A., (1997), 'Studies on Health and Health Care: A Review of Findings', Mimeo, Madras Institute of Development Studies, Chennai.

World Bank (2001), India's Future Health Systems : Issues and Options, Draft Report, World Bank, New Delhi.